# Social Media and Political Communities in Malaysia

The **ISEAS – Yusof Ishak Institute** (formerly Institute of Southeast Asian Studies) is an autonomous organization established in 1968. It is a regional centre dedicated to the study of socio-political, security, and economic trends and developments in Southeast Asia and its wider geostrategic and economic environment. The Institute's research programmes are grouped under Regional Economic Studies (RES), Regional Strategic and Political Studies (RSPS), and Regional Social and Cultural Studies (RSCS). The Institute is also home to the ASEAN Studies Centre (ASC), the Singapore APEC Study Centre, and the Temasek History Research Centre (THRC).

**ISEAS Publishing**, an established academic press, has issued more than 2,000 books and journals. It is the largest scholarly publisher of research about Southeast Asia from within the region. ISEAS Publishing works with many other academic and trade publishers and distributors to disseminate important research and analyses from and about Southeast Asia to the rest of the world.

# SOCIAL MEDIA AND POLITICAL COMMUNITIES IN MALAYSIA

EDITED BY

**JAMES CHIN • PAULINE POOI YIN LEONG**

**ISEAS** YUSOF ISHAK INSTITUTE

First published in Singapore in 2024 by
ISEAS Publishing
30 Heng Mui Keng Terrace
Singapore 119614
*E-mail*: publish@iseas.edu.sg
*Website*: http://bookshop.iseas.edu.sg

*The responsibility for facts and opinions in this publication rests exclusively with the authors and their interpretations do not necessarily reflect the views or the policy of the publisher or its supporters.*

**ISEAS Library Cataloguing-in-Publication Data**

Name(s): Chin, Ung-Ho, 1967-, editor. | Leong, Pauline Pooi Yin, editor.
Title: Social media and political communities in Malaysia / edited by James Chin and Pauline Pooi Yin Leong.
Description: Singapore : ISEAS – Yusof Ishak Institute, 2024. | Includes index.
Identifiers: ISBN 978-981-5203-14-1 (soft cover) | ISBN 978-981-5203-16-5 (PDF) | ISBN 978-981-5203-15-8 (epub)
Subjects: LCSH: Online social networks—Malaysia. | Social media and society—Malaysia. | Politics in social media.
Classification: LCC HM742 S66

Cover design by Lee Meng Hui
Index compiled by Sheryl Sin Bing Peng
Typesetting by International Typesetters Pte Ltd
Printed in Singapore by Markono Print Media Pte Ltd

# Contents

# Acknowledgements

The terrain of political debate is ever evolving in a world where information is shared at a speed never seen before and communication technology is advancing at an exponential rate. Social media's advent has changed how people interact with one another online, which has led to the growth of online communities and the modification of political narratives. Our volume, *Social Media and Political Online Communities in Malaysia*, endeavours to explore the impact of digital platforms on political discourse and critically examine the digital interactions that occur within various online communities in Malaysia.

This compilation is the culmination of extensive research and collaboration with scholars and researchers who are experts in their field and have dedicated their time and expertise to comprehensively unravel the complexities and dynamic intersection between social media and various political online communities in Malaysia. We are extremely grateful to the contributors of each chapter, whose committed dedication and scholarly rigour to shedding light on the multifaceted landscape of digital discourse in different Malaysian online communities have enriched this collection with diverse perspectives and insights on the intricate relationships between social media and political engagement. Their research, analysis and thoughtful reflections provide a comprehensive overview of the role that online communities play in influencing political opinions, shaping public discourse and impacting the democratic fabric of Malaysia. We would also like to thank the ISEAS – Yusof Ishak Institute for supporting and facilitating this book project from the initial stages to its fruition, especially Ms Lee Sue-Ann, coordinator of the Media, Technology and Society Programme, for believing in this initiative.

James would like to thank Doria, Cayla, Christa and Catrina for their patience and support throughout the duration of putting together this book.

Pauline would like to thank her parents, Francis and Josephine, and her sister and brother-in-law, Christine and Bing, for their love and support all these years as she pursues challenging academic endeavours.

It is our sincere hope that this book sparks further ongoing dialogue and inquiry into the ever-changing intersectional relationship between social media and political discourse in Malaysian online communities. We hope that readers will gain deeper insights and understanding of the role social media plays in shaping political communities in Malaysia, as well as the challenges and opportunities that arise.

*Pauline Pooi Yin Leong* and *James Chin*

# About the Contributors

**Ahmad Farouk Musa** is an academic and researcher at the Jeffrey Cheah School of Medicine and Health Sciences, Monash University Malaysia. He has a PhD in Surgery from Monash University Australia and a Master of Medicine in Surgery from Universiti Sains Malaysia. He is a doctoral candidate in Islamic Studies at Universiti Muhammadiyah Malaysia and also the founder and director of the Islamic Renaissance Front, Kuala Lumpur, a think tank focusing on *islah* (reform) and *tajdid* (renewal) in Islam.

**Ahmad Fauzi Abdul Hamid** is Professor of Political Science, School of Distance Education, Universiti Sains Malaysia (USM), Penang. He has held visiting posts with the Faculty of Social Sciences and Humanities, Universiti Malaysia Sarawak; the S. Rajaratnam School of International Studies, Nanyang Technological University, Singapore; the ISEAS – Yusof Ishak Institute, Singapore; the Southeast Asia Regional Centre for Counter-Terrorism, Ministry of Foreign Affairs, Kuala Lumpur; and the Oxford Centre for Islamic Studies, United Kingdom. A well-published author of more than 100 academic works in the form of journal articles, book chapters and research monographs, Ahmad Fauzi has been the editor-in-chief of *Kajian Malaysia: Journal of Malaysian Studies* (USM Press) since January 2019. His research has earned him airtime over international media such as Channel NewsAsia and the BBC. An elected member of USM's Senate, Ahmad Fauzi has represented Malaysia diplomatically at international meetings in Grozny, Chechen Republic, Russian Federation and Teheran, Iran.

**Azahar Kasim** is a Senior Lecturer with the School of Multimedia Technology and Communication, College of Arts and Sciences, Universiti Utara Malaysia (UUM). He specializes in Communication and Media Technology (Journalism) and received his PhD from Universiti Malaysia Kelantan. He is currently the Director of UUM's Unit of Corporate Communication. Dr Azahar had eighteen years of experience as senior and executive editor, as well as reporter with various media such as Berita Harian, Harian Metro, Watan, and other media organizations. Capitalizing on his diverse experience in news reporting and editorial, Dr Azahar is also an active researcher, consultant and trainer in public and private institutions in Malaysia. He is also an active member of various non-governmental agencies, such as the Journalist and Malay Writer National Association of Malaysia (PKWPMM) and Communication Scholar Association of Malaysia (PERSKOM).

**James Chin** is Professor of Asian Studies and the inaugural Director of the Asia Institute at the University of Tasmania. He was the founding Head, School of Arts and Social Sciences, Monash University. He is currently Senior Fellow, Jeffrey Cheah Institute on Southeast Asia, Sunway University, Malaysia; Vice President, Australian Institute of International Affairs (Tasmania) and adjunct Professor, Monash University. He was previously Senior Visiting Research Fellow, Institute of Southeast Asian Studies (ISEAS), Singapore and a Salzburg Global Freeman Fellow. Professor Chin is a leading commentator on Malaysian politics and has published extensively on Malaysia. He is widely considered to be the leading scholar on political change in Sabah and Sarawak.

**Clarence Devadass** is a Catholic priest and Director of the Catholic Research Centre in the Archdiocese of Kuala Lumpur. He holds a Doctorate in Sacred Theology, specializing in Moral Theology. He has been a Visiting Fellow at the Faculty of Divinity, University of Cambridge UK (2017) and a Visiting Research Associate with the University of Nottingham Malaysia from 2019 to 2021. He teaches, writes, publishes and speaks on matters concerning ethics and morality, moral education, virtue ethics and Asian contextual theology.

**Kavitha Ganesan** is a Senior Lecturer at the Centre for the Promotion of Knowledge and Language Learning, Universiti Malaysia Sabah. Her primary research interest is in Postcolonial Studies that examines the Malaysian Anglophonic Tradition. As an extension of her research in postcolonialism, she is currently working on projects related to the indigenous Lundayeh in Sabah, Malaysia.

**Anantha Raman Govindasamy** is an Associate Professor in Politics at the Centre for the Promotion of Knowledge and Language Learning, Universiti Malaysia Sabah. His research area focuses on Malaysian and Southeast Asian politics, specifically on minority Malaysian Indians and East Malaysian politics (Sabah and Sarawak).

**Yuen Beng Lee** is currently a professor and Deputy Dean of Research and Sustainability at the School of Arts, Sunway University. Awarded a PhD from the University of Melbourne in 2012, he has researched Malaysian cinema, communication, media and cultural studies, and creative industries. His current research interest is in localizing and implementing Sustainable Development Goals (SDGs) at the national level. He is the author of *Malaysian Cinema in the New Millennium: Transcendence beyond Multiculturalism* and co-editor of *Media and Elections: Democratic Transition in Malaysia*. A self-described free-time filmmaker, he works on short documentaries that preserve the cultural heritage and the arts and skills of vulnerable trades through the Reel Heritage Series.

**Pauline Pooi Yin Leong** is currently heading the Department of Communication, School of Arts at Sunway University. She received her PhD in Political Communication from Monash University and Master's in Mass Communication from Nanyang Technological University where she was awarded the Pearson Education Gold Medal Award for the Best Graduating Student. She also holds a Bachelor of Laws (Honours) (LLB) from the National University of Singapore. A qualified lawyer by training, she was also previously a journalist at *The Straits Times*. Professor Leong is the author of *Malaysian Politics in the New Media Age: Implications on the Political Communication Process* (2019). She was a Visiting Fellow with the ISEAS – Yusof Ishak Institute in Singapore under the Media, Technology, and Society Programme during 2021–22.

**Mohd Azizuddin Mohd Sani** specializes in politics and international relations, and is an expert in political theory and philosophy, human rights, civil liberties, media politics, democratization and Malaysian politics. He is currently the Deputy Vice Chancellor (Academic and International), Universiti Utara Malaysia (UUM). Professor Azizuddin graduated with a PhD in Politics and International Relations from Keele University, United Kingdom. He was previously a Visiting Fellow at the ISEAS – Yusof Ishak Institute, Singapore and is currently a Visiting Adjunct Professor at the School of Liberal Arts and Sciences, Taylor's University, Malaysia. Professor Azizuddin is a public advocate and contributes his expertise by writing columns in Malaysian newspapers, such as *Berita Harian* and *Sin Chew Jit Poh*. He has also been interviewed by many media agencies, both locally and internationally.

**Miew Luan Ng** currently serves as the Dean of the Faculty of Education and Liberal Arts at INTI International University, Malaysia. Her research interests cover crucial areas such as education, media education, political communication, minority press, and language and power. Her publications include Scopus-indexed journal articles such as "Chinese Cultural Preservation, Identity and Community: Examining the Roles of *Sin Chew Daily* in Bridging Chinese Education, Cultural and Religious Rights of the Chinese Community in Malaysia" (2020), "Vaxx-Confident and Vaxx-Hesitant Agents: Factors Affecting COVID-19 Vaccination Willingness among Young Adults in Klang Valley, Malaysia" (2023), "Perceived Social Media Influencers' Reputation of a Beauty Cosmetics Company: A Perspective of Customers" (2024), and book chapters such as "Chinese Newspapers, Ethnic Identity and the State: The Case of Malaysia", in *Media and the Chinese Diaspora: Community, Communications and Commerce* (2006).

**Meng Yoe Tan** is a Senior Lecturer of Media and Communications Studies at the School of Arts and Social Science, Monash University Malaysia. His research focuses on exploring how Malaysian Christians use online platforms such as blogs and social media sites to express and experience Christian community and spirituality in new ways. He has also published on how Internet practices shape religious and political communication among Malaysians in individual, institutional and national sociopolitical contexts. His ongoing curiosity is on the concept of "reality" in cyberspace, and whether spirituality can be experienced online. Apart from the above, he has also ventured into other areas of collaborative research in areas such as media and politics in Malaysia, health communication and education research.

**Jerry Yang Sheng Tan** is currently a Lecturer at the Faculty of Creative Industries, Universiti Tunku Abdul Rahman (UTAR). He is a master holder in screen studies from the University of Science, Malaysia (USM) in 2018. He has researched communication, media and society, and religious studies. His publications include a Scopus-indexed journal article "Transcending Information Delivery: How Malaysian Online News Portals Report on COVID-19 Crisis Response" (2023). He is also the co-author of the book *A Study of Traditional Chinese Religions in Malaysia: The Decline and the Path towards Revitalization* (2023). Tan is also one of the members of Yuen Beng Lee's team working on short documentaries relating to the Reel Heritage Series.

# 1

# Introduction: Politics and Social Media in Malaysia

Pauline Pooi Yin Leong and James Chin

Malaysia, like other Southeast Asian countries, has extremely active online communities. The drivers behind the rapidly growing online communities are basically youths, new technological developments such as mobile phone applications and the lowering of data costs. Young Malaysians, like their counterparts elsewhere in the world, are digital natives who grew up with smartphones and Internet access as part of their daily lives. The advent of social media applications, such as Facebook, Instagram and X (formerly known as Twitter), makes social interactions via online platforms the default mode to connect with friends, communities and the world. Furthermore, Internet connection costs have fallen dramatically. Many telecommunication companies in Malaysia offer unlimited prepaid and postpaid data access of 3GB for as low as RM30 (US$7.50) a month, which enables users to use applications such as WhatsApp and Facebook at RM1 a day. Statista Research Department (2023) found that as of May 2022, some 97.7 per cent of Malaysian respondents stated that their favourite communication application was WhatsApp. The dramatic drop in Internet costs is similarly mirrored by a fall in hardware prices. The cheapest smartphone in the Malaysian market at the end of 2022 was about RM300 (US$75) while second-hand smartphones cost around RM100 (US$25), which allows users to install and use basic applications such as WhatsApp, Telegram, X and even Facebook Lite. In fact, costs of more advanced smartphones have dropped significantly as well such that it is not uncommon for young professionals for change their smartphones once or twice a year. The Malaysian Communications and Multimedia Commission Internet Users Survey 2023 showed that the country's Internet penetration rate stood at 97 per cent of the total population at the beginning of the year, of which 81 per cent used at least one social media platform (Shamsher 2023).

According to Boyd and Ellison (2007), social networking sites are web-based services that allow people to build public or semi-public profile in a system in order to share a connection; they can also view and cross-list their relationships with others in the system. Traditionally, communities that are separated in time and space face the dilemma of bringing people together as they had to be physically present to interact. Social media has bridged this gap by providing new resources to enable people to be "together" despite being separated by time and space (Wenger et al. 2005). Online communities are virtual spaces where people and entities with shared interests congregate to communicate and exchange information and ideas (Autio, Dahlander, and Frederiksen 2013; Kim et al. 2008; Miller, Fabian, and Lin 2009; Plant 2004). According to Rheingold (1994b), virtual communities are "social aggregations that emerge from the Net when enough people carry on those public discussions long enough, with sufficient human feeling, to form webs of personal relationships in cyberspace." He added, "... virtual communities are cultural aggregations that emerge when enough people bump into each other often enough in cyberspace. A virtual community is a group of people who may or may not meet one another face to face, and who exchange words and ideas through the mediation of computer bulletin boards and networks" (Rheingold 1994a). These groups of people with shared interests interact using online technology (Rheingold 1993) and their frequent connections form a social structure (Dahlander and Frederiksen 2012).

Online communities have proliferated in tandem with the universal development of digital and mobile technologies (Faraj, Jarvenpaa, and Majchrzak 2011; Rheingold 2000). These virtual groups have many social configurations from small close-knit clusters to platforms that host billions of users (Resnick and Kraut 2011). Various technological platforms have supported the evolution of online communities, such as bulletin boards, email lists, Usenet groups and forums. The introduction of the browser and the World Wide Web's (Web 1.0) hypertext interface in 1993 enabled more people to easily access the information superhighway by just clicking and browsing the graphical interface. Online communities congregated on websites to share information and limited interaction. Web 2.0 expanded this trend by facilitating ease of networking that enabled communities to learn and collaborate globally, thus expanding the reach of peer-to-peer interactions (Wenger, White, and Smith 2009).

Such online communities have evolved to be digital "third places", as opposed to a person's first and second places which are home and work respectively, where people can informally socialize and establish relationships without any pressure. According to Oldenburg (1999), the "third place" offers individuals relief from the demands of work and home life, and provides inclusiveness and belonging by allowing individuals to participate in the group's social activities. The "third place" also strengthens community ties through social interactions, fosters commitment to local politics through public discourse, and promotes safety and security via open and visible interaction. The "third place" is a vital outlet for building and maintaining of social capital (Oldenburg 1999; Putnam 2000). While Oldenburg envisioned the third place as a physical venue or location, scholars such as Jones (2002) argue that the Internet can provide a virtual third place where community is "formed, maintained and revitalised", based on his review of Kendall (2002)'s ethnographic study of a computer-mediated community. While Soukup (2006) admits that there appears to be similarities between third places and virtual communities, there are also significant differences as the former are localized communities that are social levellers and accessible. For Turkle (1997), traditional third places differ from computer-mediated contexts because the latter's interactions are dependent on simulation, thus changing the participants' experience. Soukup (2006) suggested the term "virtual third place" as the interaction "transcends space and time and alters identity and symbolic referents via simulation". He argues that virtual localization can occur through discourse and other signifiers which become symbolic spaces. Meanwhile, Wright (2012) retheorized the concept of third place space as a non-political online discussion space where political talk can emerge, which can form "a portion of the public sphere" (Habermas 1991).

Daily political discussions are an important aspect of democratic citizenship as it is through such conversations that "citizens construct their identities, achieve mutual understanding, produce public reason, form considered opinions, and produce rules and resources for deliberative democracy" (Kim and Kim 2008). These everyday exchanges have been shown to influence people's political attitudes (Huckfeldt, Mendez, and Osborn 2004), which leads to the formation of public opinion "in every conversation in which private individuals assemble to form a public body" (Habermas 1991). Such political talk can occur in online "third spaces": public spaces beyond the home (first space) or work (second space) where people can meet and interact informally and where political talk, planning and action can occur.

The emergence of social media has advanced the expansion of online communities as these technological networks expedite the sharing of ideas, thoughts and information. The first social networking site was Six Degrees, launched in 1997, which allowed people to connect with strangers. Next came blogs, which were online diaries such as LiveJournal, launched in 1999, and WordPress which enabled anyone to "pen" their thoughts; their readers could also comment. Popular bloggers could build a community of followers. Friendster then emerged as an online community platform for people to make new friends and date. The early twenty-first century saw the appearance of LinkedIn as a social networking space for professionals to connect for career advancements. MySpace and Facebook then became popular networking sites where members can create profiles, connect with their friends' friends, share text and photos, as well as join groups with like-minded strangers who have similar interests. Other top social media sites include Reddit where users can share content, discuss topics and also vote for the most popular stories.

X, on the other hand, is a micro-blogging site where users can only post up to 280 characters, while Tumblr allows users to publish blogs, follow other bloggers as well as comment. Meanwhile, Flickr, Snapchat, Instagram, Pinterest, YouTube and TikTok focus on the sharing of visual content such as photos and videos. Online communities also exist on instant messaging groups such as WhatsApp, Signal and Telegram. Specialized online communities exist on Discord, which started from the gaming community, and Quora, which connects the average Internet user who has a question to experts in specific fields who can provide answers.

Today, online communities are *de rigueur* among Internet users. According to Ruby (2023), there are 4.9 billion social media users as of 2023 and the number is expected to rise to 5.85 billion by 2027. The average social media user, led by millennials and Gen Z, interacts with at least six platforms, spending about two hours and thirty-five minutes daily. Thus, online communities are the new "public sphere" where people constantly discuss issues of the day, which can influence the formation of "public opinion". Web 2.0 has expanded the public sphere in Malaysia by enabling more citizens to participate in the democratic process, through information dissemination, mobilization or crowdsourcing and fundraising (Leong 2015). It has also become a barometer of public opinion as it facilitates reactions from netizens about current sociopolitical issues (Leong 2021).

## THE DEVELOPMENT OF ONLINE COMMUNITIES

According to Preece (2000b), an online community consists of:

a) People who socially interact for their informational and relational needs; some may perform tasks such as leading or moderating;
b) A shared purpose or common interest such as information exchange or services which is the community's raison d'être;
c) Policies that govern the community's social interactions such as underlying guidelines, protocols, rituals, rules and laws that regulate behaviour; and
d) Technological platforms that support and facilitate social interactions virtually.

Communities are not just entities; they are a process (Fernback 1999) because they develop and evolve continuously. Their fluid nature makes online communities different from other groups as their existence and success are contingent on their members' voluntary participation and intrinsic motivation (Faraj, Jarvenpaa, and Majchrzak 2011). Successful online communities usually have a large supply of content that can entice new members to join. One way to develop online communities successfully is to identify and encourage existing group members who have the characteristics, skills and motivation to create content that will, in turn, attract new members (Resnick and Kraut 2011). The success of online communities is highly dependent on the content that is produced by its members, hence the uphill battle is to attract a critical mass of people who can create vibrant content that would attract new members and retain existing ones. Failure to do so would result in inactive and dormant groups.

Actively engaged users are the heart and soul of an online community; its lifeblood is dependent on the people who join it. Vibrant discussions lead to information exchange and the development of new ideas. Continually changing user-generated content differentiates online communities from the more static and less interactive web pages. However, members in online communities are often transient, joining and leaving at will, which may cause a high turnover rate (Dabbish et al. 2012; Ren, Kraut, and Kiesler 2007). Despite this, there is usually a core group that keeps contributing and sharing, as well as retaining the online community's "institutional knowledge" (Ransbotham and Kane 2011), which helps newcomers navigate the group. Even if there are participants who leave the virtual group, the influx of new people will help to rejuvenate the group and maintain membership levels. It is important to draw people into the community and encourage them to participate and continue coming back. Online conversations expressing ideas, comments, reactions, jokes, reflections and suggestions keep community members engaged so that they keep returning to the group. Electronic word-of-mouth from existing members can also draw new people into the group. There are many reasons why people are interested in joining an online community—some want information or support and empathy in dealing with issues, while others want to share their knowledge and ideas, debate about politics, or discuss new interests. They are those who join to have fun interacting with others, meeting new people and developing friendships (Nonnecke and Preece 1999; Preece 2000a). Sometimes, Internet anonymity encourages people to freely disclose their innermost thoughts and true self; they become hyper-personal (Lea et al. 1992; Spears, Lea, and Lee 1990; Walther 1996) and this may lead to the fast formation of deep connections (McKenna, Green, and Gleason 2002). Thus, an online community exists to serve its members' informational and relational needs (Fisher 2019).

Anyone who joins an online community is considered a participant, and the community's character can change when people join and/or leave. Dominant group members have a strong impact as they tend to direct the group conversation (Wallace 1999) and alter the overall character of the community. This means there will be other members who are silent due to shyness or fear of negative reactions, and of being misunderstood or misquoted (Nonnecke and Preece 1999). Depending on population size, tensions between groups can skew the characteristics of online communities. For the virtual group to survive, there must be reciprocity among its participants (Rheingold 1994a). According to Wallace (1999), reciprocity of self-disclosure on the Internet is powerful. People who disclose some personal information about themselves will find others reciprocating by revealing intimate details about themselves. This exchange of information helps to build relationship ties. Nevertheless, some prefer to hide their real identities behind multiple fake accounts for the purpose of trolling or cybertrooping as part of cyberwarfare. Such fabrications affect the integrity of the online community and cause distrust among its members which can negatively impact relationship ties.

While some actively participate by commenting or posting user-generated content, some prefer to lurk by just remaining silent and observing the conversations (Nonnecke and Preece 1999). Lurkers have many reasons why they do not actively participate in online groups such as their concerns about privacy and safety, as well as personal factors such as culture, motivation and emotional involvement or detachment. They may be more interested in obtaining information rather than socializing with others (Preece 2000e). Some online communities schedule invitations to professionals to lead discussion sessions so that group members can pose questions for the experts to answer. Such chats can elevate the level of conversation and change the knowledge hierarchy within the online community (Preece 2000e). Lastly, an online group is often managed by moderators or administrators, and mediators— each with different roles and tasks. Moderators or administrators will review user-generated messages and content posted in the online community to ensure that participants follow guidelines. Disciplinary action can be taken by moderators or administrators to suspend or remove participants from the online group for breaching community rules. Mediators, on the other hand, are less active and are activated to settle disputes (Preece 2000e).

Participants in online communities do not necessarily maintain their roles throughout their membership in the group. Lurkers may one day decide to be more active participants, and those already active may become group experts or be invited to become moderators. The Reader-to-Leader Framework (RLF) describes four roles in online communities:

a) Reader—visiting, reading, searching, returning
b) Contributor—posting, reviewing, rating
c) Collaborator—engaging with others and collaborating to create content
d) Leader—mentoring newcomers, setting policies, monitoring users, and promoting participation (Preece and Shneiderman 2009)

These roles are not exhaustive but are common categories of participation in online communities, and the proportion of readers who transition to leadership is minimal. According to Nielsen (2006)'s 90-9-1 rule of online participation, 90 per cent are usually lurkers who "read or observe, but do not contribute"; 9 per cent will contribute a bit over time, while the 1 per cent minority lead the group conversation. The RLF gives an overview of how online participants can transition from being a passive reader to becoming a more active contributor and collaborator that shares or generates content, to gaining leadership to drive conversations in the online community. Although the framework suggests that the progression is linear, there is also the possibility that participants can move in a non-linear fashion (Gilbert 2017).

The community's purpose can involve any or all of the following:

a) Exchange information: To broadcast information to members or obtain answers to questions, which can be uni- or multi-directional. Information exchange can occur during online conversations.

b) Provide support: To give emotional support, either verbally or non-verbally, to members.

c) Enable communication: To allow participants to socialize informally through virtual chatting either synchronously or asynchronously via light-hearted banter.

d) Discuss ideas: To generate and develop viewpoints that involve deeper reflection and analysis. The discussion pace will be slower and may become heated or go off-topic, thus requiring action from the moderator (Preece 2000f).

e) Organize real events such as a protest or demonstration. The online community becomes the most powerful tool in organizing people into real world activities.

The purpose of the online community is one factor that influences people's interactions (Wallace 1999) as well as the group's character. Patient and emotional support communities had more empathy and lower hostility, based on a research of 100 listserv and bulletin board communities (Preece and Ghozati 1998a, 1998b). In comparison, religious, political and cultural communities had more frequent aggressive comments with minimal empathy (Preece 2000e). First impressions and outward projections are important when attracting new people into the community. The group's name, description, and/or statement of purpose will assist potential members to decide whether its aims are aligned with the person's needs, and thus, is worth joining. For newcomers, knowing the community's clear purpose will deter those who are less committed as well as reduce the risk of participants being frustrated because the community does not meet their expectations (Preece 2000e). Online communities that have clearly stated objectives are more likely to attract people with similar attitudes, ideas and goals. Therefore, like-minded people are attracted to each other and are usually less hostile; this creates a stable community. Broad-based communities, on the other hand, are more likely to have participants with different expectations. This may lead to interpersonal confrontations and frustrations when these expectations are not met. However, there is some evidence that suggests that cross-posting of off-topic ideas from outside the community can positively impact the conversation (Whittaker et al. 1998). Although initially each member may have a set of beliefs that may not necessarily align with the online community's beliefs, as he or she interacts with others, they will integrate into the group by either adopting, adapting and potentially discarding prior beliefs (Davidson et al. 2019).

Traditionally, when people meet face-to-face, first impressions are formed based on non-verbal cues, including visual and aural characteristics, and content of self-disclosure. When people join online groups, they are unable to view a person's physical and aural attributes and this affects the formation process of first impressions (Walther 2013). Even photos on social media offer insufficient information about people. The social identity model of deindividuation effects (SIDE model) suggests that the absence of visual cues in groups using computer-mediated communication can cause people to become depersonalized (Lea et al. 2000). Because people cannot "see", they may not realize that people are different from them, especially when people join an online group discussion and focus on the task at hand rather than talking about personal matters (Walther and Carr 2010). Early research proposed that the lack of non-verbal cues in online groups would affect impression formation and cause communities to be impersonal and sterile (Keisler, Seigel, and McGuire 1984; Siegel et al. 1986). However, other scholars believe that meeting in online communities can eliminate the chances of prejudging someone based on appearance (Wallace 1999), which is a positive development. The absence of non-verbal cues about one's physical characteristics can magnify the attraction of members towards each other. Although they experience depersonalization, they are aware of their shared common characteristics and links which is their overarching social identity. People may have vague impressions about individuals in the group and might not sense individual differences in members, but the overarching similarity of belonging to a larger group identity may result in participants forming exceptionally strong bonds to the group itself (Walther 2013).

Online communities have some advantages that offline groups do not have. Firstly, all communications are digitalized and can be archived. This means that the behaviours of group members can be "captured forever" in cyberspace (Fineman 2014; Paul-Choudhury 2011). Secondly, online communities benefit from artificial intelligence (AI) technology that can execute searches and use algorithms to match people and content, as well as notify people about potentially interesting content and events. Each social media platform has different functions to allow community creators or founders to control the access and ability of group members to participate in the community (Resnick and Kraut 2011). Online communities can also accommodate more members compared to offline ones since they are not limited by geographical and temporal boundaries, which expands online public spaces for virtual sociability as endless numbers of communities can be formed (Brändle 2019).

Another advantage of online communities is the ability to reach and spread information among "weak tie" social connections—those whom a person does not directly know but has links to those with "strong ties" to the person, for example, a friend of a friend. People with weak ties are less similar and therefore have access to different types of information compared to a person's network of strong ties that have similar knowledge (Granovetter 1973). Social media platforms, therefore, function as intermediaries between people and their prospective weak tie connections (Wellman and Gulia 1996). People can search and join online communities on topics of interest, thus meeting those with weak ties who have different social circles and possess diverse information.

## COMMITMENT, SOCIAL PRESENCE AND COMMON GROUND

Commitment is about the "feelings of attachment or connection" of members to the community and underlies their willingness to be part of the group and contribute to it (Preece 2000a). People who are more committed tend to be better satisfied and contribute more, leading to improved performance. They are also less likely to look for alternatives and leave the group (Mathieu and Zajac 1990). However, in virtual communities, referents of belonging are flexible, which allows variations in group membership and loyalty. Netizens can be members of many online communities, playing different roles in each one. Furthermore, virtual groups often have less stringent criteria for inclusion and exclusion. Technological platforms also allow members to easily join and leave virtual groups at a click of a button, hence it is more difficult to forge a sense of commitment among online members as relationship ties among members may be weak. In this situation, online relationships are less intense compared to face-to-face ones (Brändle 2019). Online communities find it more challenging to instil commitment among their members because there are many other similar groups in cyberspace that people can join without geographical constraints. New members are also usually less committed to a community compared to established members (Resnick and Kraut 2011).

Even if bonds between online members are often weak, shallow, short-lived and merely instrumental, there is still the possibility of stronger intensive relationship ties developing over a period of months due to the emotional aspects, especially if members share a common interest, commitment or solidarity despite being strangers (Brändle 2019; Preece 2000a). Online relationships can also be strengthened if members collectively produce common resources that are openly shared in cyberspace, giving rise to the emergence of values such as trust and altruism. Unlike offline communities, relationships in virtual groups are often decentralized and horizontal. Therefore, it is possible to build relationships and a sense of community on the Internet (Brändle 2019).

To do so, online community members need to be "socially present" on the technological platform. Social presence theory (Short, Williams, and Christie 1976) discusses how media can convey a sense of the participants being physically present, with face-to-face communication as the standard of assessment. This concept originated from social psychological theories of interpersonal communication and symbolic interactionism (Biocca et al. 2001; Biocca, Harms, and Burgoon 2003; Rice 1993; Sallnäs 2005; Tu 2001). Social presence is dependent not only on spoken words but also on verbal and non-verbal cues, body language and context (Rice 1987, 1993); it affects how participants sense emotion, intimacy and immediacy (Rice 1993). Although the theory originated from non-mediated interpersonal communication, social presence is often discussed today in the context of computer-mediated communication (CMC).

Social presence is linked to the concept of immediacy, which are non-verbal behaviours such as facial expressions, eye contact and body movements that could result in more intensive closeness in communication (Wiener and Mehrabian 1968). Interpersonal communication scholars (Biocca, Harms, and Burgoon 2003; Gunawardena 1995; Gunawardena and Zittle 1997; Reio Jr. and Crim

2006; Rice 1993; Rourke et al. 2001; Sallnäs 2005; Tu 2001) have also studied social presence in the context of Argyle and Dean (1965)'s concept of intimacy, which suggests that eye contact, physical proximity, the intimacy of topics and smiles are components that develop equilibrium for intimacy. If any component changes, the other components compensate to maintain equilibrium. For example, if two people are physically close to each other, they are likely to have less eye contact.

Social presence theory was then extended to mediated communication by Short, Williams, and Christie (1976) in the field of social psychology and telecommunications, and today it is widely used in the area of CMC. In mediated communication, intimacy levels are affected by interpersonal elements such as physical distance, eye contact, smiles and personal topics. For example, in text-only systems, both task and social information function in the same single verbal/ linguistic channel which cannot transmit non-verbal cues (Walther 1994). Thus, it is not surprising that Short, Williams, and Christie (1976) found greater intimacy when people use television than audio-only communication. As for immediacy, Short, Williams, and Christie (1976) argued that it enhances social presence and that individuals can convey immediacy and non-immediacy verbally as well as non-verbally. Thus, social presence, which is "the degree of salience of the other person in the interaction and the consequent salience of the interpersonal relationships" (p. 65), is an important factor in a communication medium. Social presence influences how individuals perceive their discussions and relationships during the communication process. In their view, social presence is the unidimensional quality of the medium and varies among different media as the latter affects the nature of the communication and interacts with its purpose. While social presence is influenced by the user's subjective perceptions about the medium, it is also dependent on the medium's objective ability to transmit verbal and non-verbal cues (Short, Williams, and Christie 1976). Thus, social presence theory suggests that digital media have varying abilities to transmit social cues that facilitate social presence in computer-mediated interpersonal communication.

Short, Williams, and Christie (1976)'s study led to the development of media richness theory in relation to social presence (Kehrwald 2008). Media richness theory is similar to social presence theory but examines communication from a media perspective by describing the medium's capability for immediate feedback through conveying cues and involving various senses (Daft and Lengel 1986). Media that allow synchronous and immediate verbal and non-verbal cues during communication such as video and phone calls are high in social presence as they are very similar to face-to-face communication, hence better at facilitating social connectedness. Video calls have more social presence than voice calls (Sallnäs 2005) as it combines verbal and non-verbal cues during communication.

On the other hand, text messaging and email are asynchronous and have fewer communicative cues, which are why this form of media has a lower social presence (Nguyen et al. 2022). This may result in misunderstandings and frustration which disrupts relationship development, thus those who communicate using media with limited social presence need to work harder to compensate for missing non-verbal information. Experienced users can find ways to deal with the absence of visual cues (Rice and Barnett 1986). Social information processing (SIP) theory (Walther 1992) discusses how, despite the absence of non-verbal cues, people can form impressions and know each other individually through online platforms to a level similar to real-life interactions. In such situations, people adapt their interpersonal as well as instrumental communication using any available cues in the digital channel that they are using. In text-based CMC, social information is perceived through the language content and style characteristics, as well as the timing of messages (Walther 2013). One way is to adopt a conversational online writing style that is non-confrontational and use linguistic softeners such as phrasing a comment tentatively or choosing neutral words to avoid the perception of being aggressive (Wallace 1999).

However, not everyone has the linguistic ability and an extensive vocabulary to be able to communicate effectively. While spoken language always has emotional or physical cues through voice tone, hand or eye gestures and other visual elements, these are not present in text-based digital communication. To solve this issue, some systems have developed functions that enable participants to use icons, photographs or 3D avatars to represent themselves as a way to increase social presence. Emoticons are keyboard symbols that are combined to make pictures such as "<3" for heart (Novak et al. 2015), and emojis are pictographs of faces, objects and symbols introduced by Shigetaka Kurita in Japan in the late 1990s to provide emotional and contextual cues behind textual communication on a mobile Internet platform (Skiba 2016). For example, a smiley emoticon or emoji may be added to indicate intentions or feelings and assure the other party that the comment is well meant. Emojis and emoticons act as non-verbal surrogates to inform the message recipient of the sender's facial expression, thus delivering additional social cues to support understanding of the message (Hamza 2016) and reduce the risk of miscommunication. Therefore, text messaging conversations that have high synchronicity and use visual cues such as emoticons and emojis can also create a stronger social presence compared to asynchronous text conversations without visual cues (Hsieh and Tseng 2017; Park and Sundar 2015). In text messaging apps where traditional interpersonal social cues are limited, one can creatively use functions such as emoticons and emojis on digital communication platforms to achieve a high social presence (Baym 2015).

It is possible for people who use text-based digital communication platforms to form strong relationships if given sufficient time (Walther 1993); it just takes longer to establish the relationship as both parties need to send more messages to develop a common understanding. There is evidence that some people can develop flourishing social relationships using this form of digital communication (Spears and Lea 1992). A study by Antheunis, Valkenburg, and Peter (2010) found that interactive text-based CMC was more dynamic in forming impressions compared to static photos and self-descriptions on social media profiles.

Thus, when there is sufficient social presence or compensatory methods to overcome the absence of social cues on digital platforms, participants in the communication process can achieve common ground which is a mutual belief that they have a shared understanding and validation (Clark and Brennan 1993). People in online communities often start off as strangers and need to initially interact to establish common ground that becomes the foundation of the relationship (Spa 2004). Once common ground is achieved, then group members will have a greater commitment to each other, hence building stronger relationship ties in the online community, which boosts its growth and development.

## DIGITAL INTIMACY AND SOCIAL CAPITAL THEORY

There are three key phases in contemporary sociological studies of intimacy. First is the exercise of "free" choice in modern interpersonal relationships that promote compatibility and friendship within elective intimacies instead of familial duties (Giddens 1992). The emphasis on choice led to more fluid intimacies in the second phase with the emergence of diverse forms of social dependency based on the friendship paradigm and non-conventional partnerships, often described using terms such as "friends as family" and "families of choice" such as lesbian, gay, bisexual and transgender (LGBT) relationships (Roseneil 2000; Weeks, Heaphy, and Donovan 2001) or "personal communities" with friends, neighbours and workmates, as well as relatives (Spencer and Pahl 2006). The rise of personal communities and individual networks resulted in the third phase of "networked individualism"— from tight bonds to fluid systemic interactions based on individuals with shared interests rather than groups or places (Haythornthwaite and Wellman 1998; Wellman 2002). Networked individuals develop new social skills and strategies such as managing self-presentation and personal boundaries in digitally supported networks (Rainie and Wellman 2012). Such individuals are embedded in a "network public culture" (Boyd 2011) where modern intimacy and friendship is about choice, agency, flexibility, respect, mutual disclosure and companionship.

While scholars such as McGlotten (2013) are concerned that virtual intimacies are failures or "diminished and dangerous corruption[s] of the real thing" (see also Attwood 2006; Chambers 2013; Hobbs, Owen, and Gerber 2016, Jamieson 2013), such mediated intimacies via contemporary social media platforms can be understood through the commodification of relationships built into the digital infrastructure. Today's digitally mediated friendships emphasizes social connectedness and sharing rather than exclusiveness and privacy. Social media platforms such as Facebook promote openness and service free at the point of use but gathers its users' data for profit (van Dijck and Poell 2013); it exploits "friendship" as a powerful symbol of interpersonal democratization (Chambers 2013). The implication is that connectedness is more powerful through disclosure and reciprocity, so Facebook steers users to share highly personal information instead of having private and exclusive connections.

Bucher (2012) and van Dijck (2013) state that digital and technical norms operating on these social network sites circumscribe users' connections to each other. In fact, Bucher (2012) proposes the concept of "algorithmic friendship" to describe socio-technical dimensions of online friendship programme sociality. Berlant (2008) discusses the creation of intimate publics through mass media textual discourse as scenes of mass intimacy, identification and subjectification. She suggests that an intimate public operates "when a market opens up to a block of consumers, claiming to circulate texts and things that express those people's particular core interests and desires". Intimate publics create shared worldviews and emotional knowledge which "flourishes as a porous, affective scene of identification among strangers that promises a certain experience of belonging and provides a complex of consolation, confirmation, discipline, and discussion". Hjorth and Arnold (2013) argue that social media "constitute a new socio-technical institutionalisation of public intimacy".

Intimate encounters and self-representations on social media can generate more and/or deeper social connections as well as platform engagement such as time spent paying attention and generating data (Dobson, Carah, and Robards 2018). Bollmer (2018) states that intimacy is a "structure of feeling" that is arranged around the imagined presence of others and longings for connection, rather than direct reciprocity, and social media is able to represent, facilitate and archive people's social and emotional investments. People keep logging on in search for the "good life" promised by intimacy (McGlotten 2013), and Facebook has capitalized on this by packaging and repackaging historical digital traces of users' lives and relationships, and resurfacing these for them to review (Robards 2014). A study by Hopkins and Ryan (2014) found that the practice of sharing self-images, jokes and memes on Facebook fosters affective connections and social belonging for youths from disadvantaged rural communities who are starting university together. Facebook enables these youths to build community and support networks which results in social mobility. These studies show that intimate and everyday sharing on social media have an affective impact on its users and may lead to potentially enduring changes. According to Dobson, Carah, and Robards (2018), such social media connections, attachments and relationships, and the kind of "everyday activism" that builds digital intimacy can potentially develop constitutively into social capital.

For communities to be successful, there must be cooperation and trust. Three conditions must be in place for cooperation to exist (Kollock 1998). Firstly, the chances of individuals interacting again must be high, otherwise, people might act without thinking of the consequences of their behaviour on other members because there is no future culpability. Thus, it is important to establish common ground in ongoing relationships, which is helped when there is social presence. Online communities that see people joining and leaving without commitment and consequences are likely to have minimal cooperation and civil interactions. Registration may deter casual hopping from community to community. Secondly, members should be able to identify with each other such that it encourages responsible online behaviour as there are social consequences. Furthermore, like-minded people are inclined to share a common understanding more than those from whom they differ (Granovetter 1982; Walther 1994), and discussing a shared passion or problem may effectively foster cooperation and relationship ties. Thirdly, if people anticipate that they are likely to interact with others in the future, they are more likely to behave reasonably (Walther 1994). What is acceptable behaviour will depend on the community's purpose, members' activities and attitudes, and governing policies. For example, political communities may be more tolerant of heated remarks compared to education communities (Preece 2000c).

Trust is another factor that is needed for communities to become successful. According to Figallo (1998), trust is essential in online communities as it is the glue that holds together relationships between group members, and is the core of any community. Fukuyama (1995) stated that "trust is the expectation that arises within a community of regular, honest, and cooperative behaviour, based on commonly shared norms, on the part of the members of the community". Thus, group members should be encouraged to be responsive and reliable as this will help to build community trust.

Research on face-to-face groups where members have some similarities show that there is a state of "swift trust" where people act as though they can trust each other, even though they may not know each other personally. After interacting over time, group members learn about each other's skills, abilities and overall reliability, which leads to "enduring trust" (Meyerson, Weick, and Kramer 1996). In online groups, it may be more difficult to form swift trust due to a lack of visual and social cues unlike in offline settings. However, the SIDE theory suggests that online participants in some situations can form positive first impressions based on their similar overarching identity to the group which leads to the formation of swift trust. However, for online groups to be successful, there should also be enduring trust. While some scholars such as Handy (1995) are pessimistic about the ability of online groups to form enduring trust due to the lack of non-verbal information and social cues unlike in face-to-face communication. However, other studies show that virtual group members can make judgements on trustworthiness based on online behaviour, for example, types of messages and responses, despite the lack of non-verbal social cues (Iacono and Weisband 1997). A study by Walther and Bunz (2005) also found that rules and structured management are beneficial to group behaviour and engender trust, and that online groups can accommodate and compensate for the limited social and verbal cues in CMC.

Communities, including online ones, are a collection of interconnected social relationships (Marquis, Lounsbury, and Greenwood 2011), and cooperation and trust among group members will engender goodwill, resulting in social capital (Putnam, Feldstein, and Cohen 2004). Social relationships bring about social capital which is a valuable resource inherently embedded in social relations that can be mobilized to facilitate action, which includes trust, reciprocity, common norms and shared beliefs within the social network of relationships. Social capital is "the goodwill available to individuals or groups. Its source lies in the structure and content of an actor's social relations. Its effects flow from the information, influence, and solidarity it makes available to the actor" (Adler and Kwon 2002).

Firstly, social capital provides people with access to quality information that is relevant and timely, which gives them an advantageous position (Burt 1997, 2009; Uzzi 1997). Secondly, social capital also produces influence in a community network because of reciprocal obligations between group members and a sense of connectedness that accumulates in the social relationships (Coleman 1988) which can be utilized to perform tasks (Sandefur and Laumann 1998). Research by Steinfield, Ellison, and Lampe (2008) showed that the amount of Facebook friends is associated with one's self-reported level of social capital because of the ability to search for help and resources from others, especially those with weak ties that are present in the social media platform.

Social capital theory, therefore, reflects "a primordial feature of social life ... that social ties ... often can be used for different purposes" (Adler and Kwon 2002). Lastly, social relations can also persuade group members to comply with norms and beliefs, as well as develop a commitment to collective objectives. Thus, solidarity, which is the feeling of unity, can develop from social capital. When people share common interests or objectives, there is little need for formal controls (Sandefur and Laumann 1998).

In a study conducted on an online community in the United Subang Jaya (USJ) suburb in Klang Valley, Shafiz and Kamarul (2014) found that there are some elements of social capital as most people join an online community to get to know other members better which promotes a sense of belonging. The virtual platform also serves as a medium of communication to discuss and vote on community issues in a forum moderated by the webmaster. The online community also uses this virtual platform to decide on the appointment of its leaders. In addition, community members also help each other by offering financial help and support to others in need, or services to the handicapped and elderly. The community members also feel respected and have built some level of relationship that engenders togetherness and sociability. Most of them belong to at least one volunteer organization such as residents' associations and neighbourhood watch groups. Such acts of volunteerism are an indicator of the existence of social capital which promotes and sustains the loyalty and commitment of its members. However, the level of trust is still limited as they are unlikely to ask their virtual neighbours for assistance with daily chores and errands. Another study conducted by Wan Munira and Nabila (2011) on multi-ethnic online communities found that such groups widen communication and social networking, which contributes to the development of social capital and integration.

# CONTENT AND COMMUNITY MODERATION

No doubt social media has enabled ordinary people to create and publish content online with minimal technical skills at the touch of a button. Instantaneous communication applications also allow people to share their ideas or favourite contents to others, without any institutional or news media gatekeepers to manage the flow of information and communication. Social media platforms enable more people directly connect with each other, offering them new opportunities to speak and interact with a variety of people, and organizing them into networked publics (Baym 2015; Benkler 2006; Boyd 2011; Bruns 2008). While this enlarges the public sphere for discussion, the erosion of media gatekeeping has also resulted in the emergence of negative phenomena such as fake news, trolling and flaming (Gerbaudo 2022) as well as pornography, obscenity, violence, illegality, abuse and hate (Gillespie 2018).

Hence, the need for content moderation, which is the "organised practice of screening user-generated content (UGC) posted to Internet sites, social media and other online outlets, in order to determine the appropriateness of the content for a given site, locality, or jurisdiction" (Roberts 2017). The inappropriate content can be removed by the moderator who are either volunteers or, in a commercial context, by individuals or firms who receive remuneration. There are various moderation styles on different sites, platforms and communities, depending on the rules or community guidelines. While there are volunteer moderators who carry out their duties in their own groups or online communities, the growth of Web 2.0 sites has resulted in tech and online media companies having to resort to content moderation, especially in the comments sections. Some media firms use in-house human moderators or technological interventions such as word filtering, disallowing anonymous postings or removing the comments section (Roberts 2017). Social media platforms must, in some form or another, moderate: to protect its users and also remove offensive, vile or illegal content. However, the challenge is the drawing of the "proper boundaries of public expression" and deciding "when, how, and why to intervene" by balancing between different value systems, political ideologies and cultural wars across national, cultural and linguistic boundaries (Gillespie 2018).

Community policies are important so that moderators have guidelines that they can act upon in deciding what to retain and remove to justify their actions. These statements document the principles that have been established over time when dealing with contentious situations. Most platforms usually have two main documents: "terms of service", which is a contract that describes the obligations between the social media platforms and their users, and "community guidelines", which lays out the platform's expectations of appropriate content and behaviour (Gillespie 2018). The purpose of community guidelines is articulate the platform's ethos that will honour and protect online speech while preventing offence and abuse. It also signals to lawmakers that further regulation is unnecessary due to the platform's diligence, and to advertisers that the platform is a safe space for commercial appeals (Gillespie 2018).

As online communities on social media platforms grow larger in size by recruiting more members, there is a risk of attracting unsuitable persons who may behave inappropriately and disrupt the activities of current members, especially new users who may not be aware of group norms. Furthermore, different people may have contrasting interests that conflict. Large online discussion groups, especially those that deal with controversial topics, such as religion or politics, attract trolls who enjoy flaming conversations by posting inflammatory, irrelevant or off-topic messages that provoke emotional responses from others (Schwartz 2008). Also, Internet users can hide behind the veil of anonymity, which reduces inhibitions towards aggressive online behaviour (Preece 2000d) as people have less social accountability. Users do not need to communicate face to face; they can camouflage themselves behind the computer screen, thinking that no one knows or can trace them. They may also think that they will not encounter other members again, so they are less restrained in venting negative comments and launching ad hominem attacks by trolling or flaming (Preece 2000e). Members can also create online personas that are different from their offline identities, even to the extent of switching gender (Preece 2000d). Also, some members may prefer that the discussion stay on-topic, but others may want to interact with others whom they are familiar with on matters of mutual interest (Resnick and Kraut 2011).

Communication in online communities is technologically mediated, which means that users may not be able to detect non-verbal interpersonal cues that are present during face-to-face interactions. The prevalent mode of online communication is textual; with fewer social cues to monitor, this may lead to misinterpretations and misunderstandings. In such cases, there must be mechanisms in place to regulate the behaviour of group members by limiting inappropriate conduct that is damaging to the online community (Resnick and Kraut 2011). Community guidelines are basic policies that provide a behavioural framework for group members for social growth. As the online community grows with the increasing influx of members, it develops and forms its character and such social policies and structure set the expected code of civil conduct for participants. Achieving the balance in planning and developing social policies that are understandable and acceptable to online group members requires skill and sensitivity. Online communities are more likely to succeed when early social planning adequately discourages inappropriate behaviour while supporting its purpose and facilitating its evolution (Preece 2000b).

Therefore, some established members of their online communities help to govern the online community by becoming moderators and/or mediators. Moderators generally try to ensure reasonable behaviour and help to direct activity within the community, but their actual roles and responsibilities may vary depending on the group's moderation policy. Mediators, on the other hand, have a less active role as they are usually activated to settle disputes; they may even serve several groups at once (Preece 2000e). Moderators and mediators have the important role of preventing flaming (Preece 1998) and trolling. Moderators, especially, have other tasks such as filtering and monitoring messages to ensure that only appropriate posts are published. Unsuitable posts and spam should not be allowed to disrupt the conversation among members. The aim is to keep a high ratio of relevant messages in the online community, which is also known as the signal/noise ratio (Collins and Berge 1997; Salmon 2000). Other than managing the ebb and flow of the conversation and content and keeping peace in the community, they keep the group focused and "on-topic" as well as manage the frequently asked questions (FAQs) by directing people to the section, answering questions or updating regularly. They also manage membership by adding, removing or suspending members in the community. Moderators also manage content by allowing their publication, removing undesirable ones that breach community guidelines, or archiving old content that is no longer relevant (Collins and Berge 1997; Salmon 2000).

Nevertheless, the sheer volume of user-generated content may overwhelm human moderators and take a toll on their mental health, hence the use of artificial intelligence (AI) to improve the moderation process by using technology to filter out improper content. Automated AI systems can identify potentially harmful content, increasing the speed and effectiveness of the overall moderation procedure (Darbinyan 2022). Meanwhile, there are online groups that do not have any moderation due to lack of resources or the ideological belief in absolute free speech. However, such communities run the risk of descending into chaos which might deter potential new members, as well as potential legal liabilities due to improper comments (Grimes-Viort 2010).

Moderating online communities can be very time-consuming and exhausting as the moderator not only needs to be the group expert but also have good interpersonal and communication skills and manage the personalities of different group members. To understand people's online behaviour, one ought to have some insight into cognitive and social psychology (Wallace 1999). Moderators need to strike a balance between rigidly enforcing the community's rules and regulations and allowing freedom of speech of its members to converse in the group. A good moderator who has skills and experience (Collins and Berge 1997) will be able to negotiate walking on that tightrope, but this is not something that one learns from school as most are either self-taught or learn by observing other moderators (Feenberg 1989). Thus, not many people are willing to be moderators in online communities as it can be a thankless, unappreciated task as some members chafe at having to follow rules. In situations where there is a dispute, mediators can be called in to resolve the issue (Preece 2000e).

Moderation techniques may vary in different online communities because of their diverse purposes. For example, scholarly discussion communities (Collins and Berge 1997) are likely to have moderators who focus on ensuring that the conversation stays on track, while moderators in distance education communities would direct discussions that support learning goals and scholarly topics (Salmon 2000). On the other hand, online communities that discuss controversial political and religious issues are likely to engage in heated debates whereby moderators have to actively arbitrate. In contrast, online support communities tend to be more peaceful, and moderators can be less involved (Preece 2000e). Online communities ought to have clearly stated moderation policies that direct behaviour that the moderator and group members can refer to; this reduces confusion and claims of unfair treatment (Preece 2000e). Policies are needed to determine who is allowed to join the online community, the preferred communication style and appropriate conduct, as well as consequences for non-compliance. In some virtual communities, policy statements are formalized statements while others have suggested codes of conduct that are less formal (Preece 2000e).

Online communities often have membership requirements and screen potential new members to ensure their suitability before they can join. Completely open groups that allow anyone to join and leave may be convenient, but this opens the community to abuse as unscrupulous people may troll, spam and flame, in addition to scamming others. Thus, online communities often have a registration process for new members who need to provide a login name and password and wait for a while before their membership application is approved. This policy decision is to deter less serious or shady characters from joining the online community to create chaos and trouble (Preece 2000e). It is easier for members to voluntarily leave the virtual group at the click of a button, but there should also be policies in place should the group moderators or administrators decide to remove a person for not adhering to community guidelines. Community policies also protect members from breaching national laws in areas such as hate speech, pornography, obscenity, terrorism and other criminal offences. These guidelines give some form of legal protection for online community founders and administrators (Preece 2000e). Although this might be a deterrent in attracting newcomers, a free-for-all online community without rules might become a wild and unpleasant environment for its members.

To protect moderators from criticism, most online communities make their moderation rules public. Having guidelines for civil behaviour will reduce the risk of aggression among participants (Preece 2000a). Policies should guide behaviour in the community but be sufficiently flexible to facilitate fruitful conversations that promote sociability and relationships among its participants. Having a balance is important to support information exchange and communication (Preece 2000a).

Too much community governance may cause community members to feel like they are in a classroom with a schoolteacher imposing rules everywhere, but if there are minimal guidelines, then the online community may be affected by negative content in a toxic environment. Thus, community governance regulates behaviour to prevent crises and issues from surfacing (Preece 2000e). Online community policies and their execution shape community membership and behaviour, and subsequently influence its overall group character. This, in turn, will attract like-minded members to keep returning to the online community as well as entice new participants (Preece 2000a), which influences its evolution. Therefore, the impact of online policies and governance on participants can make or break the online community.

## DIGITAL DEMOCRACY, SOCIAL MOVEMENTS AND THE POLITICAL POTENTIAL OF ONLINE COMMUNITIES

During the early days of the Internet, scholars such as Papacharissi (2002) expanded on the Habermasian concept by calling it as a "virtual public sphere" as many of its interactive features offered new forms of democratic discourse and participation. However, the development of social media or Web 2.0 public sphere is different from Habermas (1991)'s normative model; instead of being a decentralized and networked system, it is now a highly commercialized space that is dominated by large corporate platforms such as Facebook and X, and the rise of instant messaging applications such as WhatsApp and Telegram as well as video-sharing platforms such as TikTok which revolves around simple low-intensity instantaneous interactions such as social media reactions (Gerbaudo 2022) that require minimal effort beyond pressing a button—Facebook likes, haha-s, wows and shares; X retweets and loves; YouTube likes and comments. The "popularity" of any content is measured by the aggregated collection of users' individual reactions which is then fed into social media algorithms that determine the visibility of different contents and ultimately their influence. Thus, it would seem that digital democracy has become "reactive"; online discussions on issues, incidents or statements become ongoing micro-referendums with different factions stating their positions. According to Gerbaudo (2022), social media reactions appear to resemble an ongoing public opinion poll. Despite the hope that the Internet's network-like structure would decentralize power from the elites to the citizens (Barlow 2019; Shirky 2010), Web 2.0 is experiencing enormous concentration as tech giants such as Google, Apple, Facebook and Amazon dominate the market (McChesney 2014) and in essence control the structure of online discussions and interactions.

Gerbaudo (2022) argues that the social media public sphere is plebeian rather than bourgeois because its dominant collective actors are "online crowds" rather than "publics", and that interactions are more "affective" rather than informational and cognitive because the aim is to mobilize affects and emotions. These are also known as "affective publics" (Papacharissi 2015, 2016) who congregate on social media platforms to engage in "trending topics" by using hashtags, like buttons, re-tweets, re-shares and @mention functions that "invite affective attunement, support affective investment, and propagate affectively charged expression", suggesting that logic and rationality are often secondary to emotional reactions that arise from being wired into a socially mediated event. The digital crowd are not necessarily from the same class, but gather around spaces of socialization, entertainment and informal discussion. Social media platforms offer "expanded possibilities for the formation, coordination and control of collective behaviour" (Dolata and Schrape 2016) because "like-minded" individuals can easily gather based on common interest and connected conversations. Crowd-like phenomena can emerge as online users can easily gather at short notice and engage in digitally mediated forms of collective action; they can disappear and reappear in a different form later (Gerbaudo 2022). These non-organized collective "online crowds" may lack physical proximity but are digitally experiencing a form of "crowding" (Dolata and Schrape 2016), a trend that was earlier observed by Poster (2001) who said that the Internet was becoming the new place of public crowding, replacing physical spaces like street corners, squares and taverns for social interactions. Such online crowds can quickly transform into physical crowds (Gerbaudo 2012) such as Occupy Wall Street and Black Lives Matter—social movements that emerged on the back of popular Internet hashtags and viral memes circulated by social media crowds. Similarly, Bernie

Sanders campaign during the 2016 Democratic primaries and Donald Trump's election victory the same year were spearheaded by "digital armies" of committed supporters who constantly shared content and mobilized people to participate in campaign events.

According to Tufekci (2014), social movements can be conceptualized as collective actors with "capabilities" and that digital media are instruments with affordances that enable social movements to develop certain capabilities such as engagement, protests, occupation, synchronization, visibility, publicity, logistics, coordination and attention. Social media is integral to social movement and that communication is a form of organization. Although these digital protests and movements are strong in some dimensions such as attention, coordination and publicity, they may have less impact on areas such as elections and policy changes due to lack of institutional capacity. Their ability to build an infrastructure for collective decision-making is limited because the rapid development of social media-enabled movements makes them vulnerable to "tactical freezes" when the movement starts to garner public attention (Tufekci 2017). Low intensity of online participation in social movements may weaken commitment levels and cause, leading to "slacktivism" (Gladwell 2010).

Volatility in the social media public sphere is due to technological structure of social media, which fosters a high degree of individualization or "networked atomisation". Social media are "personal media" (Papacharissi 2002) as these accounts belonging to specific individuals, rather than a collective group, that form the basic unit of the social organization (Wellman 2001). The social media public sphere has enabled individual Internet users to collectively express themselves online, and their reactions, views and sentiments can be aggregated in the form of metrics that measure public sentiments. Therefore, the reactions of online crowds can influence the political climate, resulting in politicians adjusting their positions when they encounter negative reactions online. Social media public sphere is an important arena for politicians, parties and social movements to navigate by using appropriate political strategies to harness the power of online crowds and their online reactions to build and display support for their causes.

Online communities have the potential for political purposes such as mobilization, petitions, protests and campaigns. Hence, online communities do not necessarily exist only on the Internet; some may be hybrid. Members may actually meet each other physically first, and subsequently, form an online community, or they may interact online and later meet offline. The first type can be characterized as a virtualized online community; the second as de-virtualized. Also, group members who interact online and offline are not the same, thus the hybrid structures can intersect in each community. Such online and offline interactions between its participants can help strengthen the community.

Online communities also can be categorized based on various factors: evolution versus formalized creation, digital platforms for communication (e.g., social media, webchats, forums, wikis, blogs or microblogs), or topic of focus. Therefore, the structure and organization of political online communities can be very different (Smitten 2008). The common theme in such online communities is their objective and drive in playing their role to influence the political process and sociopolitical system. Online communities can use the Internet to organize themselves internally as well as interact with the outside world. There are many ways where online communities may operate politically, for example, articulating and aggregating interests, garnering political support, as well as political socialization and recruiting of political personnel (Fuhse 2005). Interactivity is one of the important aspects of digital technology in promoting democracy in society (Endres and Warnick 2004; Heeter 1989; McMillan and Hwang 2002; Stromer-Galley 2004; Stromer-Galley and Baker 2006; Stromer-Galley and Foot 2002; Sundar, Kalyanaraman, and Brown 2003; Warnick et al. 2005) as it enables citizens to communicate horizontally among themselves, and for them to communicate vertically with elites.

In democratic discourse, anonymous expression is seen as important because it allows unpopular opinions by marginalized, disadvantaged or isolated members of a community to be published without fear of recrimination (McKenna and Bargh 1998). However, anonymity also allows people to attack others through flaming and trolling. Anonymity is both a shield and a sword—it can protect the freedom of expression of weaker minority groups, but it can also cause chaos in online communities as people express their views with minimal personal accountability (Stromer-Galley and Wichowski 2011).

Online community members may discuss the main purpose of the group on their digital platforms, as well as choose their leaders in e-polls. Virtual groups can function like a "school for democracy" because political socialization can occur due to interactions between group participants which form their political attitudes. Digital media can also be used to mobilize passive members and recruit new supporters by describing the issue at hand and requesting for financial support or political action. Political campaigns can reach out to the public through websites and social media pages that contain relevant information about the issue, current events, actions and success stories. One can also assess public opinion on current issues through online polls. Online communities can also support other campaigns by sharing or republishing content in their groups (Smitten 2008). Online campaigns can also have an offline dimension. For example, online communities can organize an online petition or email protests to politicians or authorities. Digital technology can be used to organize supporters and members for physical protests and demonstrations. Content in prominent online communities may also capture the attention of traditional media which may feature their position or content, and this may attract the attention of politicians who may be pressured to take some form of action to address the highlighted issues.

However, if the political online community is unable to clearly define or agree collectively about its objective(s), then it will not have a clear direction and plan of action, which will weaken the group. Online communities also face offline structural issues such as legislative and executive threats from the authorities who may pass obstructive laws and arrest members as they perceive these groups as disrupting the system and challenging the power structure (Smitten 2008). Furthermore, the Internet is inundated with many groups since anyone can easily start an online community. To gain attention and be taken seriously by politicians and the authorities, online communities need to build up credibility. In essence, online communities may be successful in raising public attention, but offline action needs to happen to effect political change.

Online social networking sites are often seen as revolutionary as they allow more citizen participation in the form of information dissemination and content creation. The networked population gains greater access to information and opportunities to participate in public discussions, which may result in the group taking collective action (Iosifidis and Wheeler 2015). Web 2.0 advances plurality of expression and constructs information and communication networks that diffuse centralized power and democratize political expression (Castells 2012). The networked society constitutes of autonomous connected individuals connected to digital and social media that allow for public access and creation of multidimensional range of opinions and values that can shape political behaviour and outcomes. Thus, the Internet has the potential to influence social movements by using communication for online mobilization and protest actions and has facilitated the development of epistemic communities and advocacy networks (Keck and Sikkink 1998).

## ONLINE COMMUNITIES AND SOCIAL MOVEMENTS IN MALAYSIA

In Malaysia, due to the fractured nature of its multiethnic and multireligious polity, the online community is highly polarized, reflecting the politics of the country. Malaysia has often been described as a country divided by "2Rs", which are race and religion (Loh and Chin 2023). There are permanent tensions between the major ethnic groups—Malay, Chinese and Indian. On top of this, there are political tensions between East and West Malaysia (Chin 2019). Constitutionally, all Malays are legally Muslims and Islam has a status as the official religion of the Federation. In the 2020 Malaysian census, *bumiputera* (sons of the soil), which include the Malays, constitute about 69.4 per cent of the population while the ethnic Chinese and Indians constitute about 30 per cent. Since the country achieved its independence in 1957, the ethnic Malay majority has enjoyed a constitutionally protected special status, while other ethnic minorities experienced treatment as second-class citizens (Chin 2009, 2022). The affirmative action policies called the New Economic Policy (NEP), which were put in place to support the majority Malay population in the 1970s, are widely seen by the Chinese and Indians as holding them back from their full potential. The resentment being treated as second-class citizens is reflected in the non-Malay social media across all ages and segments. The rise of political Islam in the past three decades has added another dimension to the polarization as the Malay polity adopted Islam as the core part of their political identity (Chin 2021). A significant portion of the Malay population believes that Islam should play the pivotal role in the country's public policies while increasing number of conservative Malays hold the view that Malaysia should be an Islamic state. Parti Islam Se-Malaysia (Malaysian Islamic Party—PAS) has openly advocated for Malaysia to be turned into an Islamic state. On top of the political divide by race and religion, language is also a barrier. Each of the major ethnic groups—Malay, Chinese and Indian—prefer to use their own language in political groupings and this is reflected in the social media space as well. While most Chinese and Indian Malaysians understand *Bahasa Malaysia* as they study the national language in public schools, most Malays do not understand Mandarin or Tamil. Most Malaysian Indians do not understand Mandarin as well and vice-versa.

In the Borneo states, the divide is even more complicated. In both Sabah and Sarawak, there are more than thirty indigenous groups and more than fifty languages and dialects in each of these Borneo states. The largest group in Sabah is the Kadazandusun while in Sarawak it is the Iban. Both these groups have a significant number of speakers, and this is reflected in the social media groups in these states.

Previously, such polarizing divisions were kept control as the then Barisan Nasional (BN—National Front) government controlled traditional media—newspapers, television and radio—through legislation and ownership, either direct or indirect. This meant that it could dictate the dominant public narrative to ensure that it maintained its political hegemony, and there was little room for alternative viewpoints to emerge in the public sphere. The advent of the Internet in the late 1990s broke the BN government's media dominance (Chin 2003) as the opposition strove to use new information and communication technologies (ICTs) to propagate their ideology to the public such as email listservs, online discussion lists, Usenet groups, short message service (SMS), political websites and blogs. The Internet was seen as a "liberation technology" by 2010 (Diamond 2010) as it enabled the opposition to bypass the government's strict media controls.

In Malaysia, SMS was used during the 2004 general election while sociopolitical blogs influenced the 2008 general election as they provided alternative information to the government-controlled news on traditional media. When social media developed, online communities emerged as netizens interacted regularly through technological platforms and developed relationships (Gruzd, Wellman, and Takhteyev 2011), which facilitated communication, networking and mobilization among the populace. A study conducted by Leong et al. (2020) on Bersih, a social media-enabled movement that advocated for clean and fair elections in Malaysia that eventually morphed into a transnational coalition, found that clustering and structuring emergence enabled the movement to evolve across three different phases from dispersed individuals to dispersed groups, eventually resulting in a networked group. In Bersih's situation, social media enabled a global network of active groups to be linked to a core group of city coordinators who could consolidate resources and capabilities. Unlike other digitally enabled social movements where core groups are loosely defined and unstructured, Bersih's structuring emergence, through relational and cognitive mechanisms, led movement members to assign roles to core group members which reduced conflict and maintained commitment movement (Leong et al. 2020). Social media also enabled diverse framings of the cause by different groups in Bersih to converge and align by enabling open large-scale deliberations (Leong et al. 2020), which is a critical condition for the emergence and sustainability of collective action (Benford and Snow 2000; McAdam, McCarthy, and Zald 1996). Social media also enabled Bersih's participants to highlight any event or issue that relates to its cause. A study by Lim (2017) also found that Malaysian society felt a sense of "civic responsibility" to support the Bersih movement and contribute to the public discourse by organizing and disseminating information online using their personal (and public) social networking sites. Online attention on its activities, such as the support for overseas Malaysian to vote, showcased the movement's success, which is critical for maintaining its momentum and ability for large-scale mobilization that can influence the political environment (Leong et al. 2020).

Realizing that its political dominance was being chipped away by the opposition's mastery of ICTs, the then BN government decided to jump on the bandwagon and joined its political competitors in cyberspace by establishing its New Media Unit and recruiting political bloggers; these subsequently morphed into cybertroopers who were well-versed with social networking sites. Facebook and other social media platforms such as X (formerly known as Twitter) were used in the 13th general election (GE13) in 2013, while Facebook Live and WhatsApp were prominent GE14. In a study conducted by Johns and Cheong (2021), WhatsApp's closed architecture and end-to-end encryption made it useful for activists and communities to resist and subvert state-based surveillance and control of public conversations on social media. Meanwhile, TikTok became influential during the recently concluded 15th general election (GE15) in 2022, especially on first-time voters who could automatically vote upon reaching eighteen, thanks to the passing of the Undi 18 (Vote18) Bill.

The reliance on social media as the main political communication tool in Malaysia has amplified tensions and polarization surrounding race and religion. Politicians and political parties use simplified and emotive messages in order to score political points. For example, the United Malays National Organisation (UMNO) propagated a narrative that Malay voters would sell out their race and religion if they voted against the party. During the recent 15th general election in 2022 and six state elections in 2023, PAS's TikTok campaign gained traction among the conservative Malay-Muslim votes who were exhorted that it was an "obligatory holy struggle" to defend their faith by voting not just for a political party but for an Islamic government that upholds the Quran (Leong 2023; Chin 2023). Welsh (2020) states that polarization has exacerbated because some Malaysian political parties no longer have strong grassroots connection and patronage resources after 2018. Coupled with the loss of media control of the dominant narrative, party leaders use race and religious divisive rhetoric to attract undecided voters and compensate for their loss of reliable grassroots support, which has exacerbated polarization in the country. Such simplistic messages and slogans that call on voters' support while demonizing political opponents such as "Anything but UMNO", "No to DAP [Chinese]", "Save Malaysia [from Najib and UMNO]" and "Protect Islam" are easier to communicate to the populace as it taps on their emotional insecurities and righteous indignation rather than discussing substantive issues and policy reforms.

Johns and Cheong (2021)'s study on WhatsApp showed that unverified information such as rumours and conspiracy theories flow more freely through WhatsApp groups due to insularity within a closed "socio-technical system" that result in users only trusting insiders and rejecting mainstream news and "official" accounts as inauthentic and fake. While these encrypted instant-messaging applications are "safe spaces" where activists and other political communities can retreat into to avoid state surveillance or censorship, the lack of "moderating mechanisms" meant that there are minimal checks on the validity and quality of information being circulated in these private groups, compared to social media which is more public. Furthermore, false information is easily spread through WhatsApp due to its emotive content that creates a sense of anxiety and urgency that causes users to suspend rational judgement. If the information is received from a known and trusted contact, users are more likely to believe its validity; combined with the forward function's haptic qualities and the end-to-end encryption security, they are more likely to share by forwarding to various WhatsApp groups that they belong to. The constant forwarding results in the virality of the content which may reinforce and normalize conspiratorial belief.

Increasingly, Malaysian voters obtain their news from social media echo chambers that reflect and reinforce their own beliefs, perspectives and ideologies. Memon (2017) argues that millennials obtain news and opinions mainly from social media channels, which they also use to comment and debate. Echo chambers are "a bounded, enclosed media space that has the potential to both magnify the messages delivered within it and insulate them from rebuttal" (Jamieson and Cappella 2008), a situation where people are in as a result of media supply, distribution and/or their own demand. While some netizens prefer to seek out "attitude-consistent" (Arguedas et al. 2022) information that reinforces their preexisting views, some end up in "filter bubbles" where algorithms influence the personalization of search engine results and social media feeds that create "a unique universe of information for each of us" (Pariser 2011) which contains what we agree with and hides information that we dislike to reduce cognitive dissonance. These developments fuel polarization as people become insulated from exposure to ideologically different viewpoints which will diminish mutual understanding and subsequently lead to a situation where people become so extreme that they share very little common ground. Clearly, the digital media-tization of politics in Malaysia has intensified feelings of discontent which results in increasing polarization in society.

In Malaysia, other than ethnic and religious cleavages, there is also the language divide. This is especially true of political-theme pages or groups. The end result is the creation of "language-bubble" echo chambers where people from the same language group often reinforce each other's views. While online communities who use vernacular languages are often from the same ethnic group (Malays—*Bahasa Malaysia*, Chinese——Mandarin and Indians—Tamil), those that converse primarily in English consist of members from various ethnic groups but are primarily from the middle- and upper-class groups whose preferred *lingua franca* is English, which adds to the complexity in cyberspace. This is, of course, not unique to Malaysia and is often seen in political social media spaces where users prefer to flock to pages, groups and sites that reflect and reinforce their political views, leading to increasing polarization in the political spectrum.

Meanwhile, the other 13 per cent of the Malaysian population comes from the East Malaysian states of Sabah and Sarawak where the demography is completely different. There are more than thirty official ethnic groups in Sarawak and more than forty in Sabah. Politically, these groups can be broadly divided up into three major groups: Muslim *bumiputera*, non-Muslim *bumiputera* and Chinese. This three-way divide is reflected in the online communities as well, especially in political social media groups.

## WHAT THIS BOOK IS ABOUT

The objective of this book is to explore the development of social media and emergence of politically active cyber-communities in Malaysia, with an emphasis on how the ethnic-based political parties used the cyberspace to promote their platform and agenda. As a plural society with multiethnic, multireligious citizens, there is no single online social media site or platform in Malaysia that encompasses the main public discourse. Instead, there are many social media sites that populate the Malaysian social media environment, drawing inhabitants from similar ethnicity, religion, language or region. Malaysia's polarization caused by race, religion and regional divide will play central themes in the book which aims to investigate the environment of such social media sites and cyber-communities in various ethnic, religious, language and regional groups and gain comprehensive understanding of how they operate in Malaysia's cyberspace. It is impossible to cover the entire spectrum of online communities in Malaysia, thus a small volume such as this will have to choose which community to study and understand.

What is clear from this collection of chapters is that social media is now the dominant form of political communication in Malaysia. This has led to some writers claiming that the upcoming Malaysia elections can be won by social media. This claim is not without foundation. In the 2022 presidential elections in the Philippines, Ferdinand "Bongbong" Marcos Jr., the son of the late kleptocrat Ferdinand Marcos, was able to win the elections with the biggest margin in decades. Many observers cite social media as the key reason why he won the vote despite his family's dismal human rights record and wholesale theft of the Philippines (Mendoza 2022; Arugay and Baquisal 2022). Marcos was able to use Facebook and TikTok to dominate the narratives during the campaign and this is reflected in the final results. Marcos won 31.6 million votes against his nearest opponent, Leni Robredo, who took in only 15 million votes. There is no reason to think that such a scenario cannot happen in Malaysia.

Lastly, the book hopes to contribute to the theoretical discussion on how these online communities have empowered minorities in Malaysia and allow groups to organize themselves and provide a voice to their political interests. While it is not possible to study every politically active group on cyberspace, we have a selection of case studies which we think will shed enough light on the political cyberspace in Malaysia.

Chapter Two deals with the Malay online community, politically the most important segment of Malaysia's cyberspace. Mohd Azizuddin Mohd Sani and Azahar Kasim provide an overview of Malay-language sociopolitical online sites and cyber-communities, focusing on political parties such as the United Malays National Organisation (UMNO), Parti Pribumi Bersatu Malaysia (Bersatu), Parti Islam Se-Malaysia (PAS) and their supporters. The chapter explores the differences and similarities between members of the various Malay-language online communities as well as the current sociopolitical issues that dominate the online public discussions.

In Chapter Three, Ahmad Farouk Musa and Ahmad Fauzi Abdul Hamid analysed the space occupied by the Islamists in Malaysia. The chapter focuses on the role of the Islamic Renaissance Front (IRF) as a case study of a Muslim online community that discusses and highlights reformist issues relating to the practice of Islam in Malaysia in the digital world based on Habermas's concept of the public sphere. The chapter explains IRF's transformation from using the brick-and-mortar approach to the digital tools sphere due to the COVID-19 pandemic. Through video conferencing tools and social media platforms, it has managed to reach a wider audience and give a voice to marginalized groups while promoting a progressive Islamic reform discourse that actively engages with modernity.

In Chapter Four, Yuen Beng Lee, Ng Miew Luan and Jerry Tan Yang Sheng deal with Mandarin-speaking online communities. This chapter examines various Chinese language sociopolitical online communities that exist on social media. Specifically, it focuses on cyber-groups that discuss sociopolitical issues that affect the Chinese language community. These include political parties such as the Malaysian Chinese Association (MCA) and Democratic Action Party (DAP), including its supporters. The chapter also covers Chinese language civil society and non-governmental groups such as Dong Zong and the United Chinese School Committees' Association of Malaysia.

In Chapter Five, Anantha Raman Govindasamy and Kavitha Ganesan examine the consumption and dissemination of information relating to political and socioeconomic discourse among Malaysian Indian online communities. In the chapter, they explore how the various cyber-platforms such as emails, blogs, online forums, online media and even text messages have played a crucial role in reshaping Malaysian Indians' perception on the then-ruling Barisan Nasional government, as well as specific issues such as Tamil schools, urban poverty, Hindu temples and general matters relating to good governance, corruption, human rights and ethnic supremacy in Malaysia. The authors also discuss the use of social media tools such as WhatsApp and Facebook as a source of information and platform for discussion and debate, especially among the younger generation, and this had an observable impact during the 14th general elections in 2018. In this chapter, based on documentary and close observations, the authors argue that online communities have become an alternative voice and a catalyst for Malaysian Indians' newfound voice.

In Chapter Six, James Chin looks at political communities using social media in the Borneo states of Sabah and Sarawak. He argues that many of these groups are using the social media to mobilize and reinforce state nationalism. The parochial nature of these groups means that local issues predominate discussions. For example, the issue of "PTI" or undocumented migrants is raised in all Sabah groups while this is largely absent in Sarawak groups. The common theme for both groups is the controversy over the Malaysia Agreement 1963 (MA63).

In Chapter Seven, Clarence Devadass, Pauline Pooi Yin Leong and Tan Meng Yoe examine how Christian communities in Malaysia discuss sociopolitical issues affecting mainstream Catholic and Protestant online communities, including those from the evangelical and non-denominational churches. The chapter reviews the different sociopolitical issues that arise in the online community discussions, especially in relation to the Bersih protests. The authors also analyse how the Christian online communities react to sociopolitical issues that affect the practice of their faith in social media communities as well as their ideological worldview as a minority religion in an Islamic-dominated country.

## REFERENCES

Adler, Paul S., and Seok-Woo Kwon. 2002. "Social Capital: Prospects for a New Concept". *Academy of Management Review* 27, no. 1: 17–40.

Agur, Colin. 2019. "Insularized Connectedness: Mobile Chat Applications and News Production". *Media and Communication* 7, no. 1: 179–88. https://doi.org/doi:10.17645/mac.v7i1.1802.

Antheunis, Marjolijn L., Patti M. Valkenburg, and Jochen Peter. 2010. "Getting Acquainted through Social Network Sites: Testing a Model of Online Uncertainty Reduction and Social Attraction". *Computers in Human Behavior* 26, no. 1: 100–109.

Arguedas, Amy R., Craig T. Robertson, Richard Fletcher, and Rasmus K. Nielsen. 2022. *Echo Chambers, Filter Bubbles, and Polarisation: A Literature Review.* Oxford: Reuters Institute for the Study of Journalism. https://reutersinstitute.politics.ox.ac.uk/echo-chambers-filter-bubbles-and-polarisation-literature-review.

Argyle, Michael, and Janet Dean. 1965. "Eye-Contact, Distance and Affiliation". *Sociometry* 28, no. 3: 289–304.

Arugay, Aries A., and Justin Keith A. Baquisal. 2022. "Mobilized and Polarized: Social Media and Disinformation Narratives in the 2022 Philippine Elections". *Pacific Affairs* 95, no. 3: 549–73.

Attwood, Feona. 2006. "Sexed Up: Theorizing the Sexualization of Culture". *Sexualities* 9, no. 1: 77–94.

Autio, Erkko, Linus Dahlander, and Lars Frederiksen. 2013. "Information Exposure, Opportunity Evaluation, and Entrepreneurial Action: An Investigation of an Online User Community". *Academy of Management Journal* 56, no. 5: 1348–71.

Barlow, John P. 2019. "A Declaration of the Independence of Cyberspace". *Duke Law & Technology Review* 18, no. 1: 5–7.

Baym, Nancy K. 2015. *Personal Connections in the Digital Age*. Cambridge, UK: Polity Press.

Benford, Robert D., and David A. Snow. 2000. "Framing Processes and Social Movements: An Overview and Assessment". *Annual Review of Sociology* 26, no. 1: 611–39.

Benkler, Yochai. 2006. *The Wealth of Networks: How Social Production Transforms Markets and Freedom*. New Haven, CT: Yale University Press.

Berlant, Lauren. 2008. *The Female Complaint*. Durham, NC: Duke University Press.

Biocca, Frank, Chad Harms, and Judee Burgoon. 2003. "Toward a More Robust Theory and Measure of Social Presence: Review and Suggested Criteria". *Presence: Teleoperators & Virtual Environments* 12, no. 5: 456–80.

Biocca, Frank, Judee K. Burgoon, Chad Harms, and Gates M. Stoner. 2001. "Criteria and Scope Conditions for a Theory and Measure of Social Presence". Fourth International Workshop on Presence, Philadelphia, USA.

Bollmer, Grant. 2018. "Software Intimacies (Social Media and the Unbearability of Death)". In *Digital Intimate Publics and Social Media*, edited by Amy S. Dobson, Brady Robards, and Nicholas Carah, pp. 45–58. Cham, Switzerland: Palgrave Macmillan. https://doi.org/https://doi.org/10.1007/978-3-319-97607-5_3.

Boyd, Danah M. 2011. "Social Network Sites as Networked Publics: Affordances, Dynamics, and Implications". In *A Networked Self: Identity, Community, and Culture on Social Network Sites*, edited by Zizi Papacharissi, pp. 39–58. New York and London: Routledge.

Boyd, Danah M., and Nicole B. Ellison. 2007. "Social Network Sites: Definition, History, and Scholarship". *Journal of Computer-Mediated Communication* 13, no. 1: 210–30.

Brändle, Gaspar. 2019. "Social Media and Virtual Communities". In *Core Concepts in Sociology*, edited by J. Michael Ryan, pp. 274–75. NJ: John Wiley & Sons.

Bruns, Axel. 2008. *Blogs, Wikipedia, Second Life, and Beyond: From Production to Produsage* (Vol. 45). New York: Peter Lang.

Bucher, Taina. 2012. "The Friendship Assemblage: Investigating Programmed Sociality on Facebook". *Television & New Media* 14, no. 6: 479–93.

Burt, Ronald S. 1997. "The Contingent Value of Social Capital". *Administrative Science Quarterly* 42, no. 2: 339–65.

————. 2009. *Structural Holes: The Social Structure of Competition.* Cambridge, MA: Harvard University Press.

Castells, Manuel. 2012. *Networks of Outrage and Hope: Social Movements in the Internet Age.* Cambridge, UK: Polity Press.

Chambers, Deborah. 2013. *Social Media and Personal Relationships.* New York, NY: Palgrave Macmillan.

Chin, James. 2003. "Malaysiakini.com and Its Impact on Journalism and Politics in Malaysia". In *Asia.com,* edited by K. C. Ho, Randy Kluver, and C. C. Yang, pp. 147–60. London: Routledge.

————. 2009. "The Malaysian Chinese Dilemma: The Never Ending Policy (NEP)". *Chinese Southern Diaspora Studies* 3: 167–82.

————. 2019. "The 1963 Malaysia Agreement (MA63): Sabah and Sarawak and the Politics of Historical Grievances". In *Minorities Matter: Malaysian Politics and People,* edited by Sophie Lemiere, pp. 75–92. Malaysia and Singapore: Strategic Information & Research Development Centre/ISEAS – Yusof Ishak Institute.

————. 2021. "Malaysia: Identity Politics, the Rise of Political Islam and Ketuanan Melayu Islam". In *Religion & Identity Politics: Global Trends and Local Realities,* edited by Mathews Mathew and Melvin Tay, pp 75–96. Singapore: World Scientific.

————. 2022. "Racism towards the Chinese Minority in Malaysia: Political Islam and Institutional Barriers". *Political Quarterly* 93, no. 3: 451–59.

————. 2023. "Anwar's Long Walk to Power: The 2022 Malaysian General Elections". *Round Table: The Commonwealth Journal of International Affairs* 112, no. 1: 1–13.

Clark, Herbert H., and Susan E. Brennan. 1993. "Grounding in Communication". In *Readings in Groupware and Computer-Supported Cooperative Work,* edited by Ronald M. Baecker. Burlington, Massachusetts: Morgan Kaufmann Publishers.

Coleman, James S. 1988. "Social Capital in the Creation of Human Capital". *American Journal of Sociology* 94 (Supplement): S95–S120.

Collins, Mauri P., and Zane L. Berge. 1997. "Moderating Online Electronic Discussion Groups". Paper presented at the American Educational Research Association (AERA) meeting, Chicago, IL, 24–28 March 1997.

Dabbish, Laura, Rosta Farzan, Robert Kraut, and Tom Postmes. 2012. "Fresh Faces in the Crowd: Turnover, Identity, and Commitment in Online Groups". ACM 2012 Conference on Computer Supported Cooperative Work, 11 February 2012.

Daft, Richard L., and Robert H. Lengel. 1986. "Organizational Information Requirements, Media Richness and Structural Design". *Management Science* 32, no. 5: 554–71.

Dahlander, Linus, and Lars Frederiksen. 2012. "The Core and Cosmopolitans: A Relational View of Innovation in User Communities". *Organization Science* 23, no. 4: 988–1007.

Darbinyan, Rem. 2022. "The Growing Role of AI in Content Moderation". *Forbes*, 14 June 2022. https://www.forbes.com/sites/forbestechcouncil/2022/06/14/the-growing-role-of-ai-in-content-moderation/?sh=2d4ee4314a17.

Davidson, Brittany I., Simon L. Jones, Adam N. Joinson, and Joanne Hinds. 2019. "The Evolution of Online Ideological Communities". *PLoS ONE* 14, no. 5. https://doi.org/https://doi.org/10.1371/journal.pone.0216932.

Diamond, Larry. 2010. "Liberation Technology". *Journal of Democracy* 21, no. 3: 69–83.

Dobson, Amy S., Nicholas Carah, and Brady Robards. 2018. "Digital Intimate Publics and Social Media: Towards Theorising Public Lives on Private Platforms". In *Digital Intimate Publics and Social Media*, edited by Amy S. Dobson, Brady Robards, and Nicholas Carah. Cham, Switzerland: Palgrave Macmillan.

Dolata, Ulrich, and Jan-Felix Schrape. 2016. "Masses, Crowds, Communities, Movements: Collective Action in the Internet Age". *Social Movement Studies* 15, no. 1: 1–18.

Endres, Danielle, and Barbara Warnick. 2004. "Text-Based Interactivity in Candidate Campaign Web Sites: A Case Study from the 2002 Elections". *Western Journal of Communications* 68, no. 3: 322–43.

Faraj, Samer, Sirkka L. Jarvenpaa, and Ann Majchrzak. 2011. "Knowledge Collaboration in Online Communities". *Organization Science* 22, no. 5: 1224–39.

Feenberg, Andrew. 1989. "The Written World: On the Theory and Practice of Computer Conferencing". In *Mindweave: Communication, Computers and Distance Education*, edited by Robin Mason and Anthony Kaye. Oxford: Pergamon Press.

Fernback, Jan. 1999. "There is a There There: Notes Toward a Definition of Cybercommunity". In *Doing Internet Research: Critical Issues and Methods for Examining the Net*, edited by Steve Jones, pp. 203–20. California: Sage Publications.

Figallo, Cliff. 1998. *Hosting Web Communities: Building Relationships, Increasing Customer Loyalty, and Maintaining a Competitive Edge*. New York: John Wiley & Sons, Inc.

Fineman, Meredith. 2014. "What We Post Online Is Forever, and We Need a Reminder". *Inc.*, 24 November 2014. https://www.inc.com/meredith-fineman/what-we-post-online-is-forever-and-we-need-a-reminder.html.

Fisher, Greg. 2019. "Online Communities and Firm Advantages". *Academy of Management Review* 44, no. 2: 279–98. https://doi.org/https://doi.org/10.5465/amr.2015.0290.

Fuhse, Jan. 2005. "Theorien des politischen Systems: David Easton und Niklas Luhmann. Eine Einführung". Wiesbaden, Germany: VS Verlag für Sozialwissenschaften. https://doi.org/https://doi.org/10.1007/978-3-322-80763-2.

Fukuyama, Francis. 1995. *Trust: The Social Virtues and the Creation of Prosperity.* New York: The Free Press.

Gerbaudo, Paolo. 2012. *Tweets and the Streets: Social Media and Contemporary Activism.* London: Pluto Press.

———. 2022. "Theorizing Reactive Democracy: The Social Media Public Sphere, Online Crowds and the Plebiscitary Logic of Online Reactions". *Democratic Theory* 9, no. 2: 120–38. https://doi.org/https://doi.org/10.3167/dt.2022.090207.

Giddens, Anthony. 1992. *The Transformation of Intimacy: Sexuality, Love and Eroticism in Modern Societies.* Cambridge, UK: Polity Press.

Gilbert, Sarah. 2017. "Portraits of Participation: Exploring the Relationship between Social Motivators and Facets of Participation in a Twitter-Based Community". Proceedings of the 50th Hawaii International Conference on System Sciences.

Gillespie, Tarleton. 2018. *Custodians of the Internet: Platforms, Content Moderation, and the Hidden Decisions That Shape Social Media.* New Haven, CT: Yale University Press.

Gladwell, Malcolm. 2010. "Small Change: Why the Revolution Will Not Be Tweeted". *The New Yorker*, 4 October 2010. https://www.newyorker.com/magazine/2010/10/04/small-change-malcolm-gladwell.

Goleman, Daniel. 1995. *Emotional Intelligence.* London: Bantam Books.

Granovetter, Mark S. 1973. "The Strength of Weak Ties". *American Journal of Sociology* 78, no. 6: 1360–80.

———. 1982. "The Strength of Weak Ties: A Network Theory Revisited". In *Social Structure and Network Analysis*, edited by Peter V. Marsden and Nan Lin, pp. 105–30. Beverly Hills: Sage Publications.

Grimes-Viort, Blaise. 2010. "6 Types of Content Moderation You Need to Know About". *Social Media Today*, 7 December 2010.

Gruzd, Anatoliy, Barry Wellman, and Yuri Takhteyev. 2011. "Imagining Twitter as an Imagine Community". *American Behavioral Scientist* 55, no. 10: 1294–318.

Gunawardena, Charlotte N. 1995. "Social Presence Theory and Implications for Interaction Collaborative Learning in Computer Conferences". *International Journal of Educational Telecommunications* 1, no. 2/3: 147–66.

Gunawardena, Charlotte N., and Frank J. Zittle. 1997. "Social Presence as a Predictor of Satisfaction within a Computer Mediated Conferencing Environment". *American Journal of Distance Education* 11, no. 3: 8–26.

Habermas, Jürgen. 1991. *The Structural Transformation of the Public Sphere: An Inquiry into a Category of Bourgeois Society*. Cambridge, Mass.: MIT Press.

Hacker, Kenneth L. 1996. "Missing Links in the Evolution of Electronic Democratization". *Media, Culture and Society* 18, no. 2: 213–32.

Hamza, Alshenqeeti. 2016. "Are Emojis Creating a New or Old Visual Language for New Generations? A Socio-semiotic Study". *Advances in Language and Literary Studies* 7, no. 6.

Handy, Charles. 1995. "Trust and the Virtual Organization". *Harvard Business Review* 73, no. 3: 40–50.

Haythornthwaite, Caroline, and Barry Wellman. 1998. "Work, Friendship and Media Use for Information Exchange in a Networked Organization". *Journal of the American Society for Information Science* 46, no. 12: 1101–14.

Heeter, Carrie. 1989. "Implications of New Interactive Technologies for Conceptualizing Communication". In *Media Use in the Information Age: Emerging Patterns of Adoption and Consumer Use*, edited by Jerry L. Salvaggio and Jennings Bryant, pp. 217–35. NJ: Lawrence Erlbaum Associates.

Hjorth, Larissa, and Michael Arnold. 2013. *Online@AsiaPacific: Mobile, Social and Locative Media in the Asia-Pacific*. New York and London: Routledge.

Hobbs, Mitchell, Stephen Owen, and Livia Gerber. 2016. "Liquid Love? Dating Apps, Sex, Relationships and the Digital Transformation of Intimacy". *Journal of Sociology* 53, no. 2: 271–84.

Hopkins, Susan, and Naomi Ryan. 2014. "Digital Narratives, Social Connectivity and Disadvantaged Youth: Raising Aspirations for Rural and Low Socioeconomic Young People". *International Studies in Widening Participation* 1, no. 1: 28–42.

Hsieh, Sara H., and Timmy H. Tseng. 2017. "Playfulness in Mobile Instant Messaging: Examining the Influence of Emoticons and Text Messaging on Social Interaction". *Computers in Human Behavior* 69: 405–14.

Huckfeldt, Robert, Jeanette M. Mendez, and Tracy L. Osborn. 2004. "Disagreement, Ambivalence, and Engagement: The Political Consequences of Heterogeneous Networks". *Political Psychology* 25, no. 1: 65–95.

Iacono, C. Suzanne, and Suzanne Weisband. 1997. "Developing Trust in Virtual Teams". Proceedings of the 1997 30th Annual Hawaii International Conference on System Sciences, Maui, HI.

Iosifidis, Petros, and Mark Wheeler. 2015. "The Public Sphere and Network Democracy: Social Movements and Political Change?" *Global Media Journal* 13, no. 25: 1–17.

Jamieson, Kathleen H., and Joseph N. Cappella. 2008. *Echo Chamber: Rush Limbaugh and the Conservative Media Establishment*. New York: Oxford University Press.

Jamieson, Lynn. 2013. "Personal Relationships, Intimacy and the Self in a Mediated and Global Digital Age". In *Digital Sociology: Critical Perspectives*, edited by Kate Orton-Johnson and Nicholas Prior. London: Palgrave Macmillan.

Johns, Amelia, and Niki Cheong. 2021. "The Affective Pressures of WhatsApp: From Safe Spaces to Conspiratorial Publics". *Continuum* 35, no. 5: 732–46.

Jones, S. 2002. "Review". In *Hanging Out in the Virtual Pub*, edited by Lori Kendall. Berkeley, CA: University of California Press. http://ark.cdlib.org/ark:/13030/kt367nc6m1/.

Keck, Margaret E., and Kathryn Sikkink. 1998. *Activists Beyond Borders: Advocacy Networks in International Politics*. Ithaca, NY: Cornell University Press.

Kehrwald, Benjamin A. 2008. "Understanding Social Presence in Text-Based Online Learning Environments". *Distance Education* 29, no. 1: 89–106.

Keisler, Sara, Jane Seigel, and Timothy W. McGuire. 1984. "Social Psychological Aspects of Computer-Mediated Communication". *American Psychologist* 39: 1123–34.

Kendall, Lori. 2002. *Hanging Out in the Virtual Pub*. Berkeley, CA: University of California Press.

Kim, Jae Wook, Jiho Choi, William Qualls, and Kyesook Han. 2008. "It Takes a Marketplace Community to Raise Brand Commitment: The Role of Online Communities". *Journal of Marketing Management* 24: 409–31.

Kim, Joohan, and Eun Joo Kim. 2008. "Theorizing Dialogic Deliberation: Everyday Political Talk as Communicative Action and Dialogue". *Communication Theory* 18, no. 1: 51–70.

Kollock, Peter. 1998. "The Economics of Online Cooperation: Gifts and Public Goods in Cyberspace". In *Communities in Cyberspace*, edited by Marc A. Smith and Peter Kollock. New York and London: Routledge.

Kwon, Seok-Woo, and Paul S. Adler. 2014. "Social Capital: Maturation of a Field of Research". *Academy of Management Review* 39: 412–22.

Lea, Martin, Russell Spears, Susan E. Watt, and Paul Rogers. 2000. "The InSIDE Story: Social Psychological Processes Affecting Online Groups". In *SIDE Issues Centre Stage: Recent Developments in Studies of De-individuation in Groups*, edited by Tom Postmes, Martin Lea, Russell Spears, and S. D. Reicher, pp. 47–62. Amsterdam: KNAW.

Lea, Martin, Tim O'Shea, Pat Fung, and Russell Spears. 1992. "'Flaming' in Computer-Mediated Communication: Observations, Explanations, and Implications". In *Contexts of Computer-Mediated Communication*, edited by Martin Lea. London: Harvester-Wheatsheaf.

Leong, Carmen, Isam Faik, Felix T. C. Tan, Barney Tan, and Ying Hooi Khoo. 2020. "Digital Organizing of a Global Social Movement: From Connective to Collective Action". *Information and Organization* 30, no. 4. https://doi. org/https://doi.org/10.1016/j.infoandorg.2020.100324.

Leong, Pauline P. Y. 2015. "Political Communication in Malaysia: A Study on the Use of New Media in Politics". *eJournal of eDemocracy and Open Government* 7, no. 1: 46–71.

———. 2021. "Digital Media: An Emerging Barometer of Public Opinion in Malaysia". *ISEAS Perspective*, no. 2021/38, 1 April 2021. https://www. iseas.edu.sg/articles-commentaries/iseas-perspective/2021-38-digital-media-an-emerging-barometer-of-public-opinion-in-malaysia-by-pauline-pooi-yin-leong/.

———. 2023. "Political Polarisation Marked Malaysia's Recent State Elections". *ISEAS Perspective*, no. 2023/84, 19 October 2023. https://www.iseas.edu. sg/articles-commentaries/iseas-perspective/2023-84-political-polarisation-marked-malaysias-recent-state-elections-by-pauline-pooi-yin-leong/.

Lim, Joanne B. Y. 2017. "Engendering Civil Resistance: Social Media and Mob Tactics in Malaysia". *International Journal of Cultural Studies* 20, no. 2: 209–27.

Loh, Benjamin Y. H., and James Chin, eds. 2023. *New Media in the Margins: Lived Realities and Experiences from the Malaysian Peripheries*. Singapore: Springer Nature.

Marquis, Christopher, Michael Lounsbury, and Royston Greenwood. 2011. "Introduction: Community as an Institutional Order and a Type of Organizing". *Research in the Sociology of Organizations* 33: ix–xxvii.

Mathieu, John E., and Dennis M. Zajac. 1990. "A Review and Meta-Analysis of the Antecedents, Correlates, and Consequences of Organizational Commitment". *Psychological Bulletin* 108, no. 2: 171–94.

McAdam, Doug, John D. McCarthy, and Mayer N. Zald. 1996. *Comparative Perspectives on Social Movements*. Cambridge: Cambridge University Press.

McChesney, Robert W. 2014. *Digital Disconnect: How Capitalism Is Turning the Internet against Democracy*. New York: New Press.

McGlotten, Shaka. 2013. *Virtual Intimacies: Media, Affect and Queer Sociality*. Albany, NY: State University of New York Press.

McKenna, Katelyn Y. A., Amie S. Green, and Marci E. J. Gleason. 2002. "Relationship Formation on the Internet: What's the Big Attraction?" *Journal of Social Issues* 58, no. 1: 9–31.

McKenna, Katelyn Y. A., and John A. Bargh. 1998. "Coming Out in the Age of the Internet: Identity 'Demarginalization' through Virtual Group Participation". *Journal of Personality and Social Psychology* 75: 681–94.

McMillan, Sally J., and Jang-Sun Hwang. 2002. "Measures of Perceived Interactivity: An Exploration of the Role of Direction of Communication,

User Control, and Time in Shaping Perceptions of Interactivity". *Journal of Advertising* 31: 29–43.

Memon, Shaz. 2017. "How Millennials and Social Media Changed the World". *HuffPost*, 23 March 2017. https://www.huffingtonpost.co.uk/shaz-memon/how-millennials-and-socia_b_15537484.html.

Mendoza, Maria E. H. 2022. "Philippine Elections 2022: TikTok in Bongbong Marcos' Presidential Campaign". *Contemporary Southeast Asia: A Journal of International and Strategic Affairs* 44, no. 3: 389–95.

Meyerson, Debra, Karl E. Weick, and Roderick M. Kramer. 1996. "Swift Trust and Temporary Groups". In *Trust in Organizations: Frontiers of Theory and Research*, edited by Roderick M. Kramer and Tom R. Tyler, pp. 166–95. Sage Publications.

Miller, Kent D., Frances Fabian, and Shu-Jou Lin. 2009. "Strategies for Online Communities". *Strategic Management Journal* 30: 305–22.

Nguyen, Minh Hao, Jonathan Gruber, Will Marler, Amanda Hunsaker, Jaelle Fuchs, and Eszter Hargittai. 2022. "Staying Connected While Physically Apart: Digital Communication When Face-to-Face Interactions Are Limited". *New Media & Society* 24, no. 6: 2046–67. https://doi.org/https://doi.org/10.1177/1461444820985442.

Nielsen, Jakob. 2006. "The 90-9-1 Rule for Participation Inequality in Social Media and Online Communities". Nielsen Norman Group, 8 October 2006. https://www.nngroup.com/articles/participation-inequality/.

Nonnecke, Blair, and Jennifer Preece. 1999. "Shedding Light on Lurkers in Online Communities". *Ethnographic Studies in Real and Virtual Environments: Inhabited Information Spaces and Connected Communities*, 24–26 January 1999.

Novak, Petra K., Jasmina Smailović, Borut Sluban, and Igor Mozetič. 2015. "Sentiment of Emojis". *PLoS ONE* 10, no. 12.

Oldenburg, Ray. 1999. *The Great Good Place: Cafes, Coffee Shops, Bookstores, Bars, Hair Salons and Other Hangouts at the Heart of a Community*. 2nd ed. Marlowe & Company.

Papacharissi, Zizi. 2002. "The Virtual Sphere: The Internet as a Public Sphere". *New Media and Society* 4, no. 1: 9–27.

_____. 2015. *Affective Publics: Sentiment, Technologies and Politics*. Oxford: Oxford University Press.

_____. 2016. "Affective Publics and Structures of Storytelling: Sentiment, Events, Mediality". *Information, Communication & Society* 19: 307–24.

Pariser, Eli. 2011. *The Filter Bubble: What the Internet Is Hiding from You*. New York: Penguin Press.

Park, Eun Kyung, and S. Shyam Sundar. 2015. "Can Synchronicity and Visual Modality Enhance Social Presence in Mobile Messaging?" *Computers in Human Behavior* 45: 121–28.

Paul-Choudhury, Sumit. 2011. "Digital Legacy: The Fate of Your Online Soul". *New Scientist*, 19 April 2011. https://www.newscientist.com/article/mg21028091-400-digital-legacy-the-fate-of-your-online-soul/.

Plant, Robert. 2004. "Online Communities". *Technology in Society* 26, no. 1: 51–65.

Poster, Mark. 2001. "Cyberdemocracy: Internet and the Public Sphere". In *The Information Subject: Critical Voices in Art, Theory and Culture*, edited by Mark Poster and Stanley Aronowitz, pp. 95–115. New York and London: Routledge.

Preece, Jenny. 1998. "Empathic Communities: Reaching Out across the Web". *Interactions Magazine* 2, no. 2: 32–43.

_____. 2000a. "Community Tours". In *Online Communities: Designing Usability, Supporting Sociability*, pp. 34–36. John Wiley & Sons Ltd.

_____. 2000b. "Introduction". In *Online Communities: Designing Usability, Supporting Sociability*, p. 10. John Wiley & Sons Ltd.

_____. 2000c. "Research Speaks to Practice: Groups". In *Online Communities: Designing Usability, Supporting Sociability*, pp. 169–200. John Wiley & Sons Ltd.

_____. 2000d. "Research Speaks to Practice: Interpersonal Communication". In *Online Communities: Designing Usability, Supporting Sociability*, pp. 147–67. John Wiley & Sons Ltd.

_____. 2000e. "Sociability: Purpose, People and Policies". In *Online Communities: Designing Usability, Supporting Sociability*, p. 81. John Wiley & Sons Ltd.

_____. 2000f. "Usability: Tasks, Users and Software". In *Online Communities: Designing Usabiltiy, Supporting Sociability*, pp. 109–43 John Wiley & Sons Ltd.

Preece, Jenny, and Ben Shneiderma. 2009. "The Reader-to-Leader Framework: Motiviating Technology-Mediated Social Participation". *AIS Transactions on Human-Computer Interaction* 1, no. 1: 13–32.

Preece, Jenny, and Kambiz Ghozati. 1998a. "In Search of Empathy Online: A Review of 100 Online Communities". *AMCIS 1998 Proceedings* 33.

_____. 1998b. "Offering Support and Sharing Information: A Study of Empathy in a Bulletin Board Community". Computer Virtual Environments Conference, Manchester, UK.

Putnam, Robert D. 2000. *Bowling Alone: The Collapse and Revival of American Community*. New York: Simon & Schuster.

Putnam, Robert D., Lewis Feldstein, and Donald J. Cohen. 2004. *Better Together: Restoring the American Community*. New York: Simon & Schuster.

Rainie, Lee, and Barry Wellman. 2012. *Networked Individualism: The New Social Operating System*. Cambridge, MA: The MIT Press.

Ransbotham, Sam, and Gerald C. Kane. 2011. "Membership Turnover and Collaboration Success in Online Communities: Explaining Rises and Falls from Grace in Wikipedia". *MIS Quarterly* 35, no. 3: 613–27.

Reio Jr., Thomas G., and Susan J. Crim. 2006. "The Emergence of Social Presence as an Overlooked Factor in Asynchronous Online Learning". Online Submission.

Ren, Yuqing, Robert Kraut, and Sara Kiesler. 2007. "Applying Common Identity and Bond Theory to Design of Online Communities". *Organization Studies* 28, no. 3: 377–408. https://doi.org/10.1177/0170840607076007.

Resnick, Paul, and Robert E. Kraut. 2011. "Introduction". In *Building Successful Online Communities: Evidence-Based Social Design*, edited by Robert E. Kraut and Paul Resnick. Cambridge, MA: The MIT Press.

Rheingold, Howard. 1993. *The Virtual Community: Homesteading on the Electronic Frontier*. New York: HarperPerennial.

_____. 1994a. "A Slice of Life in My Virtual Community". In *Global Networks: Computers and International Communication*, edited by Linda M. Harasim, pp. 57–80. New York: The MIT Press.

_____. 1994b. *The Virtual Community: Finding Connection in a Computerized World*. London: Minerva Press.

_____. 2000. *The Virtual Community: Homesteading on the Electronic Frontier*. Cambridge, MA: The MIT Press.

Rice, Ronald E. 1987. "Computer-Mediated Communication and Organizational Innovations". *Journal of Communication* 37: 85–108.

_____. 1993. "Media Appropriateness: Using Social Presence Theory to Compare Traditional and New Organizational Media". *Human Communication Research* 19, no. 4: 451–84.

Rice, Ronald E., and George Barnett. 1986. "Group Communication Networks in Electronic Space: Applying Metric Multidimensional Scaling". In *Communication Yearbook* 9, edited by Margaret McLaughlin. Sage Publications.

Robards, Brady. 2014. "Digital Traces of the Persona through Ten Years of Facebook". *M/C Journal* 17, no. 3. https://doi.org/https://doi.org/10.5204/mcj.818.

Roberts, Sarah T. 2017. "Content Moderation". 2 May 2017. https://escholarship.org/uc/item/7371c1hf (accessed 17 November 2017).

Roseneil, Sasha. 2000. "Queer Frameworks and Queer Tendencies: Towards an Understanding of Postmodern Transformations of Intimacy". *Sociological Research Online* 5, no. 3. http://www.socresonline.org.uk/5/3/roseneil.html.

Rourke, Liam, Terry Anderson, D. Randy Garrison, and Walter Archer. 2001. "Assessing Social Presence in Asynchronous, Text-Based Computer Conferencing". *Journal of Distance Education* 14, no. 3: 51–70.

Ruby, D. 2023. "Social Media Users — How Many People Use Social Media in 2023". Demand Sage, Inc. https://www.demandsage.com/social-media-users/#:~:text=Social%20Media%20Users%20Statistics%202023,the%20world%20as%20of%202023 (accessed 25 January 2023).

Sallnäs, Eva-Lotta. 2005. "Effects of Communication Mode on Social Presence, Virtual Presence, and Performance in Collaborative Virtual Environments". *Presence: Teleoperators and Virtual Environments* 14, no. 4: 434–49.

Salmon, Gilly. 2000. *E-moderating: The Key to Teaching and Learning Online*. London: Kogan Page.

Sandefur, Rebecca L., and Edward O. Laumann. 1998. "A Paradigm for Social Capital". *Rationality and Society* 10: 481–501.

Schwartz, Mattathias. 2008. "The Trolls among Us". *New York Times Magazine*, 3 August 2008. https://www.nytimes.com/2008/08/03/magazine/03trolls-t.html.

Shafiz, Affendi Mohd Yusof, and Kamarul Faizal Hashim. 2014. "Exploring the Formation of Social Capital in a Malaysia Virtual Community". *The Journal of Community Informatics* 10, no. 1.

Shamsher, Shivali. 2023. "Social-Media Addiction: Time for a National Policy to Regulate Internet Use?" *New Straits Times*, 12 May 2023. https://www.nst.com.my/opinion/columnists/2023/05/908758/social-media-addiction-time-national-policy-regulate-internet-use.

Shirky, Clay. 2010. *Cognitive Surplus: Creativity and Generosity in a Connected Age*. London: Penguin Press.

Short, John, Ederyn Williams, and Bruce Christie. 1976. *The Social Psychology of Telecommunications*. John Wiley & Sons.

Siegel, Jane, Vitaly Dubrovsky, Sara Keisler, and Timothy W. McGuire. 1986. "Group Processes in Computer-Mediated Communication". *Organizational Behavior and Human Decision Processes* 37: 157–87.

Skiba, Dian J. 2016. "Face with Tears of Joy Is Word of the Year: Are Emoji a Sign of Things to Come in Health Care?" *Nursing Education Perspectives* 37, no. 1: 56–57.

Smitten, Susanne In der. 2008. "Political Potential and Capabilities of Online Communities". *German Policy Studies/Politikfeldanalyse* 4, no. 4: 33–62.

Soukup, Charles. 2006. "Computer-Mediated Communication as a Virtual Third Place: Building Oldenburg's Great Good Places on the World Wide Web". *New Media and Society* 8, no. 3: 421–40. https://doi.org/10.1177/1461444806061953.

Spa, Meira van der. 2004. "Cyber-Communities: Idle Talk or Inspirational Interaction?" *Educational Technology Research and Development* 52, no. 2: 97–105.

Spears, Russell, and Martin Lea. 1992. "Social Influence and the Influence of 'Social' in Computer-Mediated Communication". In *Contexts of Computer-Mediated Communication*, edited by Martin Lea. Birmingham, UK: Harvester Wheatsheaf.

Spears, Russell, Martin Lea, and Stephen Lee. 1990. "De-individuation and Group Polarization in Computer-Mediated Communication". *British Journal of Social Psychology* 29: 121–34.

Spencer, Liz, and Ray Pahl. 2006. *Rethinking Friendship: Hidden Solidarities Today*. Princeton: Princeton University Press.

Statista Research Department. 2023. "Share of Internet Users Using Communication Apps in Malaysia 2022, by App". https://www.statista.com/statistics/973428/malaysia-internet-users-using-communication-apps/.

Steinfield, Charles, Nicole B. Ellison, and Cliff Lampe. 2008. "Social Capital, Self-Esteem, and Use of Online Social Network Sites: A Longitudinal Analysis". *Journal of Applied Developmental Psychology* 29: 434–45.

Stromer-Galley, Jennifer. 2004. "Interactivity-as-Product and Interactivity-as-Process". *The Information Society* 20, no. 5: 391–94.

Stromer-Galley, Jennifer, and Alexis Wichowski. 2011. "Political Discussion Online". In *The Handbook of Internet Studies*, edited by Mia Consalvo and Charles Ess, pp. 168–87. UK: Wiley-Blackwell.

Stromer-Galley, Jennifer, and Andrea B. Baker. 2006. "Joy and Sorrow of Interactivity on the Campaign Trail: Blogs in the Primary Campaign of Howard Dean". In *The Internet Election: Perspective on the Web in Campaign 2004*, edited by Andrew P. Williams and John C. Tedesco, pp. 111–31. Lanham, MD: Rowman & Littlefield Publishers.

Stromer-Galley, Jennifer, and Kirsten A. Foot. 2002. "Citizens' Perceptions of Online Interactivity and Implications for Political Campaign Communication". *Journal of Computer-Mediated Communication* 8, no. 1. https://doi.org/https://doi.org/10.1111/j.1083-6101.2002.tb00161.x.

Sundar, S. Shyam, Sriram Kalyanaraman, and Justin Brown. 2003. "Explicating Web Site Interactivity: Impression Formation Effects in Political Campaign Sites". *Communication Research* 30: 30–59.

Tu, Chih-Hsiung. 2001. "How Chinese Perceive Social Presence: An Examination of Interaction in Online Learning Environment". *Educational Media International* 38, no. 1: 45–60.

Tufekci, Zeynep. 2014. "The Medium and the Movement: Digital Tools, Social Movement Politics, and the End of the Free Rider Problem". *Policy & Internet* 6, no. 2: 202–8.

_____. 2017. *Twitter and Tear Gas: The Power and Fragility of Networked Protest*. New Haven, Connecticut: Yale University Press.

Turkle, Sherry. 1997. "Virtuality and Its Discontents". In *Life on the Screen: Identity in the Age of the Internet*, edited by Sherry Turkle, pp. 233–54. Touchstone Publishing.

Uzzi, Brian. 1997. "Social Structure and Competition in Interfirm Networks: The Paradox of Embeddedness". *Administrative Science Quarterly* 42: 35–67.

van Dijck, Jose. 2013. *The Culture of Connectivity: A Critical History of Social Media*. Oxford: Oxford University Press.

van Dijck, Jose, and Thomas Poell. 2013. "Understanding Social Media Logic". *Media and Communication* 1, no. 1: 2–12. https://doi.org/https://doi.org/10.17645/mac.v1i1.70.

Wallace, Patricia. 1999. *The Psychology of the Internet.* Cambridge: Cambridge University Press.

Walther, Joseph B. 1992. "Interpersonal Effects in Computer-Mediated Interaction: A Relational Perspective". *Communication Research* 57: 381–98.

———. 1993. "Impression Development in Computer-Mediated Interaction". *Western Journal of Communications* 57: 381–98.

———. 1994. "Anticipated Ongoing Interaction versus Channel Effects on Relational Communication in Computer-Mediated Interaction". *Human Communication Research* 20, no. 4: 473–501.

———. 1996. "Computer-Mediated Communication: Impersonal, Interpersonal, and Hyperpersonal Interaction". *Communication Research* 23, no. 1: 3–43.

———. 2013. "Groups and Computer-Mediated Communication". In *The Social Net: Understanding Online Behavior*, edited by Yair Amichai-Hamburger. 2nd ed. Oxford: Oxford University Press.

Walther, Joseph B., and Caleb T. Carr. 2010. "Internet Interaction and Intergroup Dynamics: Problems and Solutions in Computer-Mediated Communication". In *The Dynamics of Intergroup Communication*, edited by Howard Giles, Scott Reid, and Jake Harwood, pp. 209–20. New York: Peter Lang Publishing.

Walther, Joseph B., and Ulla Bunz. 2005. "The Rules of Virtual Groups: Trust, Liking, and Performance in Computer-Mediated Communication". *Journal of Communication* 55: 828–46.

Wan Munira, Wan Jaafar, and Nabila Jaber. 2011. "Online Social Networking, Social Capital and Social Integration: An Experience of Multi-Ethnic Online Community Members in Malaysia". *Malaysian Journal of Youth Studies* 5: 107–26. https://iyres.gov.my/malaysian-journal-of-youth-studies-2019/2011/192-vol-5-jun/1551-online-social-networking-social-capital-and-social-integration-an-experience-of-multi-ethnic-online-community-members-in-malaysia.

Warnick, Barbara, Michael Xenos, Danielle Endres, and John Gastil. 2005. "Effects of Campaign-to-User and Text-Based Interactivity in Political Candidate Campaign Web Sites". *Journal of Computer-Mediated Communication* 10, no. 3. https://doi.org/https://doi.org/10.1111/j.1083-6101.2005.tb00253.x.

Weeks, Jeffrey, Brian Heaphy, and Catherine Donovan. 2001. *Same Sex Intimacies: Families of Choice and Other Life Experiments.* New York and London: Routledge.

Wellman, Barry. 2001. "Physical Place and Cyberplace: The Rise of Personalized Networking". *International Journal of Urban and Regional Research* 25, no. 2: 227–52.

————. 2002. "Little Boxes, Glocalization and Networked Individualism". Digital Cities II – Second Kyoto Workshop on Digital Cities, Berlin.

Wellman, Barry, and Milena Gulia. 1996. "Net Surfers Don't Ride Alone: Virtual Communities as Communities". In *Communities in Cyberspace*, edited by Marc A. Smith and Peter Kollack, pp. 167–94. Oakland, CA: University of California Press.

Welsh, Bridget. 2020. "Malaysia's Political Polarization: Race, Religion, and Reform". In *Political Polarization in South and Southeast Asia: Old Divisions, New Dangers*, edited by Thomas Carothers and Andrew O'Donohue, pp. 41–52. Washington, D.C.: Carnegie Endowment for International Peace.

Wenger, Etienne, Nancy White, and John D. Smith. 2009. "Technology and Community: A Glimpse of History". In *Digital Habitats: Stewarding Technology for Communities*. Portland, Or.: CPSquare Publications. http://technologyforcommunities.com/.

Wenger, Etienne, Nancy White, John D. Smith, and Kim Rowe. 2005. "Technology for Communities". In *CEFRIO Guidebook*. http://technologyforcommunities.com/CEFRIO_Book_Chapter_v_5.2.pdf.

Whittaker, Steve, Loen Terveen, Will Hill, and Lynn Cherny. 1998. *The Dynamics of Mass Interaction*. ACM CSCW '98, Seattle, W.A.

Wiener, Morton, and Albert Mehrabian. 1968. *Language within language: Immediacy, a Channel in Verbal Communication*. Minnesota: Appleton Press.

Wright, Scott. 2012. "From 'Third Place' to 'Third Space': Everyday Political Talk in Non-Political Online Spaces". *Javnost – The Public* 19, no. 3: 5–20.

# 2

# Malay Politics and Social Media in Malaysia

Mohd Azizuddin Mohd Sani and Azahar Kasim

The proliferation of social media has ramifications for Malaysia as it is a conduit for alternative information and democratic values. The Internet increases transparency by helping people avoid censorship, thus facilitating the flow of information about the government and people. This disrupts traditional established political structures and national security. During the 14th general election (GE14) in 2018 and the 15th general election (GE15) in 2022, social media was an important instrument in promoting democracy by opening up more space for Malaysians to deliberate on political issues. Pakatan Harapan (Alliance of Hope – PH) dominated social media and managed to form the government after GE14. From post-GE14 until GE15, political parties had more freedom to campaign online. The Malay-based political parties such as the United Malays National Organisation (UMNO), Parti Islam Se-Malaysia (Pan-Malaysian Islamic Party – PAS), and Parti Pribumi Bersatu Malaysia (Malaysian United Indigenous Party – Bersatu) had the same opportunity to project themselves as champions of core issues such as Malay rights and unity. This chapter traces the impact of social media during GE14 and GE15, and examines the Malay-based parties' mouthpiece websites, Facebook accounts and TikTok to see their narratives and coverage of issues of Malay unity and rights, particularly on protests over the International Convention on the Elimination of All Forms of Racial Discrimination (ICERD) and struggle for the Muafakat Nasional (National Consensus – MN) alliance.

## INTRODUCTION

The term social media or Web 2.0 refers to a new wave of Internet-based applications that enable greater interaction between users and also applications through user-generated content (Komito and Bates 2009). This content is varied and includes photographs, videos and text comments, forming a media-rich mosaic. Sites such as Twitter, MySpace, Facebook, TikTok and many more have been developed, where individuals not only post different types of information on their own accounts, but also link to that of their friends, thus the description of social networking applications. Basically, social media can take many forms such as Internet forums, news portals, weblogs, social blogs, wikis, podcasts, pictures and videos. Social media technologies include blogs, picture sharing, vlogs, wall postings, email and instant messaging, among many others. All these digital platforms have functions that allow them to be democratically interactive in ways unlike radio, television or the highly edited letter pages of newspapers and magazines. Social media supports the democratization of knowledge and information, transforming people from content consumers into content producers. Social media is distinct from traditional media such as newspapers, television and film. While social media is a relatively inexpensive and accessible tool that enables anyone to publish or access information, traditional media generally require certain skills and resources for their operations. This is why social media has a huge potential for democratization which has led to Habermas's (2006) argument that the Internet can have a subversive effect on authoritarian regimes and could threaten their survival. This chapter traces the phenomenon of social media in Malaysia.

Prior to the 12th general election (GE12) in 2008, the incumbent Barisan Nasional (National Front – BN), a coalition of thirteen parties including a Malay-based party namely UMNO, was confident about its grip on power due to its control of print and broadcasting media through ownerships and legislation. For instance, in 2007, Media Prima Berhad, with close links to UMNO, acquired all the private television stations including TV3, NTV7, 8TV and TV9 and owns them until today. Laws such as the Printing Presses and Publications Act (PPPA) and the Communications and Multimedia Act (CMA) (previously the Broadcasting Act) regulate the media. Hence, people went to online media for dissent against the government. BN was dismissive of the influence of sociopolitical bloggers (Lian 2016) who were challenging the government's narrative on social media, labelling them as hacks. This proved to be a miscalculation on its part as BN lost control of five states—Perak, Kedah, Penang, Kelantan and Selangor—and two-thirds majority in parliament at the federal level. On 25 March 2008, then prime minister and chairman of BN, Abdullah Ahmad Badawi, acknowledged that his government had lost the online information war in GE12. He said, "We didn't think it was important. It was a serious misjudgement. We thought that the newspapers, the print media, the television were important but young people were looking at text messages and blogs. (The influence of alternative media) was painful. But it came at the right time, not too late" (*New Straits Times* 2008).

This cost Abdullah his premiership as he subsequently stepped down to allow his deputy Najib Razak to take over as prime minister and chairman of BN in March 2009. The political losses in GE12 were a shock to the BN juggernaut, and it wasted no time jumping onto the Internet bandwagon. BN politicians and parties, who were previously critical of digital media, started creating their own blogs and social media accounts. Teams of cybertroopers, persons who are paid to spread political propaganda on the Internet, especially on social media platforms, were recruited by the BN government in the cyber warfare against the opposition Pakatan Rakyat (People's Alliance – PR). On 11 January 2011, Najib proactively engaged people via Twitter and Facebook by asking them to use the hashtag #tanyanajib (#asknajib) and post questions (*The Malaysian Insider* 2011), which he tried to answer as many as possible via YouTube, according to the Prime Minister's

Department (Ho 2011). Najib's 1Malaysia campaign, which sought to promote racial harmony, or justify Malay dominance, depending on one's point of view, also had a large online presence (Fama and Tam 2010, p. 81). As the first Malaysian prime minister to have a Facebook account, Najib (2010, p. 99) said, "One of the advantages of Facebook is that it allows me to interact directly, and so I can receive immediate feedback regarding comments, reviews, and actions implemented by the government. Therefore, it is a highly effective medium of communication that helps me to gain a genuine picture of the people's opinions and requests pertaining to certain issues."

Despite Najib and the BN government's best efforts to use digital media, it still could not recover lost ground in the 13th general election (GE13) in 2013. Although BN remained in power, it could not win convincingly as the then-opposition PR managed to garner more popular votes. The efforts by BN were not sufficient to win over online sentiment, which was dominated by the opposition. Social media was seen as the "opposition's playground" (Leong 2019; Cheong 2020). It was only during GE14 in 2018 that the opposition PH, which was formed after PR collapsed when PAS left the PR, managed to topple BN's longstanding control of the country. PH was a coalition party established for the GE14 by Parti Keadilan Rakyat (People's Justice Party – PKR), Parti Amanah Negara (National Trust Party – Amanah), Democratic Action Party (DAP) and Bersatu. Clearly, social media played a significant role in weakening BN's propaganda machinery by chiselling away at its public support and turning the tide towards PH, enabling them to win the general election. Scholars have argued that this "political tsunami" is a result of the netizen movement in social media.

PH's win in GE14 was an extraordinary political development because, for the first time, an opposition alliance managed to wrest control from BN, which had administered Malaysia for sixty-one years since its independence in 1957. PH won a simple majority of 113 out of 222 parliamentary seats, two more than the required for a simple majority while BN secured seventy-nine seats only. Interestingly, the PH coalition was led by Malaysia's former premier Mahathir Mohamad, aged ninety-two years old at that time, who was appointed as the seventh prime minister of Malaysia. In fact, Mahathir was previously from BN as the fourth prime minister from 1981 to 2003 for twenty-two years. BN's defeat was made possible by a so-called "Malaysian tsunami". John Sifton, Asia Advocacy Director at Human Rights Watch, said: "Nothing less than a historic political earthquake is underway in Malaysia right now" (*Aljazeera* 2018).

The new PH government promised to bring reforms, particularly in electoral system and good governance in Malaysia. However, it faced challenges from the now BN-led opposition which used social media to launch its attacks. For example, former prime minister Najib Razak embarked on a social media campaign using the moniker *"BossKu"* (MyBoss) and the tagline *"Malu Apa BossKu"* (Why the Shame, MyBoss) as a strategy to revive his political fortunes, despite losing the previous general election. There were also attacks, especially on social media, from right-wing Malay-Muslim groups when the PH government tried to accede ICERD, which led to street protests in the capital city of Kuala Lumpur. These external attacks combined with infighting led to the collapse of the PH coalition government before it could even serve a full term. Mahathir resigned as prime minister on 24 February 2020 and a new government was formed under the new alliance. This was led by the eighth prime minister Muhyiddin Yassin, president of Bersatu, who decided to leave PH together with a splinter group from PKR, and form the new government with BN, PAS, Gabungan Parti Sarawak (Sarawak Parties Alliance – GPS) and several parties from Sabah including Parti Bersatu Sabah (United Sabah Party – PBS) in March 2020. Muhyiddin also sacked Mahathir (chairman) and his son Mukhriz Mahathir (deputy president) from Bersatu. On 7 August 2020, Muhyiddin established a new coalition party called Perikatan Nasional (National Alliance – PN) from Bersatu, PAS and Parti Gerakan Rakyat Malaysia (Malaysian People's Movement Party – Gerakan).

However, the PN-led government did not last long and collapsed in August 2021 when fifteen members of parliament (MPs) from BN decided to withdraw their support for Muhyiddin as prime minister of Malaysia. Later that month, MPs were asked by the Yang di-Pertuan Agong, the Malaysian monarch, to nominate a new prime minister. A simple majority of 114 MPs chose Ismail Sabri Yaakob from BN, the then deputy prime minister to become the ninth prime minister of Malaysia. Ismail took oath on 21 August 2021. To avoid another collapse of government and stabilize the political situation, he decided to sign a memorandum of understanding (MOU) with the opposition PH led by its chairman Anwar Ibrahim, president of PKR. Interestingly, some of the MOU content involved reform agenda, such as the implementation of Undi 18 (Vote18) which reduced the legal voting age from twenty-one to eighteen, limiting the prime minister's term in office to a maximum of two terms or ten years, and introducing anti-hopping laws. However, continued infighting within Ismail's administration between BN and PN leaders caused instability and he subsequently dissolved parliament on 10 October 2022, paving the way for the 15th general election (GE15) on 19 November 2022. Unfortunately, the result of GE15 revealed that no coalition was able to obtain a simple majority and after protracted negotiations, the PH alliance managed to form a "unity" government consisting of BN, GPS, Gabungan Rakyat Sabah (Sabah People's Alliance – GRS), Parti Warisan (Heritage Party – Warisan), Parti Bangsa Malaysia (Malaysian Nation Party – PBM) and Parti Ikatan Demokratik Malaysia (Malaysian United Democratic Alliance – Muda). The idea of a "unity" government was proposed by the Yang di-Pertuan Agong, but PN refused to join the coalition.

Malaysia has undergone tremendous upheavals since GE14 in 2018 when PH overcame formidable challenges to dethrone the BN behemoth. Thus, it is critical to study the influence of social media during GE14 and follow up with the post-GE14 period, especially on the debates about Malay issues. When BN through UMNO and PAS lost in GE14, these two Malay dominant parties were relegated to the back seat as opposition members, which raised their anxieties about the future of the Malays. To regain back lost power, they decided to join forces against the ruling PH government and continue winning the hearts and minds of the Malays by championing the community's causes, particularly on issues of Malay rights and unity. Thus, UMNO and PAS formed the alliance called Muafakat Nasional (National Consensus – MN) which focused on the issue of Malay rights. One of their objectives was to protest and condemn the PH government's proposal to accede ICERD on the grounds that the move would undermine the Malaysian constitution and the rights of the Malays.

Hence, this chapter aims to examine how social media was used to propagate issues on Malay rights by three Malay-based parties particularly UMNO and PAS, as well as Bersatu. Bersatu formed PN with PAS but failed to be part of MN with PAS and UMNO after UMNO rejected Bersatu joining MN. The findings will show how narratives about the Malay community have been operating on social media to change the political dynamics in Malaysia.

## Social Media in the 2018 General Election in Malaysia

It is undeniable that social media has contributed effectively to the democratization process in Malaysia. It is a means for political actors to engage and communicate with the public. To win elections, one has to capture the hearts and minds of netizens, particularly the youth. Clearly, with more people engaging with political parties via social media, Malaysia will become more democratic (Sani 2018).

Social media is effective for Malaysia's democracy because of high Internet penetration. Malaysia's Internet penetration had risen to 85.7 per cent in 2017 from just 70.0 per cent in 2015 (Alias 2018). This was also contributed by the increase in usage of computers and mobile phones. Households across Malaysia with computer and mobile phone access rose to 74.1 per cent and 98.1 per cent respectively in 2017, compared with 67.6 per cent and 97.9 per cent in 2015. Meanwhile, individuals using Internet aged fifteen years and above in Malaysia rose by nine percentage points to 80.1 per cent in 2017, from 71.1 per cent in 2015, according to the Department of Statistics Malaysia. As stated by the Individual and Household Survey Report on ICT Usage and Access, the percentage of individuals using computers has also increased 1.1 per cent to 69.8 per cent in 2017 compared to 68.7 per cent in 2015. Smartphone usage for Internet access has also increased to 97.7 per cent in 2017 compared to 97.5 per cent in 2015 (*New Straits Times* 2018a).

GE14 was held on 9 May 2018. This was the first time that coalition parties, namely BN, PH and the PAS-led coalition called the Gagasan Sejahtera (Ideas of Prosperity – GS) competed with each other. In the previous GE13 in 2013, PAS was part of the opposition PR to challenge BN. However, PAS decided to leave PH two years later in 2015 due to policy disagreements over Shariah law and Malay unity, and subsequently formed GS with smaller parties and non-government organizations (Sani 2015, 2018). Then prime minister Najib Razak, who was leading BN at that time, was aiming for a second mandate since winning GE13 in 2013. However, he was being challenged by his former mentor Mahathir Mohamad, who was also the longest-serving Malaysian prime minister of twenty-two years. Amid the scandals surrounding Najib, especially regarding the 1Malaysia Development Berhad (1MDB) issue, Mahathir made a comeback after retiring in 2003 to join forces with his former political foe Anwar Ibrahim (who was imprisoned at that time and later pardoned by the Yang di-Pertuan Agong and released in 2018 after Mahathir and PH won the GE14) and PH to run against Najib. The 1MDB, a state fund, was set up in 2009 through partnerships and foreign investment to promote Malaysia's development. The chairman was Najib himself. It was one of the biggest corruption scandals in the world after more than US$4.5 billion was stolen according to the US Department of Justice. This scandal was responsible for the downfall of BN government in 2018 and the arrest of Najib (who was later found guilty and imprisoned by the court in 2022), his wife (Rosmah Mansor) and close associates (Ellis-Petersen 2020). Ross Tapsell (2020, p. 12), a researcher with the Australian National University, explained: "When Malaysians discussed the election (GE14), they would invariably talk about Najib and the 1MDB wealth fund controversy".

In 2018, WhatsApp, Facebook and the smartphone were used as "weapons of the weak" to question the increasingly authoritarian rule of Prime Minister Najib Razak and the legitimacy of the corruption scandal (Tapsell 2020). This helped undermine the BN government. In GE14, social media was the most dominant medium of communication for the electorate to engage with political parties. According to the 2017 Digital News Report, prior to GE14 in 2018, WhatsApp users in Malaysia stood at 51 per cent. The report also found that Facebook and YouTube were also popular with Malaysians, with 58 per cent and 26 per cent users respectively. WeChat and Instagram share of users stood at 13 per cent (Zamani 2017). Deputy Prime Minister Ahmad Zahid Hamidi from the BN argued that the social media would play a huge role in GE14 as 80 per cent of voters in Malaysia are active users, especially youths who accessed news on social media rather than through print or broadcast. Ahmad Zahid claimed that 92 per cent of first-time young voters between eighteen and twenty-nine are active on social media (*The Borneo Post* 2017).

One essential point mentioned by Najib Razak and Ahmad Zahid was that the incumbent BN lost out on digital media to the opposition in the 2008 and 2013 general elections. In the 2008 general election, BN underestimated the impact of online media and did not realize that the opposition's dominance on social media was challenging its control of the public narrative. One reason why BN had less presence on social media in 2008 was because it was over reliant on print and broadcasting media as its campaign machinery, given its close connection and control of traditional media companies (Sani 2014a). During GE12 in 2008, sociopolitical bloggers were already using digital media to confront the ruling BN, but the incumbent government largely ignored them to its detriment. The Internet opened up public space for Malaysian citizens to deliberate on political issues and the opposition capitalized on this as a means to level the uneven playing field during campaigning in the general election (Sani 2014a; Jalli 2016).

After the "political tsunami" in GE12 in 2008 where it lost two-thirds control of parliament, BN wasted no time jumping onto the Internet bandwagon as its political parties and politicians started blogging and opening their own social media pages and accounts. It also started recruiting cybertroopers as part of its political communication machinery. Despite its best efforts, BN was unable to regain lost ground in GE13. While it managed to win in the 2013 general election, there was a huge vote swing from urban and suburban constituencies towards the opposition PR that led to BN losing the popular vote for the first time since 1969. During GE13 in 2013, social media such as Facebook, Twitter and YouTube were used extensively in campaigning compared to blogs which were more popular during the 2008 general election (Sani 2014b).

During GE14 in 2018, BN mobilized huge resources into using social media to dominate cyberspace in its campaign against the opposition PH and PAS. According to Tapsell, "They (BN) have far stronger presence on social media and on digital media in general in a variety of ways. There are far more pro-government blogs, websites, social media messaging, in short, there is a clear increase of the volume of online engagement compared to the 2013 elections. They know what they are doing this time around; they recognise the importance of new media and are engaged in a big way" (Edward 2018). Table 2.1 shows the prominence of several Malaysian political leaders from the government and opposition on social media. The data indicates that BN leaders had higher profiles on social media such as Facebook, Twitter, Instagram and YouTube compared to PH and GS politicians.

TABLE 2.1
Visibility of Malaysian Leaders on Social Media, 2018

| Leaders (party represented) | Facebook | | Twitter | | Instagram | | YouTube |
|---|---|---|---|---|---|---|---|
| | Followers | Like | Friends | Followers | Friends | Followers | |
| Najib Razak (BN) | 3,345,409 | 3,393,163 | 157 | 4,000,000 | 30 | 383,000 | 173,000 |
| Zahid Hamidi (BN) | 1,387,163 | 1,346,240 | 8,689 | 475,000 | 5,552 | 103,000 | 14,000 |
| Khairy Jamaluddin (BN) | 1,173,103 | 1,751,887 | 2,432 | 2,400,000 | 371 | 855,000 | 26,600 |
| Anwar Ibrahim (PH) | 1,598,105 | 1,631,957 | 14,200 | 1,100,000 | 3,169 | 39,900 | 236,000 |
| Wan Azizah Wan Ismail (PH) | 921,410 | 931,383 | 166 | 289,000 | 43 | 14,800 | 6,460 |
| Mahathir Mohamad (PH) | 2,550,435 | 2,567,553 | 63 | 403,000 | 7 | 76,600 | 29,700 |
| Lim Guan Eng (PH) | 453,306 | 452,972 | 412 | 418,000 | 3 | 2,224 | 22,800 |
| Hadi Awang (GS) | 348,251 | 346,983 | 4 | 39,600 | 0 | 16,700 | 23,300 |

Note: Data was collected on 29 March 2018.
Source: Sani (2018).

Najib had the greatest number of friends and followers on Facebook and Twitter while Khairy Jamaluddin, Minister of Youth and Sports, had the highest number of friends and followers on Instagram. Although Anwar Ibrahim was still imprisoned at that time after being found guilty of sexual abuse in 2015, he had the most clips on YouTube. UMNO activated all its 191 divisions to wage an online war and BN mobilized armies of cybertroopers. Then Prime Minister Najib Razak also launched a new web portal (https://therakyat.com) as a means of reaching out to the public during GE14 to counter the opposition which is skilful in cyber warfare and have attractive and interesting news or information, whether true or otherwise (Naidu 2018). However, critics argued that some of the followers were fake. For instance, Rob Waller, a UK-based software developer, exposed that Najib was among the top of a list of political leaders with fake followers. Waller used the "Fake Follower Check" and found Najib had the largest proportion of fake followers compared to seven other leaders from the United States, India, Australia, Thailand, Singapore, Japan and Vietnam (*Malaysia Now* 2021). However, it is difficult to prove and verify fake followers, although social media platforms normally take measures to remove fake accounts. The point to be highlighted here is not about fake followers, rather there is no doubt that by combining official and personalized postings, Najib was obviously one of Malaysia's most savvy social influencers (Daud 2018).

Meanwhile, Bersatu, then one of the coalition parties under PH in GE14, used memes, GIFs and short, quirky clips to increase its social media presence and woo younger voters. PH also launched an online "do-it-yourself" kit to distribute campaign materials. The DAP, another PH coalition member, utilized social media such as WhatsApp and Facebook to reach voters in rural areas following an increase in the Internet penetration rate. Amanah, also a PH coalition partner, used Facebook Live to broadcast its "Jom Channel FB Live"; it also formed "Media Oren" to reach the electorates (Sivanandam and Rahim 2018).

To control the public narrative, BN introduced the Anti-Fake News Act which came into effect in April 2018. The move was criticized because of the rush to pass the bill through parliament without sufficient deliberation or public debate, fuelling the suspicion that it was going to be used during the campaign period of the then-upcoming GE14 in 2018 (Lim 2020). Then Chairman of the Human Rights Commission of Malaysia, Razali Ismail, warned that the law could be used to exert even greater government control over free expression (*The Star Online* 2018a). However, this was denied by the then minister of youth and sports, Khairy Jamaluddin, who said that the Anti-Fake News Act was not meant to restrict freedom of expression but to prevent the spread of false news, which is detrimental to society and the country (Shahar 2018). Critics have argued that such anti-fake news laws reinforce the culture of fear in Malaysia, especially on social media. In its 2015 report, Human Rights Watch said, "a spiralling corruption scandal involving the government-owned 1MDB, whose board of advisors is chaired by Prime Minister Najib, led the government to block websites and suspend newspapers reporting on the scandal and to announce plans to strengthen its power to crack down on speech on the Internet" (Human Rights Watch 2015).

In terms of issues dominating the campaigns in GE14, a study conducted by Sani et. al. (2018) prior to the polling day on 9 May 2018 found that there were two main issues that would affect the Malaysian vote in GE14: race and religion versus economy and development. While 44.1 per cent of the 780 respondents agreed that race and religion were the most important issues, 301 respondents (or 38.6 per cent) felt that economic and development issues would influence their votes (see Table 2.2). This result means that electorates would vote based on race and religion rather than economy and development in GE14.

**TABLE 2.2**
**Issues of Race and Religion Are More Important Than**
**That of Economy and Development in GE14**

| No. | Items | Responses | Percentage |
|-----|-------|-----------|------------|
| 1. | Yes | 344 | 44.1 |
| 2. | No | 301 | 38.6 |
| 3. | Not Sure | 135 | 17.3 |

*Source*: Sani et al. (2018).

The majority of respondents (631, or 80.9 per cent) also said that social media was their main source of information about GE14 (see Table 2.3). Two things were expected. First, extensive campaigning would appear online through social media platforms more than through print and broadcasting media. And second which is related to Table 2.2, many more issues of race and religion would be disseminated online to influence electorates in GE14. This raised a concern that propagandists in all political parties would manipulate race and religion to win votes. Clearly, identity politics in Malaysia is very relevant.

This article focuses on the online campaigns of Malay-based political parties, particularly in the post-GE14 period.

TABLE 2.3
Social Media Is the Main Source of Information about GE14

| No. | Items | Responses | Percentage |
|-----|-------|-----------|------------|
| 1. | Yes | 631 | 80.9 |
| 2. | No | 128 | 16.4 |
| 3. | Not Sure | 21 | 2.7 |

Source: Sani et al. (2018).

## MALAY ISSUES ON SOCIAL MEDIA: PARTIES' MOUTHPIECES AND FACEBOOK

Interestingly, Malay issues were predominantly played out on social media after UMNO-BN became the opposition since the end of GE14 in 2018. Together with the defeated PAS in GE14, they managed to instil fear among the Malays by condemning the then newly minted PH government for allegedly liberalizing society in favour of non-Malays, thus affecting the Malay community's rights and culture. UMNO and PAS initiated two significant campaigns to reject any reform efforts by the PH government by capitalizing on the issue of protecting Malay rights and calling for Malay unity. The first campaign was the anti-ICERD movement which focused on preserving Malay rights and the special position of Malays and Indigenous people, also known as *Bumiputera* (sons of the soil), as enshrined in Article 153 of Malaysia's Federal Constitution. At this point in time, Bersatu was still part of the PH coalition party. The second campaign was the creation of Muafakat Nasional (National Consensus – MN) as a means to strengthen cooperation between opposition Malay-based parties UMNO and PAS to attack the PH government. When the PH government subsequently collapsed, Bersatu requested to join MN but was rejected by UMNO.

The next sections trace the issues of ICERD and MN as discussed on social media. We analyse both issues as propagated by UMNO,

PAS and Bersatu, through their party websites and Facebook accounts such as UMNO Online (https://umno-online.my/), *Harakah Daily* (https://harakahdaily.net/) and *Berita Bersatu* (https://bersatu.org/). Another section focuses on the coverage of both issues in the parties' official Facebook accounts, particularly articles in the Malay language. These discussions give us an understanding about the discourse in the Malay community on Malay issues, particularly in the Malay language or Malay version of publications produced by these three political parties.

## ICERD and Malay Rights

The coverage of online news portals was emotional on the issue of ICERD, with many of their sources coming from websites of political parties such as UMNO Online and PAS's *Harakah Daily*. UMNO Online (https://umno-online.my/?s=ICERD) had 248 articles about ICERD while *Harakah Daily* (https://harakahdaily.net/?s=ICERD) had 324 articles. As Bersatu was still part of the PH government at that time, its website *Berita Bersatu* (https://bersatu.org/) unsurprisingly did not published any article on ICERD. All published articles were negative about ICERD and attacked the PH administration. Clearly, UMNO and PAS took a hard-line position as the opposition and this issue was used to rally the Malays against the PH government by labelling it as anti-Malay because it allegedly used ICERD to remove the special position of the Malays and Indigenous people, although this is enshrined in the Federal Constitution.

Malaysia's ethnic-based identification can be traced to the colonial era's policy of divide and rule, which reinforced segregation rather than integration among the races. This pattern has been reinforced further by ethnic-based politics which has persisted until today. Since independence, the government has tried to strike a balance between the Malay majority and other ethnic minority groups—mainly the Chinese and Indians. Malaysia's affirmative action policies are largely influenced by the 13 May 1969 racial riots which were caused by communal tensions between the Malay and Chinese communities. Soon after the incident, the Malaysian government introduced *Dasar Ekonomi Baru* or the New Economic Policy (NEP), an affirmative action policy aimed at achieving national unity, harmony and integrity through socioeconomic restructuring to reduce poverty levels in all ethnic groups, especially the Malay community. The National Development Policy (NDP) associated with the Second Outline Perspective Plan for 1991–2000, and then by the National Vision Policy linked to the Third Outline Perspective Plan for 2001–2010 superseded the NEP and emphasized achieving rapid growth, industrialization and structural change but maintained similar affirmative action featuring the restructuring of society and greatly favoured the Malays and *Bumiputera* (Jomo 2004; Yusof and Bhattasali 2008; Lee 2021).

Debates on this issue continue today and have greatly influenced Malaysian politics (UMNO Online 2018b). Article 153 of the Federal Constitution provides for the "reservation of quotas in respect of services, permits, etc., for Malays and natives of any of the States of Sabah and Sarawak". It also empowers the Yang di-Pertuan Agong to safeguard the "special position of the Malays and natives of any of the States of Sabah and Sarawak and the legitimate interests of other communities" in the areas of "public service and scholarships, exhibitions and other educational or training privileges or special facilities". Article 153 has greatly fuelled intense debates on issues of racial equality and Malay rights and privileges in Malaysian society. Notably, Article 153 was enacted as a necessary tool for reducing racial disparity at the time of its drafting. Calls to abolish the provisions of Article 153 have been greatly contested and criticized as the issue of Malay and *Bumiputera* rights is a very sensitive matter for the Malay community. However, some commentators, such as P. Waytha Moorthy, former minister in the Prime Minister's Department under PH government, have criticized the PH government's policies and laws for being discriminatory. In a video interview with a Dutch broadcaster that went viral on social media, Waytha Moorthy defended his past claims that the Malaysian Indian community was unjustly treated by saying that "the policies by the then UMNO government had immensely prevented the majority of the Indian community to be included in the mainstream development of the nation" (*Free Malaysia Today* 2018; UMNO Online 2018a; *Harakah Daily* 2018a).

When PH won GE14, it expressed aspirations in its manifesto to promote and protect human rights in Malaysia (Whiting 2018). For example, PH aimed to enhance and empower the role and function of the Human Rights Commission of Malaysia (SUHAKAM), and to improve the National Human Rights Action Plan, which was previously under the purview of the former BN government. The PH government also wanted to improve Malaysia's representation on the ASEAN Intergovernmental Commission on Human Rights and to accede to notable international human rights conventions, including ICERD. In addition, PH also assured Malaysians that equality, multiculturalism and religious inclusion would be implemented. Those who voted for PH expected the newly elected government to quickly deliver their promises when it succeeded on becoming the government after the 2018 general election.

However, after Prime Minister Mahathir Mohamad delivered his speech at the United Nations (UN) General Assembly in September 2018, expressing the Malaysian government's plan to accede to ICERD, strong criticism and opposition emerged from the two major Malay opposition parties, PAS and UMNO, which claimed that the move would affect Malay rights and principles of Islam. The backlash came from segments of the Malay community who were fearful that their rights and privileges as guaranteed under the Constitution would be affected (*New Straits Times* 2018b). Some Malay Muslims who supported the ICERD accession were criticized for not being "true Muslims" because it was thought that the international convention would include the elimination of discrimination against the lesbian, gay, bisexual, transgender and queer (LGBTQ) community, which Muslims oppose as the practice is considered inimical to Islam (Pilus 2018). PAS leaders rejected ICERD on the premise that it promoted Western principles of human rights, which included rights for the LGBTQ community, as it is against true human nature and abandons "true ethics of humanity". Since the majority of Malaysians are Muslim, it was argued that the accession of ICERD would undermine Islamic principles as enshrined in the Constitution since Islam is recognized as the country's official religion. PAS further claimed that the promotion of LGBTQ rights and principles would eventually lead to problems occurring in the family and social institutions (Pilus 2018).

Those who were pro-Malay rights objected to the ICERD accession as they feared Malay rights would be diluted. They were concerned that once Malaysia consented to ICERD, international pressure would subsequently cause Article 153 of the Federal Constitution to be abolished, thereby negatively impacting the rights and special privileges of the Malays and *Bumiputera* of Sabah and Sarawak. The Malays who rejected ICERD subscribe to the ideology of Malay supremacy (*Ketuanan Melayu*) (Anuar 2019), which is the belief that Malays should rule Malaysia. Many politicians have utilized the idea of Malay supremacy to their advantage by politicizing the issue of the ICERD accession and making racial insinuations in their speeches against the PH government, thus further sparking opposition among the Malays.

Senior journalist A. Kadir Jasin chided local media, including social media, for its "emotional" reactions towards ICERD instead of playing its role in educating the public on the matter (Zurairi 2019). Kadir accused some media outfits of intentionally sensationalizing the issue, rather than reporting on the UN convention objectively. He explained, "It should be discussed in a wiser manner, and rationally to create understanding in society ... Media should take a more careful look, instead of reporting emotional and irrational political reactions" (Zurairi 2019). Kadir admitted that he himself had refrained from expressing his personal views on ICERD when the topic was heated, claiming that the atmosphere over the issue was "cloudy" (Zurairi 2019). The hotter the issue, the more the Malays supported and believed propaganda from UMNO and PAS.

The arguments against ICERD were fuelled by misconceptions that were exploited by the opposition UMNO and PAS. SUHAKAM (2018) has clearly asserted that the Malaysian government would be able to take special measures to guarantee the protection as prescribed under Article 153 of the Malaysian Federal Constitution on the royal prerogative of the Yang di-Pertuan Agong as well as the privileges and rights of the Malays and *Bumiputera*. This also includes the protection of Islam as the official religion of Malaysia under the Constitution. Furthermore, the majority of the fifty-five Muslim countries that are members of the Organisation of Islamic Cooperation (OIC) have either signed or ratified ICERD, with Malaysia and Brunei being the odd ones out for not doing so. Clearly, the position of Islam in Malaysia would not be threatened by the decision to accede to ICERD (*The Star Online* 2018b).

However, due to the relentless pressure whipped up by UMNO and PAS, the Malaysian government officially announced on 23 November 2018 that it would not proceed to accede ICERD. Instead, it will "continue to defend the Federal Constitution which contains a social contract that has been agreed upon by all races during the formation of the country" (*The Star Online* 2018c). The tipping point of the anti-pluralist backlash was the protest led by UMNO and PAS on 8 December 2018, which culminated in a crowd of some 50,000 people rallying in Dataran Merdeka, Kuala Lumpur, despite the PH government's earlier decision not to accede to ICERD. Protesters were dressed in white, which is one of the symbolic colours of Islam. They considered ICERD as a threat to their religion and Malay supremacy and demanded that the opposition unite to defend their rights. The movement also made effective use of social media to mobilize its followers. In Malaysia, the online protests used the hashtag *#LucutWaytha* (#SackWaytha) in reference to P. Waytha Moorthy and #TolakICERD (Reject ICERD) (Temby 2020). One of the main forces of this protest was a youth-based Islamist non-governmental organization (NGO) called the Ikatan Muslimin Malaysia (Malaysian Muslim Solidarity – ISMA) which used social media to mobilize the protestors. The movement led to a formal Malay-Muslim pact between UMNO and PAS under the banner of MN, which provided the foundation for a series of opposition by-election victories in 2019. This demonstrated the power of Malay-Muslim majoritarian politics and presaged the rise of PN, the government under Prime Minister Muhyiddin's leadership (Ignatius 2018).

## The Agenda of Muafakat Nasional (MN)

Khoo (2020) argued that political parties such as UMNO, PAS, Bersatu, Amanah, PKR and Parti Pejuang Tanah Air (Homeland Fighter's Party – Pejuang), a new party established by former premier Mahathir Mohamed after he and his supporters were removed from Bersatu, all claimed to protect Malay rights. Their numbers are a sure sign that none of them has an uncontested claim. Strictly speaking, neither Amanah nor PKR purport to be a "protector of the Malays" in the same vein that UMNO does, while PAS has often preferred to call for the protection of the Ummah or all Muslims. By forming MN, both UMNO and PAS can claim that they are protectors of Malay as well as Muslim rights. Debates and discussions on MN were posted on UMNO and PAS's official websites. UMNO Online (https://umno-online.my/page/1/?s=Muafakat+Nasional) published 1,074 articles

about MN while PAS, through *Harakah Daily*, (https://harakahdaily.
net/?s=muafakat+nasional) published 1,291 articles. The data showed
that UMNO and PAS were seriously propagating their collaboration to
their followers to get support. Bersatu, on the other hand, only had eight
articles about MN via https://berita.bersatu.org/?s=muafakat+nasional#.
Since Bersatu was not accepted into MN, it gave less attention to the
MN agenda and preferred to focus on PN as it was the most dominant
party leading that coalition.

Since their defeat in GE14 in 2018, UMNO and PAS realized
that results showed they have majority Malay support. According to
Merdeka Centre, a polling company, PH's share of the Malay vote in
GE14 was between 25 per cent and 30 per cent. BN captured between
35 per cent and 40 per cent support while PAS's share was between
30 per cent and 33 per cent (Ong 2019). Therefore, the combination of
UMNO and PAS would garner the support of at least 65 per cent of
Malays in the country. Also, instead of fighting each other, since they
are in the opposition, it would be best for them to extend the olive
branch and cooperate to defeat PH by establishing MN to shore up
support from its Malay followers. In contrast, PH was still struggling
to win the hearts and minds of the Malays, who are the majority
ethnic group in Malaysia.

MN is a political alliance between the two largest Malay-Muslim-
based opposition parties. The cooperation became official after the
five-point *Piagam Muafakat Nasional* (National Cooperation Charter)
was signed (Hussain 2019) between UMNO President Ahmad Zahid
Hamidi and PAS President Abdul Hadi Awang on 14 September 2019
at the *Himpunan Penyatuan Ummah* (Ummah Unity Rally) in Putra
World Trade Centre (PWTC), Kuala Lumpur. Its main aim was to
unite the Malay-Muslim community or *Ummah* for electoral purposes.
Despite calls for MN to be institutionalized and become more inclusive
towards BN and GS where UMNO and PAS are major component
parties respectively, there has been no formal agreement with the other
parties in both coalitions to migrate to MN. Nevertheless, a permanent
secretariat of the pact was set up at UMNO's headquarters located at
PWTC in May 2020 (UMNO Online 2020).

After the PH government collapsed, the PN government was
established. Although Bersatu had agreed to join MN, it had also
previously applied to register PN with the Registrar of Societies

(Strangio 2021), which confirmed on 14 September 2020 that PN had been registered on 7 August 2020. UMNO became upset with PN's official registration and PAS's decision to officially join the PN because this threatened its arrangement and collaboration with PAS in MN. On 3 April 2021, Wan Saiful (2020b), Bersatu's information chief, revealed that although the party had agreed to join the MN, it did not receive any official response from UMNO or PAS. It was clear that although PAS persuaded UMNO to collaborate with Bersatu in the name of Malay unity, UMNO preferred to work alone after failing in seat negotiations. In the run-up to GE15 in 2022, UMNO was unhappy with PAS and PN because it could not secure sufficient seats for its local grassroots leaders (also known as warlords) to contest, which angered them and their supporters. UMNO also perceived Bersatu as its archenemy because the latter was formed by fifteen UMNO MPs who left the party to join Bersatu after GE14, turning them into "traitors". These grievances meant that UMNO could not see itself collaborating with Bersatu. On 30 January 2022, ahead of the 2022 Johor state election and after the 2021 Melaka state election, BN decided to contest separately from PN which was represented by Bersatu and PAS. Furthermore, BN adviser and former prime minister Najib Razak disclosed that Bersatu had never been included as part of MN even though it had signed an agreement to join the alliance in August 2020. This was because Bersatu had betrayed UMNO in the 2020 Sabah state election whereby the newly formed PN coalition, which Bersatu is part of, had contested against BN in seventeen seats (*The Vibes* 2022).

UMNO, therefore, was clearly unhappy with PAS collaborating with Bersatu under the PN umbrella. In fact, if PAS decided to politically align itself with Bersatu under PN, rather than with UMNO under MN, UMNO was willing to abandon and dissolve MN. This direction was clearly stated during the UMNO General Assembly from 16 to 19 March 2022 whereby many delegates, particularly Puteri UMNO (UMNO Women's Youth wing), clearly said no to collaborating with PAS as it was disappointed that the latter contested against the former in the Johor state election. Thus, UMNO Vice President Khaled Nordin even made a statement entitled "UMNO Di Pasca Muafakat Nasional" (UMNO in post-MN) that PAS has abandoned MN, and it is no longer relevant (UMNO Online 2021a).

The irony is that MN, instead of creating a strong alliance of Malay-Muslim political parties, had in fact weakened UMNO by splitting the party into two factions. One group was led by UMNO President Zahid Hamidi and BN Advisor Najib Razak who preferred distancing UMNO from PN and Bersatu while hoping that PAS would honour its pledge under MN to work with UMNO and abandon PN. The other group, however, was led by former prime minister Ismail Sabri who favoured working with Bersatu and PAS to create a super BN-PN coalition to win the general election. One factor that led to UMNO abandoning MN completely was its convincing electoral wins in the Melaka and Johor state elections where it captured a two-thirds majority in the state assemblies. At that point in time, the PH opposition was in shambles, unable to solve their differences. UMNO thought that by contesting on its own under the BN coalition, it would be able to satisfy its grassroots leaders by giving them the opportunity to contest in the general election.

## FACEBOOK COVERING MALAY POLITICAL PARTIES

Facebook has delivered an enormous amount of political information stretching from political news to political campaigns, including targeting youths as the active users and most exposed to its platform (Himelboim, McCreery, and Smith 2013). In fact, Facebook connections and network size of political actors and public figures have a potential effect on the spread of news, engendering political engagement and opinion expression (Chan 2016). Malaysians have a strong presence on social media. With a population of about 31.2 million, the country has more than 16 million Facebook users (Lee 2016). Facebook is the major social networking site for political parties and politicians in Malaysia (Lee 2017). Our focus in this section is to study the narratives propagated by the political parties via Facebook. To understand this phenomenon, research was conducted on the official Facebook accounts of four political parties, namely UMNO, PAS, PKR and Bersatu, from 1 September 2020 to 31 December 2020 (Kasim and Zaman 2021; Zaman 2021). This research employed qualitative content analysis to examine the issues discussed as well as user-generated comments found in the political parties' official Facebook accounts. There were three main phases throughout the study: data collection, data retrieval and data analysis (Kasim and Zaman 2021; Zaman 2021).

Data gathered from UMNO, PKR, PAS and Bersatu Facebook accounts showed that all parties had a significant number of followers. PAS had the highest with 557,977 followers followed by Bersatu with 322,978 followers. Third was PKR with 144,032 followers while UMNO came in last at 42,574 followers. There was a total of 575 posts shared by all four Malay political parties on their official Facebook sites. Despite having the least followers, UMNO's Facebook account was the most active, recording the greatest number of posts at 285 (49.8 per cent) compared to PAS which had 147 posts (24.7 per cent). PKR posted 122 posts (20.5 per cent) and Bersatu had only 21 posts (3.5 per cent) during the period. The most active period of posting was the month of November 2020 (159 posts), followed by September 2020 (142 posts), December 2020 (140 posts) and October 2020 (134 posts) (Kasim and Zaman 2021; Zaman 2021).

The study found nine issues that were discussed on the Facebook postings of the four political parties: criticism of Malay political parties, elections, COVID-19, politics, economics, social issues, government, education, and religion (see Table 2.4). Unsurprisingly, the findings found that political issues were the most discussed: UMNO's Facebook account had 113 posts, while PAS's had 71, followed by PKR's at 46 and Bersatu's at 11. Again, UMNO's Facebook account highlighted more political issues compared to others because it was eager to call for a new general election. UMNO was confident that it could win a new mandate from the people because, at that point in time, the opposition was disunited and struggling to win back support from the public. UMNO dedicated 46 Facebook posts on election issues. On the other hand, the other parties were not that interested in drumming for election. PKR posted sixteen articles while PAS and Bersatu had only two posts each on the election issue. Despite UMNO having more seats than Bersatu, it was the latter that held the reins of government and controlled decision-making during the research period. This was why UMNO was pushing for an election because it wanted to gain back power to dominate and rule the country. On economic issues, UMNO also had several Facebook postings (67), followed by PKR (36), PAS (14) and none by Bersatu (Kasim and Zaman 2021; Zaman 2021).

TABLE 2.4
Issues and Facebook Coverage for Political Parties

| Issues | UMNO | PKR | PAS | Bersatu | Total |
|---|---|---|---|---|---|
| Criticism of Malay political parties | 20 | 2 | 1 | – | 24 |
| Elections | 46 | 16 | 2 | 2 | 66 |
| COVID-19 | 3 | 2 | 9 | 2 | 15 |
| Politics | 113 | 46 | 71 | 11 | 241 |
| Economics | 67 | 36 | 14 | – | 117 |
| Social issues | 25 | 11 | 4 | 3 | 32 |
| Government | 6 | 3 | 4 | 1 | 14 |
| Education | 2 | 2 | 1 | – | 5 |
| Religion | 3 | 4 | 41 | 2 | 50 |
| Total | 285 | 122 | 147 | 21 | 575 |

Sources: Kasim and Zaman (2021); Zaman (2021).

This study also identified the forms of framing in the Facebook posts by the Malay political parties. Below are some posts about MN.

## Posts about Muafakat Nasional (MN)

Despite Bersatu not being part of MN, the party and PAS seemed positive in promoting the MN agenda. PAS President Abdul Hadi Awang stated in the party's official Facebook account:

> *Keutamaan PAS adalah persiapan untuk menghadapi PRU-15 yang dijangka dalam masa terdekat, di samping komitmen untuk mengukuhkan kerjasama dalam Muafakat Nasional dan Perikatan Nasional.*
> (Translation: PAS's priorities are preparing for the 15th General Election which will happen soon, besides the commitment to strengthen cooperation between Muafakat Nasional and Perikatan Nasional) (PAS, 11 September 2020).

Bersatu President Muhyiddin Yassin also informed the public that he had met UMNO and PAS presidents in the spirit of MN.

This was received favourably by netizens, some of whom commented that cooperation between these three parties was the way to establish Malay unity (see below):

> *Muhyiddin Yassin. Semalam saya mengadakan pertemuan dengan YB Dato`*
> *Seri Haji Abdul Hadi Awang, Presiden PAS dan YB Dato` Seri Dr Ahmad*
> *Zahid Hamidi, Presiden UMNO. Kami berbincang mengenai usaha2 untuk*
> *memperkukuhkan hubungan kerjasama antara Bersatu, PAS dan UMNO.*
> (Translation: Muhyiddin Yassin. Yesterday, I had a meeting with YB Dato' Seri Haji Abdul Hadi Awang, PAS president and YB Dato' Seri Dr Ahmad Zahid Hamidi, UMNO president. We discussed about the efforts to strengthen cooperation between Bersatu, PAS and UMNO) (Bersatu, 1 December 2020).

A netizen responded on Bersatu's post in the comments section:

> *Pandangan sy, dalam keadaan sekarang Bersatu, UMNO PAS perlu*
> *bekerjasama, buang sikap ego, tamak, kejar kuasa, kejar kekayaan, sifat*
> *dendam. Kami rakyat di bawah perlukan kamu semua pemimpin MELAYU,*
> *kami akan sentiasa berdoa AGAR hubungan Bersatu, UMNO dan PAS baik.*
> (Translation: My view is that in the current situation, Bersatu, UMNO (and) PAS should collaborate, get rid of egoistic attitudes, greed, power chase, wealth pursuit and revenge. We the people below need you all Malay leaders, we will always pray for a good relationship between Bersatu, UMNO and PAS) (Bersatu, 1 December 2020).

However, UMNO was clearly reluctant to collaborate with Bersatu or allow it to join MN. It questioned PAS's loyalty and asked the latter to choose whether it wanted to be part of MN or if it preferred to be part of PN which is against BN. Below are posts from UMNO and a comment from a netizen who was disappointed with this polemic between political parties against the agenda of Malay unity.

> *PRU15 – Muafakat Nasional (BN dan PAS) atau Perikatan Nasional (PPBM*
> *dan PAS)?*
> (Translation: GE15 – Muafakat Nasional (BN and PAS) or Perikatan Nasional (Bersatu and PAS)?) (UMNO, 16 December 2020).

The following are netizens' comments on the above post:

> *Ini saja rakyat nak tahu, bukan payah pun, kata kerajaan melayu Islam,*
> *bercakap benar lah wahai pemimpin PAS dan UMNO.*

(Translation: This is just what the people want to know, it is not too difficult. You said you are a Malay-Islamic government. PAS and UMNO leaders, please speak the truth) (UMNO, 16 December 2020).

Clearly, the MN issue has divided the Malays instead of uniting them as there were mixed responses from netizens, some of whom were favourable to MN, but others were critical. One UMNO supporter commented on the party's Facebook account that MN would have good prospects if it collaborated with Bersatu, but there were those who condemned any collaboration. For instance, a netizen commented in favouring UMNO and Bersatu collaboration:

*Jika x diterima cadangan dsn, jgn la pula ditolak bajet ini. Sekurang2nye masih ade peruntukan utk rakyat. Pilih mudharat lbih kecil dri mudharat besar … perkukuhkan MN. Pertahankan PN sehingga hbis penggal …*

(Translation: If Dato' Seri Najib's proposal is not accepted, do not reject this budget. At least, there will still be some allocations for the people. Choose the lesser harm rather than the greater harm … strengthen MN. Defend PN until the end of term …) (UMNO, 10 November 2020).

Another netizen, however, preferred UMNO and Bersatu to operate separately:

*Sudah pasti undi org melayu tak dapat ke Bersatu. Dah serik dgn kerenah ph n kemudian pn. Tamak kuasa cuba selindung bawah sharurat. Apa punya minda low class sampai nk try2 dgn DYMM YDPA.*
(Translation: Of course, Malay votes will not go to Bersatu. People are fed up with PH's attitude and then PN's. Power hungry while trying to hide behind the Emergency proclamation. What a low-class thinking to the extent of trying to challenge His Majesty, the King) (UMNO, 16 November 2020).

Then there were netizens who were upset with this power tussle between Malay political parties. They believed that any infighting between Malay political parties will benefit DAP who fights for non-Malay rights. For example, a netizen responded to this post:

*DAP gembira dengan keputusan ini, teruskan usaha memecahbelahkan bangsa melayu.*
(Translation: DAP is happy with this decision, please continue with efforts to divide the Malays) (UMNO, 14 October 2020).

Clearly, Malay-based political parties are divided in their views for and against MN. Sadly, in all these political tussles, DAP was blamed for dividing the Malays. MN later was abandoned by UMNO-BN which decided to compete without collaborating with PAS or Bersatu. On the other hand, PAS and Bersatu maintained their position working together with PN. This gave the possibility of a three-cornered fight between three coalition parties—BN, PN and PH—in GE15 in 2022. Therefore, the battleground for Malay support and votes could be seen on social media regarding the issues of MN and ICERD. In the next section, we examine the political impact of social media on Malay politics in GE15.

## IMPACT OF SOCIAL MEDIA IN THE 2022 GENERAL ELECTION

The cyberspace in Malaysia has been expanded. The Malaysian Communications and Multimedia Commission (MCMC) in the 2020 Internet Users Survey found that 50 per cent of the population spent between five and twelve hours online to communicate through voice or video, text and social networking sites (MCMC 2020). Communicating via text was the main online activity, which increased from 96.5 per cent in 2018 to 98.1 per cent in 2020. Meanwhile, social networking is the second most frequent activity, rising to 93.3 per cent in 2020 from 85.6 per cent in 2018. Online publications such as e-books, e-newspapers or e-magazines became popular with an increase to 68.3 per cent in 2020 from 56.3 per cent in 2018. Smartphone Internet users have reached the highest of 98.7 per cent in 2020, compared to 93.1 per cent in 2018 (Leong 2021). Thus, according to Leong (2021), it is not surprising that "Malaysia's mainstream media today is digital, while traditional media—print, radio, and television—have been relegated to the position of 'legacy media' and are considered as mature media established by the elite corporate 'old guards'". Clearly, the political party that dominates the online media in Malaysia has a good chance to win GE15 or at least gain the most seats in the parliament. Like in the past elections, GE15 has been dominated by ethnic and religious issues and interestingly PN managed to gain many seats, even though this was still not enough for them to win the election.

The results of GE15, which was held on 19 November 2022, showed that BN's strategy of going on its own, instead of collaborating with PN, backfired as it could win only 30 seats compared to 79 seats in GE14, the worst showing in Malaysian history. Meanwhile, PN won 74 seats. UMNO-BN's previous strategy of cooperating with PAS under MN to defeat the PH backfired as it caused schisms and internal divisions which weakened the party. Clearly, UMNO did not manage the MN issue well, which contributed to its poor performance during GE15. PAS, however, benefitted tremendously from its alliance with Bersatu under PN. Not only did it increase the number of seats from 18 in GE14 to 49 in GE15, the best performance ever, it has become the biggest winner of GE15 and the dominant party in PN as Bersatu won only 25 seats in GE15. Furthermore, PN had taken Perlis, rolled over other Malay states such as Kedah, Kelantan and Terengganu, and made further inroad into Selangor, Pahang, Perak, Melaka and Penang. One of the major factors contributing to the result was the social media.

The clear winner in MN's agenda is PAS which manages to attract sizeable Malay nationalist and Islamist voters, including the ordinary Malay voters. They were angry with UMNO whom they perceived as corrupt and did not trust the so-called "DAP-led" PH. While PAS's long-term ideological indoctrination and grassroots building are crucial, the rise of PAS as the biggest party in parliament today does not necessarily mean that more Malaysian Muslims are supporting PAS's Islamist agenda. This success reflects how PAS and other right-wing groups have successfully propagated the sentiments of "Malay Muslim insecurity". Hew (2022) argues: "Hence, the challenge ahead is not only about the growth of Islamism but also the rise of right-wing Malay Muslim majoritarianism. Of course, these two trends are not mutually exclusive; instead, they complement each other. To overcome such challenges, institutional reforms must come together with the reforms of social and political values among Malaysians, especially the youth".

The big question is how social media assisted PN's performance in GE15. A study done by Milieu Insight found that Facebook remains the main platform for Malaysians aged 35 to 44 (79 per cent) to get their news about politics or election-related matters (Tan 2022).

It also said that Instagram is popular among those aged between 18 and 24 (49 per cent), and between 25 and 34 years old (49 per cent), while those aged between 45 and 54 mainly rely on radio (55 per cent), news websites (53 per cent) and newspapers (34 per cent). In terms of all age groups, TikTok was most popular among those aged between 18 and 24 years (43 per cent) (Tan 2022). Malaysia has lowered the minimum voting age to 18 from 21, resulting in more than four million youths—one-fifth of the electorate—being eligible to vote for the first time in GE15. This has brought an increase in the penetration of social media. PN has been the most aggressive in campaigning via social media, particularly through social influencers on TikTok. Generation Z (born between 1997 and 2012) made up 43 per cent of users on TikTok in Malaysia. The TikTok video of Muhyiddin Yassin went viral and garnered more than 324,700 likes, for his participation in a song called Swipe by Alyph, a Singaporean singer, despite Muhyiddin not having an official TikTok account. In the fifteen-second clip, he was seen "liking" only his PN coalition party for being "clean and stable" and "swiping" other BN and PH coalitions as a sign of rejection (Rodzi 2022).

In our research survey published on 7 November 2022 by the Centre for Testing, Measurement and Appraisal (CeTMA), Universiti Utara Malaysia, which was conducted for two months from 6 September to 5 November 2022, we found that Muhyiddin was the most popular and trusted leader. Out of 2,716 respondents nationwide, Muhyiddin managed to get a 20 per cent approval rating compared to Anwar who was closely behind at 19 per cent (Sani et al. 2022). Similarly, PN appeared to gain a lot of support through shifting its election campaigns to social media. A survey carried out by pollster Merdeka Centre, an opinion research firm, found that there is growing support for PN among Malay respondents, especially among those aged between 18 and 20, after nomination day on 5 November 2022. It said that 35 per cent of Malays preferred PN, with a "strengthening of preference" for Muhyiddin. Hisomuddin Bakar, executive director of Ilham Centre, also a polling research firm, explained: "There should be a TikTok war because the trend has shifted to TikTok, but PN dominates the platform alone because it is not utilised much by PH and BN. Due to this, PN managed to penetrate a large market of voters — young, new and first-timers. I'm not sure why BN is not aggressive, and weak on social media. This GE should've been theirs — they were the ones who decided when to dissolve the parliament, but in terms of campaigning, they're far behind" (Rodzi 2022).

As mentioned earlier, there are several factors that contributed to the rise of PN, especially PAS. Some saw it as the "green tsunami" where PAS exploited anti-corruption and anti-UMNO sentiments, ideological indoctrination and vigorous support from the grassroots among many short- and long-term factors (Hew 2022). PN ran an effective and strategic campaign with a catchy slogan "PN, the Best" and a motto of *"Prihatin, Bersih dan Stabil"* (Caring, Clean and Stable) that many voters related to. *Prihatin* highlights Muhyiddin Yassin's fatherly image as *Abah* (Father) which he developed during his premiership. Despite various criticisms, Muhyiddin has quite successfully positioned himself as the prime minister who led Malaysia through the COVID-19 pandemic. Tapping into PH and civil societies' anti-corruption campaigns, *Bersih* shows PN as a cleaner alternative to corrupt UMNO. *Stabil*, on the other hand, emulates BN's slogan and addresses the hope of many Malaysians for political stability (Hew 2022). PN's campaign messages are clear and direct, highlighting UMNO's tarnished image and DAP's problematic reputation among Malay Muslims. PN also ran effective social media campaigns on platforms such as TikTok, Facebook and WhatsApp. On TikTok, PN generated two types of content targeting different segments of young voters. The first aimed to consolidate the support of Islamist-minded youths with direct or indirect hate messages towards "un-Islamic" groups. The second persuaded ordinary youths with fun and easy-going content (Hew 2022).

During the first PH administration, right-wing groups such as Ikatan Muslimin Malaysia (Malaysian Muslim Solidarity – ISMA) actively exploited Malay Muslim insecurity and pumped up intolerant stances towards various religious, ethnic and sexual minorities such as supporting anti-ICERD campaigns. In 2022, ISMA-run Studio Kembara produced the hit propaganda nationalist film called *Mat Kilau*. Key messages from the film were (1) urging Malay Muslims to be united against foreigners; (2) emphasizing the role of Islam in Malay identity; and (3) indicating non-Muslims are not suitable to lead Muslim-majority societies (Hew 2022). Such sentiments helped not

BN but PN campaign strategies in GE15, which propagated Malays to "reclaim" the country from "un-Islamic" and "external" influences. For example, there was a message on a TikTok video urging "Those who vote for PH, should rewatch *Mat Kilau*". Besides, a posting on the PAS's official Facebook page insisted Malay Muslims learn the lessons from the film by condemning PH for allegedly undermining the agenda of Malay Muslims and suggesting PN was preferable in protecting Malay Muslim rights. While ISMA activists produced *Mat Kilau*, the film provided fertile ground for the rise of support for PN, especially PAS among the Malays (Hew 2022).

## CONCLUSION

The proliferation of social media has ramifications for Malaysia as it is a conduit for alternative information and democratic values. The Internet increases transparency by helping people avoid censorship, thus facilitating the flow of information about the government and people. This disrupts traditional, established political structures and national security. During GE14 in 2018 and GE15 in 2022, social media was an important instrument in promoting democracy by opening more space for Malaysians to deliberate on political issues which can strengthen the democratization process in the country.

It is also clear in this chapter that Malay political parties especially UMNO, PAS and Bersatu were aware that social media could help them boost their propaganda and highlight their struggle to champion issues such as the Malay agenda and rights. The analysis showed that UMNO and PAS managed to dominate the public narrative on social media, which turned the majority of the Malay-Muslim community against the PH government and subsequently led to its downfall. PAS and PN's strong performance in GE15 showed that issues of Malay survival and unity, as well as Islam were important factors in shoring up support. The use of TikTok in political campaigning during GE15 also indicates that communication medium and technology play an influential role in politics, especially during general elections. Politicians and political parties need to keep updated on the latest trends, which could include big data and artificial intelligence. Such technological developments could either make Malaysia more democratic by levelling the playing field between all parties, or they could lead to more authoritarianism if cyberspace is dominated by those with the most resources.

## REFERENCES

Alias, Alzahrin. 2018. "Malaysia's Internet Penetration Is Now 85.7%". *New Straits Times*, 19 March 2018. https://www.nst.com.my/business/2018/03/346978/malaysias-internet-penetration-now-857-cent.

Aljazeera. 2018. "Malaysia's Opposition Pulls Off Shocking Election Win". 10 May 2018. https://www.aljazeera.com/news/2018/05/malaysia-opposition-pulls-shocking-election-win-180509184811723.html.

Anuar, Kamilia Khairul. 2019. "Analysing Malaysia's Refusal to Ratify the ICERD". Oxford Human Rights Hub, 7 January 2019.

*Berita Bersatu*. 2022. "Muafakat Nasional". https://berita.bersatu.org/?s=muafakat+nasional#

Bernama. 2020. "Bersatu Officially Invited to Join Muafakat Nasional". *New Straits Times*, 31 July 2020. https://api.nst.com.my/news/politics/2020/07/612938/bersatu-officially-invited-join-muafakat-nasional.

———. 2022. "Delegates Call for UMNO-PAS Cooperation in Muafakat Nasional to be Reviewed". *The Malaysian Reserve*, 19 March 2022. https://themalaysianreserve.com/2022/03/19/delegates-call-for-umno-pas-cooperation-in-muafakat-nasional-to-be-reviewed/.

*Borneo Post, The*. 2017. "GE14: Big Battle on Social Media". 17 December 2017. http://www.theborneopost.com/2017/12/17/ge14-big-battle-on-social-media/.

Chan, Michael. 2016. "Social Network Sites and Political Engagement: Exploring the Impact of Facebook Connections and Uses on Political Protest and Participation". *Mass Communication and Society* 19, no. 4: 430–51.

Cheong, Niki. 2020. "Disinformation as a Response to the 'Opposition Playground' in Malaysia". In *From Grassroots Activism to Disinformation: Social Media in Southeast Asia*, edited by Sinpeng Aim and Ross Tapsell. Singapore: ISEAS – Yusof Ishak Institute.

Daud, Sulaiman. 2018. "PM Najib Is One of M'sia's Most Savvy Social Influencers, Shows Focus on Online Campaigning". *Mothership*, 12 January 2018. https://mothership.sg/2018/01/najib-malaysia-politics-social-media-influencer-online-campaign/.

Edward, Jonathan. 2018. "BN Now Winning Social Media War, Academic Says". *The Malay Mail Online*, 26 January 2018. https://www.malaymail.com/

news/malaysia/2018/01/26/bn-now-winning-social-media-war-academic-says/1563123.

Ellis-Petersen, Hannah. 2020. "1MDB Scandal Explained: A Tale of Malaysia's Missing Billions". *The Guardian*, 28 July 2020. https://www.theguardian. com/world/2018/oct/25/1mdb-scandal-explained-a-tale-of-malaysias-missing-billions.

Fama, P.A., and C.M. Tam. 2010. "From Citizens to Netizens — Social Media and Politics in Malaysia". In *Social Media and Politics: Online Social Networking and Political Communication in Asia*, edited by Philip Behnke. Singapore: Konrad-Adenauer-Stiftung.

*Free Malaysia Today*. 2018. "Waytha Stands by Past Comments after 10-Year-Old Clip Makes the Rounds". 18 November 2018. https://www.freemalaysiatoday. com/category/nation/2018/11/18/waytha-stands-by-past-comments-after-10-year-old-clip-makes-the-rounds/.

Habermas, Jürgen. 2006. Habermas acceptance speech in the Bruno Kreisky Prize for the advancement of human rights. *Viennese paper Der Standard*, 10–11 March 2006. http://www.signandsight.com/features/676.html.

*Harakah Daily*. 2018a. "Ratifikasi ICERD: Mengimbas Kembali". 11 December 2018. https://harakahdaily.net/index.php/2018/12/11/ratifikasi-icerd-mengimbas-kembali/.

———. 2018b. "ICERD: Perkara 153 telah banyak dikompromi". 8 December 2018. https://harakahdaily.net/index.php/2018/12/08/icerd-perkara-153-telah-banyak-dikompromi/.

———. 2021. "Umno Selangor mahu Muafakat Nasional diperkukuh". 11 December 2021. https://harakahdaily.net/index.php/2021/12/11/umno-selangor-mahu-muafakat-nasional-diperkukuh/.

———. 2022a. "Bersama Muafakat Nasional mempertahankan Perikatan Nasional". 2 January 2022. https://harakahdaily.net/index.php/2022/01/02/bersama-muafakat-nasional-mempertahankan-perikatan-nasional/.

———. 2022b. "Muafakat Nasional". https://harakahdaily.net/?s=muafakat+nasional.

———. 2022c. "ICERD". https://harakahdaily.net/?s=ICERD.

Hew, Wai Weng. 2022. "From Islamist to Muslim Majoritarianism: The Rise of PAS in GE15". *Stratsea*, 9 December 2022. https://stratsea.com/from-islamist-to-muslim-majoritarianism-the-rise-of-pas-in-ge15/.

Himelboim, Itai, Stephen McCreery, and Marc Smith. 2013. "Birds of a Feather Tweet Together: Integrating Network and Content Analyses to Examine Cross-Ideology Exposure on Twitter". *Journal of Computer-Mediated Communication* 18, no. 2: 154–74.

Ho, Shaun. 2011. "PM's Twitter, Facebook Invitations Draw a Flood of Questions". *The Star*, 11 January 2011.

Human Rights Watch. 2015. *Creating a Culture of Fear: The Criminalization of Peaceful Expression in Malaysia*. New York: Human Rights Watch.

Hussain, H. 2019. "The Umno-PAS 'New Deal'". *The Malaysian Insight*, 14 September 2019. https://www.themalaysianinsight.com/g/183399.

Ignatius, Dennis. 2018. "Mahathir and the ICERD Affair". *Free Malaysia Today*, 13 December 2018. https://www.freemalaysiatoday.com/category/opinion/2018/12/13/mahathir-and-the-icerd-affair/.

Jalli, Nuurrianti Binti. 2016. "The Effectiveness of Social Media in Assisting Opinion Leaders to Disseminate Political Ideologies in Developing Countries: The Case of Malaysia". *Malaysian Journal of Communication* 32, no. 1: 233–60.

Jomo, K. S. 2004. *The New Economic Policy and Interethnic Relations in Malaysia*. Geneva: United Nations Research Institute for Social Development (UNRISD).

Kasim, Azahar, and Hasniza Kamarul Zaman. 2021. "Social Media Analysis on Malay Political Parties in Malaysia: Study on the Issues and Comments Facebook". *International Journal of Law, Government and Communication* 6, no. 26: 127–37.

Khoo, Boo Teik. 2020. *Malay Politics: Parlous Condition, Continuing Problems*. Trends in Southeast Asia, no. 17/2020. Singapore: ISEAS – Yusof Ishak Institute.

Komito, Lee, and Jessica Bates. 2009. "Virtually Local: Social Media and Community among Polish Nationals in Dublin". *Aslib Proceedings: New Information Perspectives* 61, no. 3: 232–44.

Lee, Cassey. 2017. "Facebooking to Power: The Social Media Presence of Malaysian Politicians". *ISEAS Perspective*, no. 2017/74, 5 October 2017.

Lee, Hwok Aun. 2021. "Fifty Years of Malaysia's New Economic Policy: Three Chapters with No Conclusion". *Economics Working Paper 2021-07*. Singapore: ISEAS – Yusof Ishak Institute. https://www.iseas.edu.sg/wp-content/uploads/2021/07/ISEAS_EWP_2021-7_Lee.pdf.

Lee, Kah Leng. 2016. "Facebook Opens Malaysian Office". *The Star Online*, 5 May 2016. https://www.thestar.com.my/tech/tech-news/2016/05/05/facebook-officially-opens-malaysia-office/.

Leong, Pauline Pooi Yin. 2019. *Malaysian Politics in the New Media Age: Implications on the Political Communication Process*. Singapore: Springer.

―――. 2021. "Digital Media: An Emerging Barometer of Public Opinion in Malaysia". *ISEAS Perspective*, 2021/38, 1 April 2021.

Lian, Hah Foong. 2016. *Power Games: Political Blogging in Malaysian National Elections*. Singapore: ISEAS – Yusof Ishak Institute.

Lim, Gabrielle. 2020. "Securitize/Counter-Securitize: The Life and Death of Malaysia's Anti-Fake News Act". Data and Society, 25 March 2016. https://datasociety.net/library/securitize-counter-securitize/.

*Malay Mail*. 2022. "No One Has Declared Dissolution of Muafakat Nasional, Says PAS Deputy President", 21 March 2022. https://www.malaymail.com/news/malaysia/2022/03/21/no-one-has-declared-dissolution-of-muafakat-nasional-says-pas-deputy-presid/2048712.

*Malaysia Now*. 2021. "Social Media Tables Turn On Najib after Muhyiddin's Ouster", 2 March 2021. https://www.malaysianow.com/news/2021/08/22/social-media-tables-turn-on-najib-after-muhyiddins-ouster.

Malaysian Communications and Multimedia Commission (MCMC). 2020. "Internet Users Survey". https://www.mcmc.gov.my/skmmgovmy/media/General/pdf/IUS-2020-Report.pdf.

*Malaysian Insider, The*. 2011. "Najib Takes Questions on Facebook and Twitter". 11 January 2011. http://www.themalaysianinsider.com/malaysia/article/najib-takes-question-on-facebook-and-twitter/.

Mutalib, Mohd. Hafiz Abd. 2021. "Kita setuju jemputan masuk MN, tapi tidak ada respons". *Utusan Malaysia*, 3 April 2021. https://www.utusan.com.my/nasional/2021/04/kita-setuju-jemputan-masuk-mn-tapi-tidak-ada-respons/.

Naidu, S. 2018. "Malaysian Politicians Gear Up for Online Battle ahead of GE14". *Channel News Asia*, 9 January 2018.

Najib, Tun Razak. 2010. *Najib's Answers*. Kuala Lumpur: Institut Terjemahan Negara Malaysia and MPH Publishing.

*New Straits Times*. 2008. "Internet Served a Painful Lesson". 26 March 2008.

———. 2018a. "Malaysia's Internet Penetration Is Now 85.7%". 19 March 2018. https://www.nst.com.my/business/2018/03/346978/malaysias-internet-penetration-now-857-cent.

———. 2018b. "Why Malaysia Backpedalled on ICERD Ratification". 24 November 2018. https://www.nst.com.my/news/nation/2018/11/434078/why-malaysia-backpedalled-icerd-ratification.

Ong, Kian Ming. 2019. "Winning the Malay and Bumiputera Votes, One Step at a Time...". *Malaysiakini*, 7 February 2019. https://www.malaysiakini.com/news/463053.

Parti Islam Se-Malaysia (PAS) Pusat. 2020. https://www.facebook.com/paspusat.

Parti Keadilan Rakyat. 2020. https://www.facebook.com/KeadilanRakyat.

Parti Pribumi Bersatu Malaysia. 2020. https://www.facebook.com/pribumibersatuofficial.

Pilus, Fairul Asmaini Mohd. 2018. "Pas: All Muslims Have a Duty to Oppose ICERD". *New Straits Times*, 22 November 2018. https://www.nst.com.my/news/nation/2018/11/433566/pas-all-muslims-have-duty-oppose-icerd.

Rodzi, Nadirah H. 2022. "Malaysia GE15: Battleground TikTok". *Straits Times*, 17 November 2022. https://www.straitstimes.com/asia/se-asia/tiktok-trumps-flag-wars-malaysia-s-parties-battle-on-social-media-to-woo-young-voters.

Sani, Mohd Azizuddin Mohd. 2014a. "The Social Media Election in Malaysia: The 13th General Election in 2013". *Kajian Malaysia* 32, no. 2: 123–47.

_____. 2014b. "Malaysia's 13th General Election: Political Partisanship in the Mainstream Print Media". *Asia Pacific Media Educator* 24, no. 1: 61–75.

_____. 2015. *Islamization Policy and Islamic Bureaucracy in Malaysia*. Trends in Southeast Asia, no. 5/2015. Singapore: ISEAS – Yusof Ishak Institute.

_____. 2018. "Battle Royale on Social Media in the 2018 General Election in Malaysia". *Asian Politics and Policy* 10, no. 3: 556–60.

Sani, Mohd Azizuddin Mohd, Nor Idayu Mahat, and Ummu Atiyah Ahmad Zakuan. 2018. "Netizens' Perception on the GE14: Parties, Leadership and Issues". Unpublished Research Report. Sintok: Universiti Utara Malaysia.

Sani, Mohd Azizuddin Mohd, Nor Idayu Mahat, Ummu Atiyah Ahmad Zakuan, A. Kasim, R. Muhammad, Z. H. Adnan, and M. A. Muis. 2022. *Sentimen Masyarakat terhadap PRU15 di Malaysia*. Sintok: Centre for Testing, Measurement and Appraisal (CETMA), Universiti Utara Malaysia.

Shahar, Fairuz Mohd. 2018. "Anti-Fake News Bill Not Meant to Restrict Freedom of Speech: Khairy". *The New Straits Times*, 29 March 2018. https://www.nst.com.my/news/government-public-policy/2018/03/350702/anti-fake-news-bill-not-meant-restrict-freedom-speech.

Sivanandam, Hemananthani, and Rahimy Rahim. 2018. "Going Big on Social Media". *The Star Online*, 9 January 2018. https://www.thestar.com.my/news/nation/2018/01/09/going-big-on-social-media-for-more-stories-political-parties-embrace-digital-platforms-to-woo-voters/.

*Star Online, The*. 2018a. "Anti-Fake News Bill Can Be Used to Muzzle Media, Warns Suhakam". 28 March 2018. https://www.thestar.com.my/news/nation/2018/03/28/suhakam-voices-objection-to-anti-fake-news-bill/#AIk63IfTIT564xAL.99.

_____. 2018b. "Malay Rights Protected by Constitution". 27 November 2018. https://www.thestar.com.my/news/nation/2018/11/27/malay-rights-protected-by-constitution-g25-icerd-will-not-affect-islams-position-either/.

_____. 2018c. "Govt Not Ratifying ICERD". 24 November 2018. https://www.thestar.com.my/news/nation/2018/11/24/govt-not-ratifying-icerd-we-will-continue-to-defend-federal-constitution-says-pms-office/.

Statista. 2017. "Number of Facebook Users in Malaysia 2019–2028". https://www.statista.com/statistics/490484/number-of-malaysiafacebook-users/.

Strangio, Sebastian. 2021. "UMNO Withdraws Its Support". *The Diplomat*, 8 July 2021. https://thediplomat.com/2021/07/umno-withdraws-its-support-for-malaysian-ruling-coalition/.

SUHAKAM (Human Rights Commission of Malaysia). 2018. Press Statement No. 45 of 2018 on ("Accession to ICERD"). 31 October 2018. http://www.

suhakam.org.my/wp-content/uploads/2018/11/Press-Statement-No.-45-of-2018-ICERD.pdf.

Tan, J. 2022. "Malaysia GE15 Social Chatter: Which Political Parties and Brands Are Trending?" *Marketing-Interactive*, 26 October 2022. https://www.marketing-interactive.com/malaysia-ge15-social-chatter.

Tapsell, Ross. 2020. *Deepening the Understanding of Social Media's Impact in Southeast Asia*. Trends in Southeast Asia, no. 4/2020. Singapore: ISEAS – Yusof Ishak Institute.

TechTarget. 2017. "Big Data Analytics". March 2017. https://searchbusinessanalytics.techtarget.com/definition/big-data-analytics.

Temby, Quinton. 2020. "Social Media and Polarization in the 'New Malaysia'". *ISEAS Perspective*, no. 2020/21, 27 March 2020.

UMNO. 2020. https://www.facebook.com/UMNOmedia.

UMNO Online. 2018a. "Kenyataan Waytha Isu ICERD: Kerajaan PH Jangan Cuba Tipu Rakyat". 12 December 2018. https://umno-online.my/2018/12/12/kenyataan-waytha-isu-icerd-kerajaan-ph-jangan-cuba-tipu-rakyat/.

_____. 2018b. "Himpunan Aman Anti-ICERD 812 Pastikan Perlembagaan Persekutuan Terus Terluhur". 9 December 2018. https://umno-online.my/2018/12/09/himpunan-aman-anti-icerd-812-pastikan-perlembagaan-persekutuan-terus-terluhur/.

_____. 2020. "Zahid, Hadi Jejak Masuk Pertama Kali Di Pejabat Muafakat Nasional". 14 May 2020. https://umno-online.my/2020/05/14/zahid-hadi-jejak-masuk-pertama-kali-di-pejabat-muafakat-nasional/.

_____. 2021a. "UMNO Di Pasca Muafakat Nasional – Khaled Nordin". 9 November 2021. https://umno-online.my/2021/11/09/umno-di-pasca-muafakat-nasional-khaled-nordin/.

_____. 2021b. "UMNO Selangor Mahu Muafakat Nasional Diperkukuh Di Negeri Itu". 11 December 2021. https://umno-online.my/2021/12/11/umno-selangor-mahu-muafakat-nasional-diperkukuh-di-negeri-itu/.

*Vibes, The*. 2022. "Bersatu Not Part of Muafakat as It Betrayed Umno during Sabah Polls". 30 January. https://www.thevibes.com/articles/news/53246/bersatu-not-part-of-muafakat-as-it-betrayed-umno-during-sabah-polls-najib.

Wan Saiful, Wan Jan. 2020a. *Parti Islam SeMalaysia (Pas): Unifier of the Ummah?* Trends in Southeast Asia, no. 14/2020. Singapore: ISEAS – Yusof Ishak Institute.

_____. 2020b. *Why Did Bersatu Leave Pakatan Harapan?* Trends in Southeast Asia, no. 10/2020. Singapore: ISEAS – Yusof Ishak Institute.

Whiting, Amanda. 2018. "Human Rights in Post-Transition Malaysia". *The Round Table* 107, no. 6: 1–3.

Yusof, Zainal Aznam, and Deepak Bhattasali. 2008. "Economic Growth and Development in Malaysia: Policy Making and Leadership". Working Paper 57726. Washington, D.C.: The International Bank for Reconstruction and Development/The World Bank. http://documents.worldbank.org/curated/en/183111468050085348/Economic-growth-and-development-in-Malaysia-policy-making-and-leadership.

Zaman, N. H. K. 2021. "Analisis Media Sosial Parti Politik Melayu Di Malaysia: Kajian Terhadap Kandungan Dan Komen Facebook". Unpublished Research Paper. Sintok: School of Multimedia Technology and Communication.

Zamani, Anis Amira. 2017. "Social Media Crucial in Malaysia's 14th General Election". *Bernama*, 5 December 2017. http://pru14.bernama.com/news.php?id=1416843.

Zurairi, A. R. 2019. "Media Erred by Focusing on 'Emotional' Backlash against ICERD, Says Kadir Jasin". *Malay Mail*, 21 February 2019. https://www.malaymail.com/news/malaysia/2019/02/21/media-erred-by-focusing-on-emotional-backlash-against-icerd-says-kadir-jasi/1725363.

# 3

# Islamic Reform through the Digital Media: A Case Study of Islamic Renaissance Front, Kuala Lumpur, based on Habermas's Concept of Public Sphere

Ahmad Farouk Musa and
Ahmad Fauzi Abdul Hamid*

The COVID-19 pandemic had a major impact on civil society worldwide as government authorities implemented draconian social movement controls to curb the spread of the virus by restricting all public gatherings. The Islamic Renaissance Front (IRF), a think tank in Malaysia that is actively engaged in spearheading Islamic reform, promptly reacted by embracing digital media to navigate the ensuing disruptions in order to ensure the continuity of its mission—that of bringing social change towards a democratic and inclusive religious society through intellectual discourse. This chapter first explains the impact of COVID-19 as the driving force behind the shift of the IRF's modus operandi from the physical brick-and-mortar setting to the digital sphere characterized by video conferencing tools and social media platforms. Next, it justifies the use of digital media as a sustainable strategy to reach a wider audience, give a voice to marginalized groups and promote a progressive Islam that actively engages with modernity. Finally, it discusses the future of Islamic reform discourse in the digital age, especially the extent of its influence on society and the state. This chapter uses Jürgen Habermas's concept of public sphere as an analytical framework.

## INTRODUCTION

The spectrum of Islamic discourse in Malaysia consists of growing Islamic streams in Malaysia-Indonesia, where conservative Islamic traditionalism and Islamic revivalism groups nudge each other to establish a discourse that is deeply rooted in the tradition of the Malay community (Azhar Ibrahim 2014). While the Islamic traditionalist group that has existed for centuries in the Malay realm emphasizes individual piety and the hereafter over worldly progress, the Islamic revivalist group that emerged in the 1970s took the form of a *da'wah* movement that aims at "Islamizing" society, that is, cleansing society of secular influences deemed un-Islamic. Within the revivalist trend is the *Wahhabi-Salafi*[1] offshoot that gained traction in the early twenty-first century and acquired more grounds with the changing political climate.

The Wahhabi school of thought is well known for its doctrinal rigidity and uncompromising puritanism. It was founded by the reformer of Najd in present-day Saudi Arabia, Muhammad ibn Abd al-Wahhab (d. 1792), who struck a strategic alliance with local warrior Muhammad ibn Saud (d. 1765) in 1744, thereby laying the basis for the first Saudi state. Under Wahhabism, this religious state strove to cleanse the Islamic faith from *shirk* (idolatry) and *bid'a* (innovations), blaming the undesirable influence of Sufism—the mystical strand of Islam—for admitting alien accretions into the faith. Heretical Muslims were invariably excommunicated. Interrupted by the Sunni Ottomans in 1819 and 1891, the Saudi-Wahhabi alliance forcibly established the third Saudi state in 1926 when Abd al-Aziz ibn Saud and pro-Wahhabi warriors called the Ikhwan conquered the Hijaz. The Kingdom of Saudi Arabia was proclaimed in 1932. Salafism is the contemporary movement reasserting the ideals of the pious generations of the first 300 years following the death of Prophet Muhammad in 633. Essentially a Saudi-derived reincarnation of Wahhabism, Salafism traces its roots to Ibn Taymiyyah. Despite their similarities, Salafis deplore the use of the term "Wahhabi", which they perceive as derogatory, to describe their movement of reform.

This conservative orientation in Malaysia has resulted in lethargy and civilizational stagnation, besides undermining Muslims' intellectual strength (Ahmad Farouk Musa 2017). Such an approach causes society to be not only passive but also more dogmatic and insular, with an intolerant mindset towards communities of other faiths, if not different denominations within Muslim communities themselves.

Against this backdrop arose a group of Islamic reformists who sought to bring a rival discourse to oppose the conservative narratives; they called for *islah* (reform) and *tajdid* (renewal) so that people would return to the values taught by the *Qur'ān* and the *Sunna* (traditions of the Prophet). This faction coalesced from ideas mobilized by Jamal al-Din al-Afghāni (1839–97) and Muhammad Abduh (1849–1905) in Egypt.[2] These two pioneers of Islamic modernism grounded in the rational school of Salafism emphasized the need for Muslims to "restate the basic ideas of Islam in such a way as to open the door for the influence of new ideas and for the acquisition of modern knowledge" (Rahman 1966, p. 217). Abduh's reformism was based on the call towards freedom of thought and the restoration of *ijtihad* (independent reasoning) to elevate the dignity of religion, reason and science (Ahmad Nabil Amir 2012). These reformers sought a thorough reform agenda that was not limited to the religious and moral spheres of life. Recognizing the scientific and political power of the modern West, they eschewed the rejectionist tendencies of religious conservatives as well as the secularist policies of Western-oriented elites. In their view, modernity posed no serious threat to an Islam that was correctly understood and interpreted. They maintained that the original message of Islam that had provided the ideal blueprint for traditional Muslim society remained eternally valid. Unlike conservative Muslims or the literalist Wahhabis, they asserted the need to revive the Muslim community through a process of reinterpretation or reformulation of their Islamic heritage in light of contemporary realities. In other words, Islamic modernists from this school of thought did not simply seek to restore the past to the time of *al-salāf al-sālih* (the pious predecessors). Rather, they called for an Islam-inspired response to the political, cultural and scientific challenge of the West and modern life. They attempted to show the compatibility of Islam with modern ideas and institutions, whether they be reason, science and technology, or democracy, constitutionalism and representative government (Esposito 1984).

In the Malay archipelago, the idea of Islamic reformism was driven by figures of *Kaum Muda* such as Kyai Ahmad Dahlan, Haji Abdul Malik Karim Amrullah (Hamka), Teungku Muhammad Hasbi Ash-Shiddieqy, Syed Sheikh al-Hadi, Sheikh Tahir Jalaluddin and Pendeta Za'ba, among others, not to mention the third president of PAS Burhanuddin al-Helmy;[3] the latter, like many other progressive Islamists of his generation, tried to graft together the streams of Islamist and nationalist thought with the intention of prioritizing a broad and universalist understanding of nationalism that went beyond the narrow confines of ethnocentrism and race-centred politics. In this manner, *Kaum Muda* called for the spirit of *islah* (reform) and *tajdid* (renewal) for Muslims to free themselves from religious obscurantism, *bid'a* (innovations) and *khurāfāt* (superstitious beliefs). As expected, the call for reformism was met with fierce resistance, especially from the *Kaum Tua*. Consisting mainly of *ulama* (religious scholars) closely aligned with the sultans, this group zealously defended the adherence to centuries-old traditional religious customs of the community without questioning if they were in line with the teachings of the *Qur'ān* and the *Sunna* (traditions of the Prophet).

However, following the death of prominent *Kaum Muda* reformist figures, the call for Islamic reformism gradually faded away. Steering into the twenty-first century, the situation became even more challenging as Islamic revivalist movements actively spread their Islamic conservatism agenda to society. This highlighted the dire need from Islamic reformists for a competing discourse that reflects a more humanist and rationalist understanding of Islam. In this beleaguered era of growing conservatism, Ahmad Farouk Musa, influenced by the ideas of *Kaum Muda*, continued the tradition of Islamic reformism by establishing a think tank known as the Islamic Renaissance Front (IRF) in Kuala Lumpur, Malaysia. In the spirit of the twenty-first century, IRF spearheaded intellectual Islamic discourses fertile for enlightenment through active involvement in the public arena using various means to reach the masses; these include academic presentations, seminars, conferences, dialogues and study groups, besides book publishing. However, the COVID-19 pandemic put a halt to most of its physical activities. In an attempt to further its mission, IRF took the initiative to shift its operations from the physical to the digital media space. This means being active in public discussions on social media, posting articles on websites, sharing readings through emails and adopting other online manoeuvres that keep the discourse alive and thriving.

This chapter focuses on IRF as its main subject; it analyses the approach and impact of IRF as an Islamic think tank engaged in the discourse of Islamic reformism through the digital media during the COVID-19 era. As its analytical tool, this chapter utilizes the concept of the public sphere propounded by Jürgen Habermas. This concept is relevant since it influences the formation of public opinion. The rationale for choosing IRF instead of other Islamic organizations as the subject of study is simple: IRF is perhaps the most active organization in Malaysia that has been coherently and consistently advocating Islamic reformism. The ideas promoted by IRF are in line with the tradition of Islamic reformism espoused by Jamāl al-Din al-Afghāni and Muhammad Abduh—two influential Muslim scholars whose ideas still reverberate within the hearts of Muslims yearning for change and an Islamic awakening. Indeed, IRF has even established the Abduh Study Group which is devoted to the study and application of Muhammad Abduh's thoughts and ideas in the modern context.

## ORGANIZATIONAL BACKGROUND

Islamic Renaissance Front (IRF) is an intellectual movement and a think tank in Malaysia that focuses on youth empowerment and promotes Muslim intellectual discourse. Based in Kuala Lumpur, it was established on 12 December 2009 and launched by Swiss-born Muslim academic, philosopher and public figure Tariq Ramadan.[4] As an intellectual movement, its main thrust is to promote democracy, liberty and social justice (IRF 2021b). In his speech on 8 December 2019 to commemorate the 10th Anniversary Celebration of the IRF's establishment, Ahmad Farouk Musa, the founder of IRF, stated: "[I]t all started with the realization that the Muslim umma is lacking the most important component in their lives, the utilization of their rational faculty" (Ahmad Farouk Musa 2020).

According to Ahmad Farouk Musa (2020), this phenomenon is due to the pervasive culture of *taqlid*—the blind following of scholars of the past without questioning or examining the premises and assumptions of their arguments to understand how and why they reached a certain conclusion. Thus, *taqlid* has stymied the life of contemporary Muslims, so much so that they could aptly be called *muqallid* (blind followers) rather than *muttabi'* (those who follow religious evidence).

With that in mind, IRF is motivated by three goals: (1) to promote ideas of Islamic reform (*islah*) and renewal (*tajdid*) for a modern, pluralistic world; (2) to revitalize the dynamism of Muslim intellectual discourse in Malaysia; and (3) to contribute to the establishment of an inclusive and just Malaysian nation. The organization advocates reforms that focus on the realm of religious thought and is critical of conservative Islamic thought such as Salafi-Wahhabism derived from the hard-line teachings of Muhammad ibn Abd al-Wahhab (1703–92), the spiritual founder of Saudi Arabia today (Ahmad Fauzi and Che Hamdan 2016).[5] Therefore, since its establishment, IRF has focused its main reform agenda towards promoting *islah* (reform) and *tajdid* (renewal). IRF founder Ahmad Farouk Musa (2014) stated: "One should understand that the essence of reformist thinking is rooted in the principle of not changing the Muslims of today into the *muqallid* (blind followers) of the previous Muslims. By sticking to the principles, we must find out how to live in our own time." The principles of *islah* and *tajdid* are clearly spelt out by Tariq Ramadan in his book *Radical Reform: Islamic Ethics and Liberation* (2008):

> *Tajdîd*, as it was understood by the classical tradition of scholars and schools of law, is thus a renewal of the reading, understanding, and, consequently, implementations of texts in light of the various historic-cultural contexts in which Muslim communities or societies exist ... The notion of *islah* implies bringing the object (whether a heart, an intellect, or a society) back to its original state, when the

said object was still considered to be pure and good: it is indeed a matter of improving, of curing, through re-forming, through reform.

Thus, IRF's reformist agenda, which is deeply anchored in Islamic religious thought, aims at developing critical thinking and reasoning, with the hope that Muslims would abandon the *taqlid* practice of the past or present and return to the principle of *maslaha* (universal good). Admittedly, this approach is bound to face opposition and challenges from conservatives who are more concerned with Islamic rituals. As an intellectual movement, IRF strives to correct the mindset of Muslims—especially those living in multicultural, pluralistic societies—by advocating the values of democracy, freedom, liberty and social justice while condemning prejudice and racism. In other words, IRF promotes pluralism and freedom of thought in society, besides democracy and human rights (Ahmad Fauzi and Che Hamdan 2016).

To achieve its goals, IRF partakes in intellectual discourses to create social awareness of its cherished values. To that end, programmes such as seminars, conferences, forums, public lectures, workshops, roundtable discussions and summer schools are routinely organized. Some of the renowned figures invited by the IRF include Tariq Ramadan, Azzam Tamimi, Nader Hashemi, Anas At-Tikriti, Jeffrey Kenney, James Piscatori, Robert Hefner, Ebrahim Moosa and Mohsen Kadivar. Other noteworthy academics who have presented at IRF events are Asma Afsaruddin, Abdullahi Ahmed An-Naim, Abdullah Saeed, Heba Raouf Ezzat, Zainal Abidin Bagir, Mustafa Akyol, Ziauddin Sardar and Shabbir Akhtar. By inviting scholars of diverse backgrounds, expertise and viewpoints, IRF hopes to enlighten the Muslim community by exposing them to agreements, nuances and disagreements since these are all part and parcel of the learning process.

IRF has also expanded its social enlightenment efforts through book publishing. For instance, IRF regularly publishes translations of relevant foreign language books originally in English and Arabic into Malay to make them more accessible to Malaysians who are more comfortable with the Malay language. Among the Malay translated books published by IRF are the following:[6]

- *Reformasi Radikal: Etika Islami dan Pembebasan* (from Tariq Ramadans's *Radical Reform: Islamic Ethics and Liberation* that forms the bedrock of IRF's reform and renewal agenda)

- *Rekonstruksi Pemikiran Keagamaan Dalam Islam* (from Muhammad Iqbal's *The Reconstruction of Religious Thought in Islam*, a major philosophical work which reflects on the perennial conflict between science, religion and modernity)
- *Pertelingkahan Politik dalam Kalangan Para Sahabat* (from the Arabic book by Mohamed El-Moctar El-Shinqiti on the early years of political altercations among the companions of the Prophet that led to schisms among Muslims until today)
- *Muktazilah dan Persoalan Kebebasan Insan* (from the Arabic text by Muhammad Imarah on the first rational school in Islam—the Mu'tazilites, who are the most probable progenitors of IRF)
- *Islam, Sekularisme dan Demokrasi Liberal: Membentuk Teori Demokrasi Untuk Masyarakat Muslim* (from *Islam, Secularism, and Liberal Democracy: Toward a Democratic Theory for Muslim Societies* by Nader Hashemi, which analyses the relationship between religion, secularism and democracy and argued that the road to liberal democracy must traverse the gates of religious politics)
- *Tertutupnya Pemikiran Kaum Muslimin* (from *The Closing of the Muslim Mind* by Robert R. Reilly who argued that the deplorable state of Muslims nowadays is probably the result of the crushing defeat of the rationalists [Mu'tazilites] at the hands of the traditionalists [Ash'arites])

With the COVID-19 pandemic, all these books, including those that were out of print, have been converted into digital e-books and are now readily available to the public at a nominal price. Meanwhile, IRF has also gathered writings from its own core members on various contemporary issues and published them in a three-volume series called *Wacana Pemikiran Reformis* (A Discourse on Reformist Thought). The previous Malaysian Home Minister in 2017 initially banned two of the three volumes, but the decision was reversed by the Court of Appeal after a lengthy and arduous legal challenge.[7] All IRF reading materials, which are mostly written by Islamic modernist scholars, carry one recurring theme: that Muslims cannot escape the realities of the global political, economic and social transformations, and need to come to terms with social concepts and categories that are often dismissed as "secular" (Ahmad Fauzi and Che Hamdan 2016).

## CONCEPTUAL FRAMEWORK: DIGITAL MEDIA AS A PUBLIC SPHERE IN THE DISCOURSE OF ISLAMIC REFORM IDEAS

Even before the COVID-19 pandemic, the advent of the Industrial Revolution 4.0 (IR 4.0) had transformed society as digital technology became entrenched in daily life activities. IR 4.0 relies on the network integration of value creation dynamics related to the integration of basic physical systems and software with branches from economic sectors and other development sectors (Ustundag and Cevikan 2018). This translates to value systems, such as the value of currencies, commodities and business dealings, operating independently from physical forms of measurement by undergoing a transformational exchange of values into digital form.

The development of IR 4.0 has also influenced the development of intellectual discourse which formulates ideas affecting the dynamics of social systems. The values embedded in intellectual discourse, such as social justice, democracy, freedom, liberty, pluralism and other similar universal values, do not simply appear just as social values that exist physically; they result from the development of the digital world which requires active interaction to allow the absorption of such ideas into society. This is even more evident with the COVID-19 pandemic, which has accelerated the transformation of the real world into the digital world. Seizing this opportunity, IRF sought to influence the digital public sphere by exposing them to the Islamic reform agenda premised on *islah* and *tajdid*. Therefore, before analysing IRF's modus operandi in promoting the Islamic reform agenda, this section will explore the conceptualization of public sphere as conceived by Habermas.[8] Jürgen Habermas (1929–present) is a German philosopher and sociologist whose scholarship is concerned with critical theory and pragmatism. His involvement with the Frankfurt School[9] focused heavily on the foundations of epistemology and theories of the social sciences. His writings influenced the fields of not only philosophy, but also political thought, law, sociology, communication studies, developmental psychology and theology.

## What is Public Sphere?

The concept of "public" is closely related to democratic ideas that call for the involvement of society in public affairs (Papacharissi 2002). In this sense, the public is actively involved in giving opinions or expressions of feelings in matters that affect either them or part of the social community. The public sphere, according to Jürgen Habermas, refers to "a realm of our social life in which something approaching public opinion can be formed. Access is guaranteed to all citizens. The citizens act as a public when they deal with matters of general interest without being subject to coercion" (Habermas 1964). The public sphere, Habermas explains in his book *The Structural Transformation of the Public Sphere* (1991, p. 176), is "made up of private people gathered together as a public articulating the needs of society with the state". Echoing Habermas, Taylor (1992, p. 220) also defines the public sphere as the "common space in which members of society are deemed to meet through a variety of media: print, electronic, and also face-to-face encounters; to discuss matters of common interest; and thus, to be able to form a common mind about these".

Simply put, the public sphere embodies individuals who act to form a public opinion that furthers the interests of society. Public sphere provides space for the community to jointly engage in public debate critically (Habermas 1991). The community gathers to express their opinion openly, where the opinions have collective support from the community. According to Habermas (1964), society behaves as a public body when the expression of opinions and feelings is done through guarantees of freedom of assembly and freedom to speak out on matters related to the public interest. Such issues are discussed via mass communication channels which are the medium for exchange and delivery of information by members of the public body. Thus, the media—which include television, radio, newspapers and digital media—can help shape public opinion in the public realm, which is rooted in a free-flow network of messages in the form of news, broadcasts, films and digital content that are polemical, informative, educational and entertaining (Habermas 2006).

According to Fuchs (2014), the public sphere connects politics, economy and culture which in turn creates an overlap between the three sections with the public sphere, forming the sociopolitical, socioeconomic and sociocultural spheres. As the most basic spheres related to civil society, these three domains have a direct impact on daily life practices, institutions and national policy. Accordingly, all issues related to the three sectors are often a public debate, which explains why the public spheres formed often are in the group of three environments (sociopolitical, socioeconomic and sociocultural).

As such, critical public debates are often driven by actors representing certain groups, particularly on issues debated in the public sphere. In this regard, Habermas (2006) has listed five key actors who often appear in an established public sphere, namely (1) lobbyists who represent special interest groups; (2) advocates of public interest groups or certain marginal groups who lack representation to communicate their voices effectively; (3) experts who have scientific or professional knowledge in specific fields and are invited to submit recommendations; (4) moral entrepreneurs who generate public attention for neglected issues; and (5) intellectuals (such as writers or academics) who have achieved a personal reputation in a number of fields and those who engage spontaneously in public discourse with the clear aim of promoting the public interest. These five groups have the credibility to influence public opinion thanks to their social status or qualification to speak on issues involving the public interest. They usually become representatives of the public in voicing certain issues, especially for communities that are negatively impacted by certain government policies.

Thus, the public sphere plays a key role in creating a communication channel that merges the various voices of civil society into a public opinion that can influence policymakers. For Habermas (1964), the public sphere is an idea that calls for a rationalization of power through the medium of public discussion among private individuals. Private individuals debate matters of public interest in a free, rational and impartial manner (Curran 2000). The public sphere depends on the quality of the discourse and the quantity of its involvement (Grbeša 2004), where the involvement of many people as a society in politics will make the existence of such a public sphere even closer (Schudson 1992).

## Digital Media as Public Sphere

Papacharissi (2002, p. 11) argues that the existence of cyberspace, which Jones (1997) considers as a "new public space", should be distinguished from the "new public sphere". He stated, "As a public space, the internet provides yet another forum for political deliberation. As a public sphere, the internet could facilitate discussion that promotes a democratic exchange of ideas and opinions." In this regard, the Internet should function as a space to discuss and exchange opinions and ideas in the public sphere. For example, social media, which was originally a place for casual social interaction, has morphed into a platform for expressing opinions and exchanging views in the digital community, which enables the formation of public opinion. McGregor (2019) revealed that journalists have used social media as a medium to shape voting data into public opinion through news writing. Through social media, journalists get an insight into the issues being debated by the digital community, thus giving them a glimpse into the forms of various public opinion in society.

Digital media plays a crucial role as a public sphere in intellectual discourse. The COVID-19 pandemic has brought a new network to human communication systems, where most of the daily affairs and interpersonal communication are carried through digital media (Vargo et al. 2020). Therefore, digital media has shifted the conduct of human affairs from offline to online. By creating a communication relationship without the need for any physical encounter, it has altered human thinking and behaviour. This development shows the effect of the digital revolution that created a space for whoever is actively involved in decision-making at the community level. Jenkins (2006) believed that the digital revolution has somehow empowered the global community to acquire greater freedom of expression and become more influential towards the political and social environment. Therefore, digital media has created a cultural connectivity that enabled individuals to be more conscious of their political power, and that somehow has encouraged a democratic culture that involves mass discussion to create an influence towards public perception (Mahlouly 2013). IRF was cognizant of this development regarding the influence of digital media especially during the COVID-19 era, since the communication between the communities was more open to different forms of discourses that have the potential to create new values and norms in society.

To further its Islamic reform agenda, the IRF has capitalized on digital media—a public domain that provides space for intellectual discourse and shapes the views of the digital community, forming public opinion that can indirectly affect public policy (Burstein 2003). In effect, IRF public discourses are aimed not only at promoting the idea of Islamic reform (*islah*) and renewal (*tajdid*) in a modern, pluralistic world, but also at offering in-depth policy analyses towards promoting a peaceful, harmonious, inclusive and just Malaysian society (IRF 2021a). To form and influence public policy, a comprehensive understanding of the concepts of *islah* and *tajdid* is necessary. This is because the discourse of Islamic reformism is often strongly opposed by a conservative society that has long lived in a tradition of non-humanist religious practice and understanding. Consequently, since digital media has become a new world to the global community in the twenty-first century, the IRF has enthusiastically embraced it as the ideal public sphere to shape society's public opinion on the issue of Islamic reformism.

## IMPACT OF COVID-19: TRANSITIONING FROM PHYSICAL TO DIGITAL ACTIVITY

As the COVID-19 pandemic became a worldwide issue, IRF had to change its modus operandi from physical to virtual programmes. This was because Malaysia's then prime minister Tan Sri Muhyiddin Yassin imposed a draconian Movement Control Order on 18 March 2020 which entailed the closure of all public premises and a ban on the holding of any physical activities in public (*New Straits Times* 2020). In addition, since the fall of the Pakatan Harapan government led by Tun Mahathir Mohamad in February 2020 and its replacement, the Perikatan Nasional government under Tan Sri Muhyiddin Yassin, Malaysia was embroiled in political unrest that rocked the country (Razak Ahmad and Zakiah Koya 2020). These two main challenges halted many of IRF's planned programmes in the physical space (Ahmad Muziru Idham 2020).

Consequently, IRF moved its public discussion on social media by posting and disseminating articles on its official website or via email respectively. It also subscribed to Zoom application to conduct its interactive intellectual activities online. The online shift had the advantage of increased networking with academics from various countries around the world (Ahmad Muziru Idham 2020)—such as Iran, Bosnia, Germany and Albania—who were invited to speak. This helped IRF to build an international network of academic contacts and expand its outreach overseas as these programmes attracted the attention of people from the speakers' own countries to participate in IRF discourses. We shall therefore look at the impact of IRF discourses in three main areas since the onslaught of COVID-19: discourse, advocacy and international engagement.

## Discourse

In terms of discourse, IRF has consistently advocated on issues related to democracy and human rights in all its programmes. Some of the themes discussed in the IRF webinars during the pandemic-driven 2020 include authoritarianism in Arab countries, genocide of the Uighur community in China, *Charlie Hebdo* and xenophobia, and demonstrations against the monarchy in Thailand. As an Islamic organization, IRF took the stance to voice out these human rights violations at the international level. While the immediate aim was to put pressure on local authorities to resolve these critical issues, more importantly, it conveyed a message to the universal community that the Islamic discourse must transcend borders. In other words, Islamic discourse should not be confined to religion and spirituality; it must extend to humanitarian issues through the lens of humanist and progressive Islamic values. IRF also routinely conducted biweekly webinars in 2020. Based on web analytics, the IRF official website received a total of 37,973 visitors throughout 2020, 73 per cent of which (that is, around 27,741) were new visitors. Meanwhile, live broadcasts on IRF's Facebook page drew a minimum audience of 1,000 visitors. The most viewed video was the webinar "Post-COVID-19: Should There Be a New Economic Model? With Dr Jomo Kwame Sundaram", which received a total of 39,100 views.

Apart from organizing programmes, IRF also published articles on its official website.[10] In 2020, a total of thirty articles were published in Malay and English; they were either original or translated articles, usually a response to current events or an exposition of Islamic reform movements across the archipelago. Indeed, IRF truly believes in the power of the written text to spread its reform ideas for three good reasons: firstly, Islam is *par excellence* a religion of the pen, with God calling on mankind to read in His very first mandate; secondly, history has proven that the spread of Martin Luther's ideas across Northern Europe was hastened with the advent of the printing press hundreds of years ago; and thirdly, translation of Islamic reformist ideas from outside into the local vernacular inevitably improves the quality of local intellectual discourses. The emergence of *Baitul Hikmah* (House of Wisdom) during the Abbasid era illustrates this point; it flourished because of the cross-fertilization of ideas following the concerted effort in translating manuscripts from Greek and Latin into Arabic.

One of the writings that attracted a lot of attention was a piece by Asma Afsaruddin titled *Jihad and the Qur'ān: Classical and Modern Interpretations* and was translated into Malay by Ahmad Muziru Idham.[11] The translated article was posted on the IRF website in response to the satirical cartoon published by *Charlie Hebdo* in October 2020 in France (BBC News 2020; *New York Times* 2020; Cobbe 2020). As a result of its ongoing commitment to combating extremist ideas within the global community, including those from so-called Muslim extremists, the IRF sought to correct any misunderstanding of the Islamic concept of *jihad* so as to discourage activities that promote gratuitous violence. Undeniably, Islamic discourse in the information age is more complex because it warrants not only resistance to conservatism but also an even more robust fight against radicalism that arises from overly narrow religious interpretations. Therefore, providing a more progressive discourse of Islamic reformism is pivotal when addressing those challenges in order to show that Islam is based equally on reason, not faith alone.

## Advocacy

In terms of advocacy, IRF has always been active in increasing community networking through various social media such as

Facebook, Instagram, Twitter and YouTube. Besides using its website to announce upcoming programmes or publish articles promoting its Islamic reform agenda, IRF also has a global email database; each email account holder receives IRF programme announcements or new articles via its mailing list. IRF regularly shares articles on current world affairs, especially those related to democracy, human rights and Islamic reformism.

To improve its advocacy strategy, IRF produced posters featuring quotes from Islamic scholars such as Nurcholish Madjid or excerpts from its own published books. Such approaches appeal to social media users—especially those on Instagram—who are usually more interested in fast and easy reading; in turn, this accelerates the dissemination of ideas to the digital community. For its efforts, IRF was recognized by SEAN-CSO[12] (2020) as one of the most influential and impactful religious organizations in Southeast Asia. As a network of civil society organizations, SEAN-CSO brings together organizations from Thailand, the Philippines, Malaysia, Indonesia and Australia by mobilizing advocacy work to achieve the mutual goal of preventing violent extremism across Southeast Asia. IRF's interactive advocacy strategy using digital media has been effective in spreading its Islamic reformism agenda, as evidenced by web analytics showing an increasing number of visitors across all of its platforms. By continually disseminating its ideas locally and internationally, IRF tries to interact closely with the community to ensure they clearly understand its discourse.

## International Engagement

IRF has collaborated with several international organizations for optimal exposure. These organizations include Islam and Liberty Network in Turkey, Forces of Renewal Southeast Asia (FORSEA) in Cambodia, together with Religious of the Sacred Heart (RSCJ) Indonesia/ Parahyangan Catholic University and Universitas Islam Negeri Sunan Gunung Djati (UIN SGD), which are both based in Indonesia.

Furthermore, IRF's discourse on the Uighurs was covered on the Foreign Affairs portal which reports on international issues (Coca 2020). Asia Sentinel, a Hong Kong-based news portal, also quoted IRF among several other NGOs who criticized the Malaysian government for abusing its power to arrest dozens of activists protesting Muhyiddin Yassin's appointment as the prime minister (Asia Sentinel 2020). In 2020, IRF joined the International Coalition for Democratic Renewal (ICDR), a global initiative that brings together intellectuals, activists and politicians who are concerned with the simultaneous expansion of power and influence of authoritarian regimes that lead to the weakening of democratic systems from within. The ICDR aims to reaffirm the fundamental principles of democracy, condemn authoritarian opponents of democracy and show solidarity with the courageous individuals who fight for freedom in undemocratic systems around the world.

## IRF and Its Impact on the Public Sphere

By discussing issues that are pertinent locally and regionally, IRF has been able to actively engage with the international community at both the individual and collective levels. A summary of IRF's efforts can be seen in Appendix A, with details of webinars conducted and articles published in an attempt to mobilize efforts and build a discourse in the public sphere. IRF's impact in the pandemic era indicates that its discourses have had a significant influence, with the general public becoming increasingly aware of the discussed issues. For instance, the scholarly opinions on Malaysian university education generated from IRF's webinar "Do our universities need revamp?" are prominently featured on the popular Times Higher Education portal.[13] The social consciousness formed from the public sphere not only nurtures and strengthens public opinion, but also acts as an agent that brings democracy to its true reality (Tiwari 2006).

In the midst of movement restrictions in the pandemic era, IRF did not halt its fight for democracy and human rights, with its emphasis on the sanctity of life, justice, freedom of choice, property and privacy—all of which are fundamental and inviolable rights in Islam (Berween 2002). By prioritizing online social communication, IRF could spread ideas of Muslim reformism through social media, such as Facebook, Twitter, Instagram and YouTube, especially during the COVID-19 pandemic as people used digital media to stay in touch with family members, relieve anxiety and boredom at home, and keep abreast of the latest information on public health (Padilla and Blanco 2020).

## POST COVID-19: THE FUTURE OF ISLAMIC REFORM DISCOURSE IN DIGITAL MEDIA AND ITS INFLUENCE ON PUBLIC SPHERE

The discourse of Islamic reformism advanced by IRF provides an antithesis to the discourse of contemporary Islamist movements calling for the establishment of a "genuine" Islamic society that both implement Sharia law and approve the use of political actions in the process (Roy 2002). In the context of a modern state involving an increasingly complex system of statehood and plural society, such a project is deemed not only irrelevant but also dangerous: Islamism, with its intolerance of non-Muslim ethos, reduces religion to a tool of power to control society whenever it takes centre stage (Tibi 2012).

On the contrary, the discourse of Islamic reformism advocated by IRF seeks to nurture values of democracy, human rights, inclusiveness, tolerance and pluralism—consistent with the true teachings of Islam. Concurrently, it brings a viable alternative so that the discourse of Wahabbi-Salafist Islamism does not dominate the public sphere. This strategy is in line with post-Islamist movements and figures in Indonesia who emphasize that Muslims should strengthen democratic institutions and promote critical reasoning without rejecting the good things that come from the West (Abdillah 1996).

### Congruence of IRF with Appropriate Aspects of Modernity

Islamic reformism, as propounded by IRF, is an inclusive concept. Rather than being confined to spiritual discussions by the Muslim community alone, IRF's Islamic discourse includes political deliberations on democracy, human rights and cultural pluralism that go beyond labels of race and religion. In fact, IRF's references are not limited to the Islamic tradition; it incorporates appropriate ideas from the West that do not violate Islamic tenets. At the same time, IRF has pioneered the idea of integrating ulama *an-nusus* (textual scholars) and ulama *al-waqi'* (contextual scholars) as expressed by Tariq Ramadan (2008) so that any discourse includes both experts in matters of Islamic revealed knowledge and "secular" knowledge such as medicine, engineering, architecture and philosophy, among others. This allows for every decision on worldly matters to be of real benefit to society while being congruent with Islamic values, which accords with the concept of *raḥmatan lil-ālamin*[14] and *maqāsid al-shari'a*[15] (Ahmad Farouk Musa and Ong 2019). This approach is perceived to be more in harmony with aspects of modernity without romanticizing the history of past Islamic civilizations (Umayyad Abbasid and Ottoman) while opening a path for reform that is more relevant to our contemporary times.

## Availability of IRF's Discourse in the Public Sphere

Since its establishment in 2010, IRF has held all its discourses in public places. Offline programmes such as public forums, study groups and summer schools took place in physical spaces while online activities were held in the digital space. The latter include webinars as well as articles and books published, translated or shared by the IRF (refer to Appendix B). Unlike offline programmes which end after delivery, online programmes endure as they remain accessible to the community beyond their delivery date. This helps the discourse of Islamic reformism to spread organically as people continuously access, discuss, debate and share them in the public sphere; these ideas eventually influence and form public opinion as a result of social interactions that, according to Habermas, arise from the flow of communication against specific issues in the public sphere (Kaiser et al. 2018). Most importantly, active IRF discourse on Facebook pages is seen to offer an additional advantage as visitors engage with each other through comments and responses that keep the debates alive. According to Yetkinel and Çolak (2017), Facebook has become a new public sphere in the twenty-first century because of its free and open function for anyone debating any issue. Since Facebook can be accessed free of charge, it allows the global community to be actively involved in any discussion without any border or boundary between them. The community can choose the time as well as the different ways they wish to contribute to the discussion. The function of Facebook as a free and open medium in itself reflects a digital network that allows social communication in the global arena to effect changes in the social structure and community's power through active participation in online discussions towards the formation of a more robust society (Yetkinel and Colak 2017). We, in the IRF, place reason and human freedom at a very high position due to our belief that any critical discussions among society members on knowledge and the political situation surrounding them would lead to a more equitable community. Hence, Facebook and any other free and open digital media enhance the Islamic reformation discourses which enable society to interact within them effectively.

## Effectiveness of IRF's Discourse

Schilirò (2021) noted that the COVID-19 pandemic has accelerated the process of IR 4.0 through the multi-sector transformation in digital technology and Internet consumption that replaced conventional industries. This phenomenon helps build a wide network of contacts and information sharing with the international community. Thanks to its presence on Facebook which has an open access feature that allows greater participation in its live broadcast, IRF discourses have gained substantial international coverage. Simultaneously, greater collaboration with overseas organizations and renowned academics has enhanced the influence of IRF regionally and internationally. This wider presence has firmly established IRF as a prominent voice in the public sphere. With the digital transformation brought by COVID-19 wherein various sectors conduct their affairs more rapidly, effectively and ubiquitously in cyberspace, IRF is expected to build a stronger discourse of Islamic reformism through the digital media to forge public opinions. Consequently, despite the dissipating condition of the COVID-19 pandemic and the resumption of daily activities in conventional fashion, we foresee that digital media will remain the main communication medium. This bodes well for the future of the IRF as it continues its mission of assuring greater Islamic discourses in the public sphere as a foil to the rise of Islamic conservatism in Malaysia.

# CONCLUSION

The COVID-19 pandemic has impacted both the country's development industry sector as well as human behaviour, with increased interaction within the virtual digital world. To stay relevant, IRF adapted its modus operandi and used digital media to promote its inclusive, pluralistic and democratic ideas for the common good in a multicultural society such as Malaysia. As a civil society organization, IRF regularly speaks out on issues related to democracy and human rights, including global humanitarian crises to reach the authorities and policymakers so that they may act to resolve those issues. Indeed, the strand of Islamic reformism advocated by IRF analyses societal problems in context rather than on rigid and stagnant textual interpretations. According to Mohd Syazreen Abdullah (2017), this discourse of religious plurality and togetherness must be made the focus of Islamic humanism—something the IRF considers a high priority in an increasingly complex, digital post-pandemic world.

Bringing the Islamic reformism discourse to the digital public sphere certainly has its own challenges, especially from Islamist groups that aspire to establish an Islamic state that practises *Shari'a* law through the centralization of power. This stands in sharp contrast to the idea of Islamic reformism driven by IRF, which strives to create public awareness regarding the importance of having a clearer understanding of Islam, especially the higher purpose of the *Shari'a* towards human flourishing. IRF also seeks to correct the mistaken insular notion that anything outside the Islamic heritage is hostile to Islam. Indeed, the Prophet himself had an ecumenical, open-minded and pragmatic approach when establishing the early Muslim community in Madinah. Narrow-mindedness imprisons Muslims into a siege mentality, paving the way to fanaticism and religious bigotry. Through its discourse of Islamic reformism, IRF hopes to influence the public sphere in pluralistic Malaysia to create a more open society that accepts rather than tolerates differences. Only then can Islam—a universal religion and way of life meant for the whole universe—be the torchbearer for human flourishing and civilizational progress.

> *"... for it is by turns that We apportion unto men such days [of fortune and misfortune] ..."*
> [Al-Qur'ān; Sura Āl-i'Imran: 140]

# APPENDIX A

## List of Webinars Conducted

| NO. | TOPIC | PANELISTS | DATE |
|---|---|---|---|
| 1. | WEBINAR: What Does the Coronavirus Pandemic Teach Us about Democracy and Authoritarianism? | Nader Hashemi (University of Denver) | 02-04-2020 |
| 2. | WEBINAR: COVID-19 and the Rule of Law | Shad Saleem Faruqi (University of Malaya) | 18-04-2020 |
| 3. | WEBINAR: Freedom of Religion in a Time of COVID-19: A Case of Competing Rights? | Shad Saleem Faruqi (University of Malaya)<br><br>Andrew Khoo (Bar Council Malaysia) | 25-04-2020 |
| 4. | WEBINAR: Post-COVID-19: Is There Going to Be a New World Order? | Chandra Muzaffar (JUST)<br><br>Emir Hadzikadunic (Ambassador of Bosnia & Herzegovina to Malaysia) | 02-05-2020 |
| 5. | WEBINAR: Post-COVID-19: Should There Be a New Economic Model? | Jomo Kwame Sundaram (Malaysian economist) | 09-05-2020 |
| 6. | WEBINAR: Post-COVID-19 New Normal: A Perspective | HE Maria Castillo Fernandez (Ambassador and Head of Delegation of the EU to Malaysia) | 16-05-2020 |
| 7. | WEBINAR: Will COVID-19 Pandemic Affect the Sustainability of UNSDGs? | Stefan Priesner (UN Resident Coordinator for Malaysia) | 06-06-2020 |
| 8. | WEBINAR: COVID-19 & the Rise of Xenophobia: Analysis & Solution | Ahmad Fauzi Abdul Hamid (Universiti Sains Malaysia)<br><br>Azhar Ibrahim (National University of Singapore) | 20-06-2020 |
| 9. | WEBINAR: Is COVID-19 Pandemic Strengthening Authoritarianism in the Arab States? | Heba Raouf Ezzat (Ibn Haldun University) | 04-07-2020 |
| 10. | WEBINAR: COVID-19 & Malaysia's Current Political Impasse | Mohd Azizuddin Mohd Sani (Universiti Utara Malaysia) | 08-08-2020 |

| | | | |
|---|---|---|---|
| 11. | WEBINAR: *Memperingati Cak Nur* (Remembering *Cak Nur*) | Budhy Munawar Rachman (University of Paramadina) <br><br> Ahmad Gaus AF (University of Paramadina) <br><br> Gerardette Philips (Parahyangan University) | 16-08-2020 |
| 12. | WEBINAR: Is the South China Sea the New Battleground for US-Chinese Exceptionalism? | Chandra Muzaffar (JUST) <br><br> Sharifah Munirah Alatas (National University of Malaysia) | 13-09-2020 |
| 13. | WEBINAR: Is the Plight of the Uighurs Just Western Propaganda? | Olsi Jazexhi (University of Durres, Albania) <br><br> Dolkun Isa (World Uyghur Congress) | 26-09-2020 |
| 14. | WEBINAR INTERNASIONAL: *Risale-i-Nur & Toleransi: Membangun Dialog Antariman dalam Perspektif Bediuzzaman Said Nursi (1876–1960)* (Risale-i-Nur & Tolerance: Fostering an Interfaith Dialogue through the Perspective of Bediuzzaman Said Nursi [1876–1960]) | Theol. Leonardus Samosir (Parahyangan Catholic University) <br><br> Asep Muhyiddin, M.Ag (Universitas Islam Negeri Sunan Gunung Djati Bandung, Indonesia) <br><br> Azrul Asmadi (IRF) | 30-09-2020 |
| 15. | WEBINAR: Reading Session on "Be Careful with Muhammad!" | Shabbir Akhtar (University of Oxford) | 17-10-2020 |
| 16. | WEBINAR: *Isu Protes Pekerja & Hak Demokrasi Rakyat Indonesia: Analisis Dan Cadangan* (Workers Protest & the Democratic Rights of the Indonesians: Analyses and Recommendations) | Piet Khaidir Hizbullah (Muhammadiyah, Indonesia) <br><br> Syafiq Hasyim (Nahdlatul Ulama, Indonesia) <br><br> Azrul Asmadi (IRF) | 01-11-2020 |
| 17. | WEBINAR: A Conversation: What Is Happening in Thailand Now? | Maung Zarni (Forces of Renewal Southeast Asia) <br><br> Edmund Bon Tai Soon (former Malaysian Representative to the ASEAN Intergovernmental Commission on Human Rights) <br><br> Sriprapha Petcharamesree (Mahidol University, Thailand) <br><br> Hishamuddin Rais (Malaysian political activist) | 21-11-2020 |

| | | | |
|---|---|---|---|
| 18. | WEBINAR: Post-Trump Era: Will There Be Any Change in the US Foreign Policy? | HE Gholam Ali Khosroo (former Iranian Ambassador to the United Nations)<br><br>Rashila Ramli (National University of Malaysia)<br><br>Chandra Muzaffar (President of JUST) | 12-12-2020 |
| 19. | WEBINAR: "China's Debt-Trap Diplomacy: Is ASEAN a Victim?" | Ramon Guillermo (Centre for International Studies, University of the Philippines)<br><br>Didi Kirsten Tatlow (Senior Fellow, German Council on Foreign Relations)<br><br>Maung Zarni (Forces of Renewal Southeast Asia)<br><br>Syed Hamid Albar (former Senior Minister in the Malaysian government) | 09-01-2021 |
| 20. | WEBINAR: *Pembelajaran Dalam Talian Era COVID-19: Isu dan Cabaran ke Arah Kesetaraan dalam Pendidikan* (Online Learning in the Era of COVID-19: Issues and Challenges towards Equity in Education) | M. Bakri Musa (Surgeon at St. Louise Regional Hospital, California & author of *Liberating the Malay Mind*)<br><br>Madeline Berma (Fellow, Academy of Sciences Malaysia & Commissioner for the Human Rights Commission of Malaysia) | 30-01-2021 |
| 21. | WEBINAR: *Pandemik COVID-19: Membela golongan yang hilang peluang pendidikan (learning loss) akibat wabak pandemik* (COVID-19 Pandemic: In Defence of the People Who Had Learning Loss from the Pandemic) | Jomo Kwame Sundaram (Senior Advisor, Khazanah Research Institute; Fellow, Academy of Sciences Malaysia)<br><br>Madeline Berma (Fellow, Academy of Sciences Malaysia; Commissioner of the Human Rights Commission of Malaysia) | 20-02-2021 |
| 22. | WEBINAR: Book dissection on "Reopening Muslim Minds: A Return to Reason, Freedom, and Tolerance" with Mustafa Akyol | Mustafa Akyol (Writer & Journalist, Senior Fellow at the Cato Institute's Center for Global Liberty and Prosperity) | 28-08-2021 |

| 23. | WEBINAR: Book dissection on "Islam, Authoritarianism, and Underdevelopment: A Global and Historical Comparison" with Ahmet T. Kuru | Ahmet T. Kuru (Porteous Professor of Political Science, San Diego State University & FORIS scholar at Religious Freedom Institute) | 22-09-2021 |
|---|---|---|---|
| 24. | Webinar on: The Quest for a Historical Muhammad: A Critical Appraisal | Mun'im Sirry (University of Notre Dame, Indiana, USA) | 12-03-2022 |
| 25. | WEBINAR: "Was Russia Intervention in Ukraine the Result of Western Aggression? Impact on the Muslim World from the Balkans to the Nusantara" | Olsi Jazexhi (International Islamic University of Malaysia) Emir Hadzikadunic (Universiti Teknologi MARA) | 26-03-2022 |
| 26. | WEBINAR: *Memperingati Bapak Bangsa, Buya Syafii Maarif (Mei 31, 1935 – May 27, 2022) bersama Dr Azhar Ibrahim & Dr Piet Hizbullah Khaidir* | Azhar Ibrahim (National University of Singapore) Piet Hizbullah Khaidir (Sekolah Tinggi Ilmu al-Qur'an & Sains Al-Ishlah) | 30-07-2022 |

## List of Articles Published

| NO | TOPIC (MALAY VERSION) | AUTHOR | DATE |
|---|---|---|---|
| 1. | Muhammad Asad, Risalah Al-Qur'an, Dan Dunia Melayu | Ahmad Syafii Maarif | 01-01-2020 |
| 2. | Prakata Penterjemah buku Muktazilah dan Persoalan Kebebasan Insan | Ahmad Nabil Amir | 05-01-2020 |
| 3. | Kata Pengantar buku Muktazilah dan Persoalan Kebebasan Insan | Faisol Fatawi | 05-01-2020 |
| 4. | Uraian buku Muktazilah dan Persoalan Kebebasan Insan oleh Dr Muhammad Imarah | Ahmad Farouk Musa | 30-01-2020 |
| 5. | Bahaya Menolak Akal dan Memberhalakan Teks – Uraian buku Muktazilah dan Persoalan Kebebasan Insan oleh Dr Muhammad Imarah | Piet Hizbullah Khaidir | 30-01-2020 |
| 6. | Jawapan kepada MUAFAKAT seputar Isu JAIS & Syiah | Ahmad Farouk Musa | 04-02-2020 |
| 7. | Dilema Antara Keagamaan Dan Kemanusiaan Pada Musim Pandemik | Ahmad Muziru Idham | 07-05-2020 |

| | | | |
|---|---|---|---|
| 8. | Wawancara dengan International Quran News Agency (IQNA) Mengenai Ali Shariati dalam memperingati Ulangtahun Kematiannya yang ke-43 | 18 June 2020 | Ahmad Muziru Idham (Translator) | 18-06-2020 |
| 9. | Konsep Jihad dalam aL-Qur'an menurut Tafsiran Klasik dan Moden – Bahagian I | Asma Afsaruddin Translator: Ahmad Muziru Idham Adnan | 27-09-2020 |
| 10. | Konsep Jihad dalam aL-Qur'an menurut Tafsiran Klasik dan Moden – Bahagian II | Asma Afsaruddin Translator: Ahmad Muziru Idham Adnan | 02-10-2020 |
| 11. | Pandangan Muhammad Asad Tentang Syariah | Ahmad Nabil Amir | 11-10-2020 |
| 12. | Pemikiran Za'ba Dan Kesannya Kepada Kebangkitan Perjuangan Nasionalisme Melayu | Ahmad Nabil Amir & Tasnim Abdul Rahman | 11-01-2021 |
| 13. | Pengaruh Rasionalisme Abduh Dalam Pemikiran Harun Nasution – Bahagian I | Ahmad Nabil Amir | 05-05-2021 |
| 14. | Muhammad Asad Antara Agama Dan Politik | Talal Asad Ahmad Muziru Idham (Translator) | 30-05-2021 |
| 15. | Islam dan Kebebasan Agama Berinstitusi | Ahmed T. Kuru Hamdan Mohd Razali (Translator) | 30-07-2021 |
| 16. | Dr Burhanuddin al-Helmy dan PAS | Ahmad Nabil Amir | 21-08-2021 |
| 17. | Dr Burhanuddin al-Helmy dan PAS – Bahagian II | Ahmad Nabil Amir | 10-01-2022 |
| 18. | Nostalgia Kolonial Macron: Projek Islamik anti-Muslim | Penulis asal: Salman Sayyid Terjemahan: Ahmad Muziru Idham | 17-02-2022 |
| 19. | Para Penterjemah: Marmaduke Pickthall, Yusuf Ali, dan al-Qur'an – Bahagian I | Penulis asal: Steve Noyes Terjemahan: Ahmad Muziru Idham | 14-05-2022 |
| 20. | Para Penterjemah: Marmaduke Pickthall, Yusuf Ali, dan al-Qur'an – Bahagian II | Penulis asal: Steve Noyes Terjemahan: Ahmad Muziru Idham | 15-05-2022 |
| 21. | Pohon Kebajikan Ahmad Syafii Maarif: Keislaman-Keilmuan-Kemanusiaan | Muhammad Abdullah Darraz | 18-07-2022 |
| 22. | Fazlur Rahman dan Interpretasi Teks al-Qur'an | Ahmad Nabil Amir & Ahmad Muziru Idham | 09-08-2022 |

| NO. | | AUTHOR | DATE |
|---|---|---|---|
| 23. | SCRIPT – Wawasan Anwar Ibrahim Bagi Malaysia Yang Lebih Baik: Sebuah Ulasan | Nageeb Gounjaria & Ahmad Farouk Musa | 22-11-2022 |
| 24. | Kemanusiaan Dalam Beragama: Persoalan Asas & Kritikan Sosial | Abdul Rahman Sayuti | 19-12-2022 |

| NO. | TOPIC (ENGLISH VERSION) | AUTHOR | DATE |
|---|---|---|---|
| 1. | Speech delivered by Ahmad Farouk Musa, on 8 December 2019, during the 10th Anniversary of the Islamic Renaissance Front, Kuala Lumpur | Ahmad Farouk Musa | 01-01-2020 |
| 2. | Mercy or No Mercy for Xinjiang's Muslims! | Ghulam Farooque Kaka | 02-02-2020 |
| 3. | On the Brink of War? | Chandra Muzaffar | 08-01-2020 |
| 4. | BFM 89.9 Interview: AMANAH's Political Identity Crisis | BFM 89.9 Interview with Ahmad Farouk Musa, transcribed by Saifullah Bhatti | 22-01-2020 |
| 5. | Annual report of the United Nations High Commissioner for Human Rights and reports of the Office of the High Commissioner and the Secretary-General on the human rights situation in Palestine and other occupied Arab territories | Human Rights Council, 43rd session | 16-02-2020 |
| 6. | Time to Empower Voters to Recall Political Frogs | Thomas Fann | 10-03-2020 |
| 7. | Who Deserves an Apology? | Jacqueline Ann Surin | 22-03-2020 |
| 8. | Coming "Cold War" between the USA and China, If It Escalates into an Armed Conflict, May Result in the Collapse of Modern Civilization | Osman Softic | 02-05-2020 |
| 9. | Freedom of Religion and the COVID-19 Pandemic | Shad Saleem Faruqi | 05-05-2020 |
| 10. | An Interview with the International Quran News Agency (IQNA) on Ali Shariati in commemorating the 43rd Anniversary of his death | Interview was conducted by Mohsen Haddadi (MH) from IQNA News Agency with Ahmad Farouk Musa | 18-06-2020 |
| 11. | Beirut Blast | Chandra Muzaffar | 09-08-2020 |

| 12. | Killing for the Sake of Something Called ... ART: The Charlie Hebdo Affair | Shabbir Akhtar | 01-10-2020 |
|-----|---------------------------------------------------|-----------------------------------------------------|-------------|
| 13. | Freedom of Expression or Freedom to Incite Hatred and Violence? | Lucy J. Aguilar | 30-10-2020 |
| 14. | Déjà Vu in France: Change Attitudes | Chandra Muzaffar | 01-11-2020 |
| 15. | The Paradox between Shoe Diagram and Sound Mind | Muhammad Irwan Ariffin | 18-11-2020 |
| 16. | 25 Years On, the Dayton Peace Agreement Is a Ticking Time Bomb | Emir Hadzikadunic | 21-11-2020 |
| 17. | Dayton Peace (Dis)agreement, 25 Years On | Emir Hadzikadunic | 15-12-2020 |
| 18. | Muhammad Abduh's Influence in Southeast Asia – Part I | Ahmad N. Amir, Abdi O. Shuriye & Jamal I. Daoud | 20-12-2020 |
| 19. | No Credible Alternative to the US Grand Strategy in Europe | Emir Hadzikadunic | 23-12-2020 |
| 20. | Muhammad Abduh's Influence in Southeast Asia – Part II | Ahmad N. Amir, Abdi O. Shuriye & Jamal I. Daoud | 03-01-2021 |
| 21. | Muhammad Abduh's Influence in Southeast Asia – Part III | Ahmad N. Amir, Abdi O. Shuriye & Jamal I. Daoud | 07-01-2021 |
| 22. | Leadership Manoeuvres: The Real Reason | Chandra Muzaffar | 12-01-2021 |
| 23. | Winning Votes through Identity Politics | Chandra Muzaffar | 05-02-2021 |
| 24. | Magellan, Inquisition and Globalisation | Felice Noelle Rodriguez & Jomo Kwame Sundaram | 16-03-2021 |
| 25. | Syria: The Price of Resistance | Chandra Muzaffar | 22-03-2021 |
| 26. | Our Humanity; Our Identity | Chandra Muzaffar | 01-05-2021 |
| 27. | US, NATO and the Question of Russia | Emir Hadzikadunic | 01-06-2021 |
| 28. | Muhammad Abduh and His Epistemology of Reform: Its Impact on Rashid Rida – Part I | Ahmad N. Amir | 03-07-2021 |
| 29. | Islam and Institutional Religious Freedom | Ahmet T. Kuru | 07-07-2021 |
| 30. | Muhammad Abduh and His Epistemology of Reform: Its Impact on Rashid Rida – Part III | Ahmad N. Amir, Abdi O. Shuriye & Jamal I. Daoud | 07-09-2021 |

| 31. | Tunisian Coup: What We Can Learn from History | Osman Softić | 31-07-2021 |
| 32. | Humiliating Defeat in Afghanistan | Chandra Muzaffar | 28-08-2021 |
| 33. | Dismantling the "Ulema-State" Is Crucial for the Future of Muslim-Majority Countries | Ahmet T. Kuru | 11-10-2021 |
| 34. | Navigating through Four Types of Malay Muslims in Malaysia | Mohd Tajuddin Mohd Rasdi | 25-01-2022 |
| 35. | Macron's Colonial Nostalgia: Anti-Muslim Islamic Project | Salman Sayyid | 14-02-2022 |
| 36. | Ukraine: Understanding the Concern of the Other | Chandra Muzaffar | 28-02-2022 |
| 37. | Is Bosnia-Herzegovina Next on Russia's Radar? | Emir Hadzikadunic | 12-03-2022 |
| 38. | The Russian Invasion of Ukraine through My Burmese Eyes | Maung Zarni | 16-03-2022 |
| 39. | The Role of Islam in Foreign Policymaking – Part I | Emir Hadzikadunic | 23-03-2022 |
| 40. | The Role of Islam in Foreign Policymaking – Part II | Emir Hadzikadunic | 29-03-2022 |
| 41. | American Political Opportunism and Washington's Long Overdue Genocide Determination | Maung Zarni | 02-04-2022 |
| 42. | Pakistan's Political Conundrum: Who Conspired to Oust the Imran Khan Government and Why? | Osman Softić | 07-04-2022 |
| 43. | Liberal Fundamentalists and Imranophobia | SherAli Tareen | 11-04-2022 |
| 44. | The Role of Islam in Foreign Policymaking – Part III | Emir Hadzikadunic | 17-04-2022 |
| 45. | The Role of Islam in Foreign Policymaking – Part IV | Emir Hadzikadunic | 28-04-2022 |
| 46. | Preface to the Unpublished Letters of Muhammad Asad | Fadlullah Wilmot | 09-05-2022 |
| 47. | Penang Malays: Icons of Reform and Tolerance | Ahmad Fauzi Abdul Hamid | 11-05-2022 |
| 48. | Myanmar: Executing Dissent | Chandra Muzaffar | 01-08-2022 |
| 49. | No Human Right to Smoke and Vape | Shad Saleem Faruqi | 11-08-2022 |

| 50. | Western Myanmar as a Genocide Triangle: The Military-Controlled State, Separatist Buddhist Rakhine Nationalists and Rohingya Genocide Victims – Part I | Maung Zarni | 29-09-2022 |
|---|---|---|---|
| 51. | Western Myanmar as a Genocide Triangle: The Military-Controlled State, Separatist Buddhist Rakhine Nationalists and Rohingya Genocide Victims – Part II | Maung Zarni | 06-10-2022 |
| 52. | SCRIPT – Anwar Ibrahim's Vision for a Better Malaysia: A Review | Nageeb Gounjaria & Ahmad Farouk Musa | 10-10-2022 |
| 53. | Islamic Values and Lessons from Malaysia | Ermin Sinanović | 18-10-2022 |
| 54. | The Absence of Principles Marks a Half-Century of Burma's Opposition | Maung Zarni | 29-11-2022 |
| 55. | Blurb for "The Unpublished Letters of Muhammad Asad" | Abdar Rahman Koya & Ahmad Farouk Musa | 21-12-2022 |

# APPENDIX B

## List of IRF Books Published

| No. | Title | Author | Translator | Year |
|-----|-------|--------|-----------|------|
| 1. | *Risalah Al-Qur'an Juz 'Amma*<br>(A translation of the final chapter of *The Message of the Qur'an*, famously known as *Juz 'Amma*)<br><br>Link: https://bit.ly/3CSOMor | Muhammad Asad | Ahmad Nabil Amir | October 2021 |
| 2. | *Risalah Al-Qur'an – Set Lengkap (3 Jilid)*<br>(A translation of *The Message of the Qur'an –* full set in three volumes)<br><br>Link: https://bit.ly/3H8tDsS | Muhammad Asad | Ahmad Nabil Amir | October 2021 |
| 3. | *Risalah Al-Qur'an – Jilid I*<br>(A translation of *The Message of the Qur'an – Volume I*)<br><br>Link: https://bit.ly/3bPaSw4 | Muhammad Asad | Ahmad Nabil Amir | October 2021 |
| 4. | *Risalah Al-Qur'an – Jilid II*<br>(A translation of *The Message of the Qur'an – Volume II*)<br><br>Link: https://bit.ly/2YlyiWC | Muhammad Asad | Ahmad Nabil Amir | October 2021 |
| 5. | *Risalah Al-Qur'an – Jilid III*<br>(A translation of *The Message of the Qur'an – Volume III*)<br><br>Link: https://bit.ly/3qmHPlu | Muhammad Asad | Ahmad Nabil Amir | October 2021 |
| 6. | *Muktazilah dan Persoalan Kebebasan Insan*<br>(A translation of *al-Mu'tazilah wa Musykilah al-Hurriyyah al-Insāniyah –* The Mu'tazilites and the Issues of Freedom of Mankind)<br>Link: https://bit.ly/3EMzpOA | Muhammad Imarah | Ahmad Nabil Amir | December 2019 |
| 7. | *Antologi Seminar Pemikiran Reformis – Jilid I*<br>(*Compendium of Seminar on Reformist Thought – Volume I*)<br><br>Link: https://bit.ly/3kgaGKZ | Editor: Ahmad Farouk Musa | – | December 2019 |

| | | | | |
|---|---|---|---|---|
| 8. | *Ke Arah Reformasi Islam: Kebebasan Sivil, Hak Asasi dan Undang-Undang Antarabangsa* (A translation of *Toward an Islamic Reformation: Civil Liberties, Human Rights, and International Law*)<br><br>Link: https://bit.ly/3k9nh2o | Abdullahi Ahmed an-Naim | Ahmad Nabil Amir | May 2019 |
| 9. | *Pertelingkahan Politik dalam Kalangan Para Sahabat* (A translation of *al-Khilāfāt as-Siyāsiah baina as-Shahābah* – Political Altercations among the Companions of the Prophet)<br><br>Link: https://bit.ly/3ERBf0J | Mohamed El-Moctar El-Shinqiti | Muhammad Thufail Sayuti | April 2019 |
| 10. | *Jalan Ke Mekah* (A translation of *The Road to Mecca*)<br><br>Link: https://bit.ly/3EPZpZA | Muhammad Asad | Mukhriz Mat Rus | January 2019 |
| 11. | *Golongan Muslim Pertama: Sejarah dan Memori* (A translation of *The First Muslims: History and Memory*)<br><br>Link: https://bit.ly/3mR5uPn | Asma Afsaruddin | Mohamad Basil Hazman Baharom | July 2018 |
| 12. | *Seruan Islah Syed Shaykh al-Hady* (A translation of *The Real Cry of Syed Shaykh al-Hady*)<br><br>Link: https://bit.ly/3wn4tS8 | Editor: Alijah Gordon | Shuhaib Ar Rumy Ismail | July 2018 |
| 13. | *Rachid Ghannouchi: Seorang Demokrat Dalam Wacana Islamisme* (A translation of *Rachid Ghannouchi: A Democrat Within Islamism*)<br><br>Link: https://bit.ly/3bOh7QL | Azzam Tamimi | Ahmad Nabil Amir & Muhammad Syamil Dzulfida | March 2018 |
| 14. | *Reformasi Radikal: Etika Islami dan Pembebasan* (A translation of *Radical Reform: Islamic Ethics and Liberation*)<br><br>Link: https://bit.ly/3o5qgdl | Tariq Ramadan | Ahmad Muziru Idham | January 2018 |
| 15. | *Apa Yang Aku Yakini* (A translation of *What I Believe*)<br><br>Link: https://bit.ly/3obvSTE | Tariq Ramadan | Ahmad Nabil Amir | December 2017 |

| | | | | |
|---|---|---|---|---|
| 16. | *Sumbangan Imam Muhammad Abduh kepada Sains dan Teknologi* (Contribution of Muhammad Abduh to Science and Technology)<br><br>Link: https://bit.ly/2ZZjopq | Ahmad Nabil Amir | – | December 2017 |
| 17. | *Manhaj Islah Imam Muhammad Abduh* (A translation of *Al-Manhaj al-Islahi li 'l-Imam Muhammad Abduh* – The System of Reformation of Imam Muhammad Abduh)<br><br>Link: https://bit.ly/3nYzfwY | Muhammad Imarah | Muhammad Thufail Sayuti | December 2017 |
| 18. | *Rekonstruksi Pemikiran Keagamaan Dalam Islam* (A translation of *The Reconstruction of Religious Thought in Islam*)<br><br>Link: https://bit.ly/3bP4816 | Muhammad Iqbal | Maryam Zakiah | October 2017 |
| 19. | *Tertutupnya Pemikiran Kaum Muslimin* (A translation of *The Closing of the Muslim Mind*)<br><br>Link: https://bit.ly/3mOISiu | Robert R. Reilly | Shuhaib Ar Rumy Ismail | September 2017 |
| 20. | *Agama Lawan Agama* (A translation of *Religion vs. Religion*)<br><br>Link: https://bit.ly/3BWRJCN | Ali Shariati | Ahmad Nabil Amir | April 2017 |
| 21. | *Wacana Pemikiran Reformis – Jilid III* (*A Discourse on Reformist Thought – Volume III*)<br><br>Link: https://bit.ly/3CRVRW4 | Editor: Ahmad Farouk Musa | – | March 2017 |
| 22. | *Islam Di Persimpangan Jalan* (A translation from *Islam at the Crossroads*)<br><br>Link: https://bit.ly/301ufiU | Muhammad Asad | Ahmad Nabil Amir | August 2016 |
| 23. | *Islam, Sekularisme dan Demokrasi Liberal: Membentuk Teori Demokrasi Untuk Masyarakat Muslim* (A translation from *Islam, Secularism, and Liberal Democracy: Toward a Democratic Theory for Muslim Societies*)<br><br>Link: https://bit.ly/3CSYaIB | Nader Hashemi | Hazman Baharom | July 2016 |

| | | | | |
|---|---|---|---|---|
| 24. | *Special Edition:*<br>*The Real Cry of Syed Shaykh al-Hady*<br><br>Link: https://bit.ly/3o4O3Kt | Editor:<br>Alijah<br>Gordon | – | April<br>2016 |
| 25. | *Islam Tanpa Keekstreman: Berhujah Untuk*<br>*Kebebasan*<br>(A translation of *Islam without Extremes: A*<br>*Muslim Case for Liberty*)<br><br>Link: https://bit.ly/3wlKraO | Mustafa<br>Akyol | Nur Ashraff<br>Mohd Noor | January<br>2016 |
| 26. | *Wacana Pemikiran Reformis – Jilid II*<br>(*A Discourse on Reformist Thought – Volume*<br>*II*)<br><br>Link: https://bit.ly/3BS3P04 | Editor:<br>Ahmad<br>Farouk<br>Musa | – | October<br>2014 |
| 27. | *Wacana Pemikiran Reformis – Jilid I*<br>(*A Discourse on Reformist Thought – Volume I*)<br><br>Link: https://bit.ly/3wkmGzS | Editor:<br>Ahmad<br>Farouk<br>Musa | – | June<br>2012 |

## Notes

* The authors would like to express their unreserved gratitude to Ahmad Muziru Idham Adnan who made this work possible, thanks to his ardent commitment and tireless research. In addition, Ahmad Fauzi Abdul Hamid would like to thank the Oxford Centre for Islamic Studies, United Kingdom, for hosting him as a scholar-in-residence from 17 January 2021 to 20 June 2021, during which he pursued the research titled "Islamism in the Era of New Malaysia: The Amorphous Struggle between Liberal and Conservative Forces", out of which ideas for the present chapter materialized. Finally, the authors would like to express their gratitude to Nageeb Gounjaria for proofreading and editing the manuscript.

1.  Taken together, Wahhabi-Salafism is the strongest current in contemporary Islamist political thought and activism (Husain 1995).
2.  Jamal al-Din al-Afghāni (d. 1897) and his closest ally, the Eygptian modernist Muhammad Abduh (d. 1905) and his disciple Rashid Rida (d. 1935) represent another modern and rational school of Salafism. This Salafiyya school promotes rational thinking besides the primary sources, viz. the *Qur'ān* and *Sunna*.
3.  Under Dr Burhanuddin's leadership, PAS developed into a radical Islamic party that was nationalistic, anti-colonialist and anti-imperialist in its outlook. The party articulated concerns related to economic independence, the struggle against colonialism and Western hegemony, as well as the need to promote a dynamic and issue-based form of popular, activist Islam (Noor 2002).
4.  Professor Tariq Ramadan (1962–present) is the grandson of Hassan al-Banna (1906–49), the founder of the Muslim Brotherhood, an Islamic movement in Egypt. He was previously Professor of Contemporary Islamic Studies at the Faculty of Theology and Religion, University of Oxford.
5.  See also endnote 1.
6.  Refer to Appendix B for the complete list of books published by IRF.
7.  *Free Malaysia Today*, "Appeals Court Quashes Home Ministry's Ban on 3 Books on Islam", 13 February 2020, https://www.freemalaysiatoday.com/category/nation/2020/02/13/appeals-court-quashes-home-ministrys-ban-on-3-books-on-islam/.
8.  Habermas's famous theory is "communicative action", which he discusses in his book *The Theory of Communicative Action* (1981). Among his other famous books are *The Structural Transformation of the Public Sphere* (1962), *On the Logic of the Social Sciences* (1967), *The Philosophical Discourse of Modernity* (1985) and *Between Facts and Norms: Contributions to a Discourse Theory of Law and Democracy* (1992).
9.  Frankfurt School is a social theory and inter-discipline critical philosophy which is correlated with the Institute for Social Research that was established

in Goethe University Frankfurt in the year 1923. It was also known as the Critical Theory which was a philosophical and sociological movement that forms the community's theories based on Marxism, and later Hegelian that forms neo-Marxism. Their way of thinking was based on dialecticism that questions the contradiction which existed within the community. Among the famous scholars within this Frankfurt School or the Critical Theory are Max Horkheimer (1895–1973), Theodor Adorno (1903–69), Herbert Marcuse (1898–1979), Walter Benjamin (1892–1940), Friedrich Pollock (1894–1970), Leo Löwenthal (1900–1993) and Eric Fromm (1900–1980). In the 1970s, Jürgen Habermas strengthened the Frankfurt School with the analytical philosophical trend, including analytical linguistic structuralism and hermeneutics. Habermas transformed Frankfurt School into a more global entity which influenced other academic disciplines in Europe.

10. Refer to https://irfront.net.

11. The translation of the writing was published in two parts. Refer to the following links: Part 1 (https://irfront.net/post/articles/konsep-jihad-dalam-al-quran-menurut-tafsiran-klasik-dan-moden-bahagian-i/) and Part 2 (https://irfront.net/post/articles/konsep-jihad-dalam-al-quran-menurut-tafsiran-klasik-dan-moden-bahagian-ii/).

12. SEAN-CSO is an acronym for South East Asian Network of Civil Society Organizations. Such recognition at the regional level showcases the impact of IRF's advocacy work which has gained international attention.

13. "Malaysian Universities In Dire Need of Reform, Say Scholars", Times Higher Education, 2 November 2021, https://www.timeshighereducation.com/news/malaysian-universities-dire-need-ofreform-say-scholars.

14. *Rahmatan lil-ālamin* denotes blessings to the entire universe; it is not limited to mankind alone.

15. *Maqāsid al-shari'a* is the higher or overarching intention, purpose or meaning intended by the *shari'a*.

## REFERENCES

Abdillah, Masykuri. 1996. "Theological Responses to the Concepts of Democracy and Human Rights: The Case of Contemporary Indonesian Muslim Intellectuals". *Studia Islamika* 3, no. 1: 1–41.

Afsaruddin, Asma. 2020. "Konsep Jihad dalam aL-Qur'an menurut Tafsiran Klasik dan Moden". Kuala Lumpur: Islamic Renaissance Front. https://irfront.net/post/articles/konsep-jihad-dalam-al-quran-menurut-tafsiran-klasik-dan-moden-bahagian-i/ (Part 1) and https://irfront.net/post/articles/konsep-jihad-dalam-al-quran-menurut-tafsiran-klasik-dan-moden-bahagian-ii/ (Part 2) (Original work published 2020).

Ahmad Farouk Musa. 2014. "Islah dan Tajdid menerusi lensa IRF". In *Wacana Pemikiran Reformis: Jilid II*, edited by Ahmad Farouk Musa. Kuala Lumpur: Islamic Renaissance Front.

———. 2017. "Kata Pengantar Editor". In *Wacana Pemikiran Reformis: Jilid III*, edited by Ahmad Farouk Musa. Kuala Lumpur: Islamic Renaissance Front.

———. 2020. Speech delivered by Ahmad Farouk Musa, on 8 December 2019, during the 10th Anniversary of the Islamic Renaissance Front, Kuala Lumpur. https://irfront.net/post/articles/speech-delivered-by-ahmad-farouk-musa-on-8th-december-2019-during-the-10th-anniversary-of-the-islamic-renaissance-front-kuala-lumpur/.

Ahmad Farouk Musa, and Marilyn Ong Siew Ai. 2019. "The Intersections between the Concept of Islam Rahmatan Lil-Ālamin and the United Nations' Sustainable Developmental Goals (SDG)". Presented at the International Conference on Nation Building 2019: Connecting Government, Business, and Civil Society towards the Development of a High-Income Nation, 26 and 27 November 2019 at Majestic Hotel, Kuala Lumpur, Malaysia.

Ahmad Fauzi, Abdul Hamid, and Che Hamdan Che Mohd Razali. 2016. *Middle Eastern Influences on Islamist Organizations in Malaysia: The Cases of ISMA, IRF and HTM*. Trends in Southeast Asia, no. 2/2016. Singapore: ISEAS – Yusof Ishak Institute.

Ahmad Muziru Idham. 2020. "IRF Annual Report 2020". Unpublished report. Kuala Lumpur: Islamic Renaissance Front.

Ahmad Nabil Amir. 2012. "Abduh Sang Reformis". In *Wacana Pemikiran Reformis: Jilid I*, edited by Ahmad Farouk Musa. Kuala Lumpur: Islamic Renaissance Front.

Asia Sentinel. 2020. "Shaky Malaysian Government's Clampdown Grows", 14 July 2020. https://www.asiasentinel.com/p/shaky-malaysian-governments-clampdown.

Azhar Ibrahim. 2014. *Contemporary Islamic Discourse in the Malay-Indonesian World: Critical Perspectives*. Petaling Jaya: Strategic Information and Research Development Centre.

BBC News. 2020. "Charlie Hebdo: Magazine Republishes Controversial Mohammed Cartoons", 1 September 2020. https://www.bbc.com/news/world-europe-53985407.

Berween, M. 2002. "The Fundamental Human Rights: An Islamic Perspective". *The International Journal of Human Rights* 6, no. 1: 61–78.

Burstein, Paul. 2003. "The Impact of Public Opinion on Public Policy: A Review and an Agenda". *Political Research Quarterly* 56, no. 1: 29–40.

Cobbe, Elaine. 2020. "Satirical Paper Charlie Hebdo Reruns Muhammad Cartoons as 14 Go on Trial for Paris Attacks". *CBS News*, 2 September

2020. https://www.cbsnews.com/news/charlie-hebdo-reruns-muhammad-cartoon-trial-paris-attacks/.

Coca, Nithin. 2020. "The Long Shadow of Xinjiang". *Foreign Affairs*, 10 September 2020. https://www.foreignaffairs.com/articles/china/2020-09-10/long-shadow-xinjiang.

Curran, James. 2000. "Rethinking Media and Democracy". In *Mass Media and Society*, edited by James Curran and Michael Gurevitch. London: Arnold Publishing.

Esposito, John. 1984. *Islam and Politics*. New York: Syracuse University Press.

Fuchs, Christian. 2014. "Social Media and the Public Sphere". *TripleC* 12, no. 1: 57–101.

Grbeša, M. 2003. "Why If At All Is the Public Sphere a Useful Concept?" *Politička Misao*, 40, no. 5: 110–21.

Habermas, Jünger. 1964. "The Public Sphere: An Encyclopedia Article". *New German Critique* 3 (Autumn 1974): 49–55.

———. 1991. *The Structural Transformation of the Public Sphere: An Inquiry into a Category of Bourgeois Society* [translation]. Cambridge, Massachusetts: The MIT Press.

———. 2006. "Political Communication in Media Society: Does Democracy Still Enjoy an Epistemic Dimension? The Impact of Normative Theory on Empirical Research". *Communication Theory* 16, no. 4: 411–26.

Husain, Mir Zohair. 1995. *Global Islamic Politics*. New York: HarperCollins.

IRF (Islamic Renaissance Front). 2021a. "Introduction". https://irfront.net/about-irf/introduction/.

———. 2021b. "Vision and Mission Statement". https://irfront.net/about-irf/vision-and-mission-statement/.

Jenkins, Henry. 2006. *Convergence Culture: Where Old and New Media Collide*. New York: New York University Press.

Jones, Steven G. 1997. "The Internet and Its Social Landscape". In *Virtual Culture: Identity and Communication in Cybersociety*, edited by Steven G. Jones, pp. 7–35. Thousand Oaks, CA: Sage Publications.

Kaiser, Jonas, Birte Fähnrich, Markus Rhomberg, and Peter Filzmaier. 2018. "What Happened to the Public Sphere? The Networked Public Sphere and Public Opinion Formation". In *Handbook of Cyber-Development, Cyber-Democracy, and Cyber-Defense*, edited by Elias G. Carayannis, David F. J. Campbell, and Marios P. Efthymiopoulos. New York: Springer Nature.

Mahlouly, Dounia. 2013. "Rethinking the Public Sphere in a Digital Environment: Similarities between the Eighteenth and the Twenty-First Centuries". *eSharp* 20, no. 6: 1–21.

McGregor, Shannon C. 2019. "Social Media as Public Opinion: How Journalists Use Social Media to Represent Public Opinion". *Journalism* 20, no. 8: 1070–86.

Mohd. Syazreen Abdullah. 2017. "Tafsir Reformis: Membentuk Masyarakat Agama yang Pluralis". In *Wacana Pemikiran Reformis: Jilid III*, edited by Ahmad Farouk Musa. Kuala Lumpur: Islamic Renaissance Front.

*New Straits Times*. 2020. "Covid-19: Movement Control Order Imposed with Only Essential Sectors Operating". 16 March 2020. https://www.nst.com.my/news/nation/2020/03/575177/covid-19-movement-control-order-imposed-only-essential-sectors-operating.

*New York Times*. 2020. "Charlie Hebdo Republishes Cartoons That Prompted Deadly 2015 Attack". 1 September 2020. https://www.nytimes.com/2020/09/01/world/europe/charlie-hebdo-cartoons-trial-france.html.

Noor, Farish. 2002. *The Other Malaysia: Writings on Malaysia's Subaltern History*. Kuala Lumpur: Silverfish Books.

Padilla, Daniel A. G., and Leonardo T. Blanco. 2020. "Social Media Influence in the COVID-19 Pandemic". *International Braz J Urol* 46, no. 1: 120–24.

Papacharissi, Zizi. 2002. "The Virtual Sphere: The Internet as a Public Sphere". *New Media & Society* 4, no. 1: 9–21.

Rahman, Fazlur. 1966. *Islam*. Chicago: The University of Chicago Press.

Ramadan, Tariq. 2008. *Radical Reform: Islamic Ethics and Liberation*. Oxford: Oxford University Press.

Razak Ahmad, and Zakiah Koya. 2020. "Pakatan Harapan Govt Collapse". *The Star*, 24 February 2020. https://www.thestar.com.my/news/nation/2020/02/24/pakatan-harapan-govt-collapses.

Roy, Olivier. 2002. *Globalised Islam: The Search for a New Ummah*. London: Hurst & Co.

Schilirò, Daniele. 2021. "Digital Transformation, COVID-19, and the Future of Work". *International Journal of Business Management and Economic Research* 12, no. 3: 1945–52.

Schudson, Michael. 1992. "Was There Ever a Public Sphere? If So, When? Reflections on the American Case". In *Habermas and the Public Sphere*, edited by Craig Calhoun. Cambridge, Mass: MIT Press.

Sean-CSO. 2020. "The Influences of Religion in Southeast Asia (Part II)". Newsletter. https://www.sean-cso.org/2020/10/08/newsletter-september-2020-the-influences-of-religion-in-southeast-asia-part-ii/.

Taylor, Charles. 1992. "Modernity and the Rise of the Public Sphere". *The Tanner Lectures on Human Values* 14: 203–60.

Tibi, Bassam. 2012. *Islamism and Islam*. New Haven & London: Yale University Press.

Tiwari, Richa. 2006. "Habermas's Views on the Significance of the Public Sphere in a Democracy". *The Indian Journal of Political Science* 67, no. 3: 639–50.

Ustundag, Alp, and Emre Cevikcan. 2018. *Industry 4.0: Managing Digital Transformation*. Switzerland: Springer International.

Vargo, Deedra, Lin Zhu, Briana Benwell, and Zheng Yan. 2020. "Digital Technology Use during COVID-19 Pandemic: A Rapid Review". *Human Behaviour and Emerging Technologies* 3, no. 1: 13–24.

Yetkinel, Ömer, and Metin Çolak. 2017. "The Effects of Transformation of Public Sphere with the New Media in Academy". *EURASIA Journal of Mathematics, Science and Technology Education* 13, no. 8: 5009–18.

# 4

# Mapping the Malaysian Chinese Cyber-Community

Yuen Beng Lee, Miew Luan Ng and Jerry Yang Sheng Tan

## INTRODUCTION

As the second largest ethnic community in Malaysia, the Chinese have been actively involved in Malaysian politics even before the nation's independence.[1] As part of the four pillars of the Malaysian Chinese community, politics, alongside education, guilds and associations, and media, are central, indispensable and inseparable (Ng and Lee 2018, 2020). The Malaysian Chinese community has primarily supported the Malaysian Chinese Association (MCA), which has been part of the Barisan Nasional (National Front – BN) coalition. BN, mainly comprising of the United Malays National Organisation (UMNO), MCA and Malaysian Indian Congress (MIC), formed the ruling government since 1957.

Since the 13th general election in 2013, Malaysian Chinese voters have mainly supported the Pakatan Harapan (Alliance of Hope – PH) coalition helmed by Anwar Ibrahim (Marzuki Mohamad and Ibrahim

Suffian 2023). This shift in support from BN saw less than 19 per cent of the Chinese voters supporting them. This trend continued in the 14th general election in 2018, in which 88 per cent of Malaysian Chinese voters supported PH as the coalition came into power for the first time. In 2020, however, the PH government lost power to the Perikatan Nasional (National Alliance – PN) coalition.

This change in government was triggered by an event dubbed the "Sheraton Move", where several PH Members of Parliament (MPs) joined the opposition parties (Lee 2022). This defection, allegedly due to infighting, caused UMNO and Parti Islam Se-Malaysia (Pan-Malaysian Islamic Party – PAS) to form the PN coalition which had the aim of forming a complete Malay-Muslim unity government. The eventual withdrawal of Mahathir Mohamad's party, Parti Pribumi Bersatu Malaysia (Malaysian United Indigenous Party – Bersatu), from PH led to his resignation as prime minister. As both PH and PN claimed they had the majority support of MPs to form the government, the Malaysian monarch, Yang di-Pertuan Agong, stepped in and asked every MP about their preferred prime minister candidate. Eventually, Muhyiddin Yassin, president of Bersatu, was appointed the eighth prime minister of Malaysia.

From March 2020 till August 2021, Malaysian Chinese voters were negative about PN as only 16 per cent were happy with its government (Marzuki Mohamad and Ibrahim Suffian 2023). During Muhyiddin's tenure as prime minister, Malaysia faced the COVID-19 pandemic, depreciation of the Malaysian ringgit, food security crisis, economic downturn and various lockdowns known as the Movement Control Orders (MCOs) (Povera, Harun, and Arumugam 2020). Despite handing out economic and financial assistance, only 47 per cent of Malaysian Chinese voters were satisfied with the government's pandemic management (Marzuki Mohamad and Ibrahim Suffian 2023).

In August 2021, Malaysia witnessed another shift in federal governance when Ismail Sabri Yaakob became the ninth prime minister due to a power shift in PN despite retaining power as the federal government. Ismail Sabri continued implementing his predecessor's MCO regulations that prevented Malaysians from moving freely and kept them confined to their homes for undefined periods. As experienced globally, schooling, working and other non-essential services took place online from home. When he was senior minister for security, Ismail Sabri faced various "backlash" from the Malaysian Chinese community due to inconsistencies in the MCO regulations for the 2021 Chinese New Year celebrations (Syed Jamal Zahiid 2021a). These regulations were mocked by individuals who created and spread online memes questioning the rationale of such regulations (Syed Jamal Zahiid 2021b). This incident was not the first time Ismail Sabri courted controversy with the Malaysian Chinese community. In 2015, he urged the Malay community to boycott Chinese traders to force them to lower the prices of goods (Yiswaree 2015).

Prime Minister Ismail Sabri launched the *"Keluarga Malaysia"* concept. Loosely translated as "Malaysian Family", it is based on family unity, putting aside political, racial, ethnic and religious differences. Based on these values, *Keluarga Malaysia* should appeal to all Malaysians. On 27 August 2021, Ismail Sabri announced that his government must present a "report card" detailing and evaluating their first 100 days in office to prove themselves and help overcome the country's pandemic, social and cultural issues, and political problems. The forming of the Cabinet, based on *Keluarga Malaysia*, would be committed and proactive to overcoming challenges faced through cross-party work.

In an interview on 2 October 2021, Ismail Sabri mentioned that in addition to the above, ministers' performance would be gauged through the feedback posted on social media to better understand the feedback, sentiment and perception of Malaysians about his government. These would account for the overall achievement scores of his Cabinet members (*Malay Mail* 2021). Ismail Sabri was also asked for his opinion about the perception of non-Malays about his administration and whether any extra efforts would be made to better gain support from them—especially from the Malaysian Chinese community. Ismail Sabri stated that he has yet to carry out a detailed study about the perception and support from the Chinese community as it was too early to gauge it then. He added that such sentiments could be positive but may gradually change.

Focusing on the Malaysian Chinese community, this chapter examines the sociopolitical issues faced by this community and their online discussions during the first 100 days of the Ismail Sabri government.

# THE MALAYSIAN CHINESE ETHNIC AND CYBER-COMMUNITY

At approximately seven million individuals, the Malaysian Chinese community remains one of the largest concentrations of Chinese outside of mainland China (Chang 2018). As the second largest ethnic group in Malaysia, Malaysian Chinese comprise of various dialect groups such as Hokkien, Hakka and Cantonese, based on their ancestors' point of origin from China. In line with the British colonial policies that saw the migration of Chinese migrants from China and formation of a Malaysian multiethnic society, a report by the Asian Strategy and Leadership Institute (ASLI) forecasts that Malaysian Chinese will account for less than 20 per cent of the population by 2030 (*Malay Mail* 2017). The same report stated that the population of Malaysian Chinese has significantly reduced from 37.2 per cent since the nation's independence to 24 per cent in 2017. In 2021, the population of the Malaysian Chinese community stood at 22.4 per cent, in contrast to the ethnic compositions of *Bumiputera* (69.8 per cent), Indians (6.8 per cent) and Others (1.0 per cent) (Department of Statistics Malaysia 2021).[2] Should the decline continue, the Malaysian Chinese language newspaper *Sin Chew Daily* (SCD) has estimated that by 2030, the Malaysian Chinese will only be 18.9 per cent and 18.4 per cent by 2040. Despite this decline, the Malaysian Chinese community remains integral to the multiethnic population and nation-building efforts. These efforts continue to be discussed online by the Malaysian Chinese cyber-community.

The Malaysian Chinese cyber-community is significant as cyber-communities contribute to civil life by connecting to, linking with and supporting traditional types of communities—the Malaysian Chinese community (Martin, Anheier, and Toepler 2010). Based on a Malaysian Communication and Multimedia Commission survey, the Malaysian Chinese community accounts for 22.4 per cent of Internet users in Malaysia (MCMC 2020b). This represents a 4.6 per cent increase from 17.8 per cent in 2014. They remain the second largest ethnic group of Internet users in Malaysia after the Malays. This number is significant because the Malaysian Chinese cyber-community offers a space transcending time and physicality that is inclusive, free from hegemonic structures, social oppression and marginalization, yet allows for a diversion from a genuine identity (Lieber 2018). Therefore, members can hide their real identities by remaining anonymous and becoming a textual or virtual representation based on texts, images, sounds and various forms of digital media (Mitra 2020). The main feature of a cyber-community is to provide a space to disseminate knowledge and information according to the interests of its members (Kim, Shim, and Martin 2008). It is within this borderless, self-regulated space where no single governing body or centralized controlling authority exists; like-minded community members are free to experience the community benefits without restrictions and to discuss matters of importance across time and space (Mitra 2020).

The Malaysian Chinese cyber-community provides a platform of contestation or imagined space (Lee 2012), where members, through social media sites such as Facebook and video-sharing sites like YouTube, share information. In this study, Facebook is the most popular among the Malaysian Chinese cyber-community. According to Malaysia Digital Report 2023, Facebook ranked second among the country's most-used social media platforms. Local Facebook users occupy 84.8 per cent of the total Internet users and 59.3 per cent of the Malaysian population. Because Malaysians are socialized politically through social media, which shapes their political attitude (Michael and Chin 2021), this explains why SCD and the *Malaysiakini* (Chinese version) focus on maintaining their 2.5 million and 1 million Facebook followers respectively. These platforms are also where Malaysian Chinese can exist and connect online without physicality to create informational and emotional conversations across multiple communities, spaces, affiliations and professions (Wang, Tucker, and Haines 2013). As community members can hide their true identities through pseudonyms due to the lack of physical contact other than a video camera, they may not be subjected to consequences or persecution caused by their actions through laws such as the Sedition Act 1948 or the Printing Presses and Publications Act 1984. It is also easier for deception, misrepresentation and lies to occur, thus making cyber-communities a potentially dangerous platform (Mitra 2020).

## ISSUES FACED BY THE MALAYSIAN CHINESE COMMUNITY DURING THE ISMAIL SABRI GOVERNMENT

In 2021, as Malaysia struggled with the COVID-19 pandemic and economic and political uncertainty, Malaysians witnessed three changes in federal governance in two years: a by-election in Melaka and the Sarawak state elections. In December 2021, Malaysian Chinese politicians from across the political divide and other politicians responded to the news reports concerning a quote about the Malaysian Chinese in Mahathir Mohamad's memoir *Capturing Hope: The Struggle Continues for a New Malaysia*. The Malaysian media reported that Mahathir wrote, "The Chinese eat with chopsticks; they don't eat with their hands" (Channel News Asia 2021). He further explained that Malays and Indians adopted Malaysia's tradition of using hands to eat. Meanwhile, eating with chopsticks was viewed as an identity brought over from China. It was seen as a continual traditional practice deemed as "unMalaysian" and divisive (Channel News Asia 2021).

In the same month, a Malaysian High Court ruled that Chinese and Tamil languages in vernacular schools did not contravene the Federal Constitution (Rahmat Khairulrijal 2021). The ruling states that the existence of vernacular schools is protected in the Malaysian Federal Constitution, in reply to a lawsuit brought by the Federation of Peninsular Malay Students (GPMS), the Islamic Education Development Council (Mappim) and the Confederation of Malaysian Writers Association (Galena). These parties filed this lawsuit, claiming that vernacular schools reduced the chances of employment for non-*Bumiputera* students because they needed to be able to converse in Bahasa Malaysia.

Although the above incidents did not occur during the first 100 days of the Ismail Sabri government, they have coloured the perception of Malaysian Chinese towards him. As a senior UMNO politician, Ismail Sabri, a lawyer by training, has been actively involved in politics since the 1980s. In 2015, as the then minister of agriculture and agro-based industries, Ismail Sabri posted, but it was later removed from his Facebook page, the need for Malays to boycott Malaysian Chinese businesses (Lee 2015), which was a response to falling oil prices in an effort to force Chinese businesses to reduce prices. Ismail Sabri was quoted as urging the Malays to use their "powers" as the majority to force the "minority" Malaysian Chinese to lower their prices of goods. Ismail Sabri explained that his comments were directed at errant Chinese businesses that refused to lower prices as an act of oppression against the Malays. Singling out local coffee shop franchise Old Town White Coffee, he stated that the company had anti-Islamic links and was partly owned by politician Ngeh Koo Ham.

In December of the same year, Ismail Sabri officiated the exclusive *Bumiputera* Mara Digital Mall building in Selangor (Carvalho 2015). With plans to open one in every state, establishing these malls exclusive to *Bumiputera* entrepreneurs was seen as an alleged response to a fight at a famous mall, Plaza Low Yat, often seen as dominated by Malaysian Chinese traders (Hakim Hassan 2020).[3] The mall, which later expanded (but has since ceased operations) to Pahang and Johor, was purposed as an alternative challenge to other digital malls while offering *Bumiputera* entrepreneurs chances of venturing into the business of information technology. In countering criticisms that this initiative was "racist", Ismail Sabri defended that this venture was helping *Bumiputera* entrepreneurs.

In February 2021, Ismail Sabri was again heavily criticized online following the announcement of standard operating procedure guidelines for the Chinese New Year (Syed Jamal Zahiid 2021a). As senior minister for security in the then Muhyiddin Yassin government, Ismail Sabri had announced the guidelines for reunion dinners and house visits during the Chinese New Year in the midst of MCO, which included protocols on how reunion dinners should only be allowed among family members currently living in the same house. There were bans on interstate travel and temple activities, although night markets were allowed to operate. These announcements led to memes and remarks on social media by Malaysians from various ethnic groups about how reunion dinners could be held at the night market instead of the confines of the home. These criticisms were echoed by politicians across the political divide and Chinese associations claiming that they were not consulted before the announcements. These guidelines were deemed culturally insensitive towards the Chinese community as it mistakenly mentioned the reunion dinner being held on the first and second days of the Chinese New Year, whereas it is traditionally held on the eve. The above incidents are linked explicitly to economic and cultural issues of the Malaysian Chinese community and are matters of deep concern as they are related to Chinese politics, education and culture, which are seen as the pillars of the Malaysian Chinese community (Ng and Lee 2018).[4]

## *AO XIANG TIAN JI*, *MALAYSIAKINI* (CHINESE VERSION) AND *SIN CHEW DAILY* (SCD) SOCIAL MEDIA

To understand the issues of importance to the Malaysian Chinese cyber-community, this chapter analyses three social media platforms frequently visited by the Malaysian Chinese—*Ao Xiang Tian Ji*, *Malaysiakini* (Chinese version) and the Facebook pages of *Sin Chew Daily* (SCD). SCD and *Malaysiakini* are Malaysian news organizations and *Ao Xiang Tian Ji* is managed by Ang Woei Shang, a lawyer, political analyst and commentator. These platforms were selected based on consistent news delivery and posts, popularity and reach, and proper organization and maintenance of their social media content concerning the Malaysian Chinese community.

### *Ao Xiang Tian Ji* (AXTJ)

*Ao Xiang Tian Ji* (AXTJ) (翱翔天际。谈古今。论道理) provides analyses and discussions on Malaysian political issues and current affairs on Facebook, YouTube and Instagram. Site owner Ang Woei Shang shares his daily views and analyses on Malaysian politics through "RealTalk Live". As a host and analyst, he held his shows on YouTube Live, with over 50,000 subscribers and 1,500,000 views, generally for two hours in the evenings for Chinese-speaking audiences. Politicians are sometimes invited to the "AXTJ the Guest" segment or "Special Live". On Facebook, Ang shares his interviews on Malaysian political issues with his followers and on Chinese radio station Ai FM. The FB post attracted more than 40,000 followers. He occasionally responds to the comments and interacts with viewers via chatroom, allowing them to hold different opinions.

## *Malaysiakini* (Chinese Version)

Steven Gan and Premesh Chandran founded *Malaysiakini*, which provides daily news in Chinese, Malay, English and Tamil. This news portal is seen as "independent journalism" as it is not linked to any political party or commercial interests; it supports justice, human rights, democracy, freedom of speech and good governance (Steele 2023) and positions itself as a faster, more accurate and independent news provider, emphasizing diverse views and information. *Malaysiakini*'s X (formerly known as Twitter) account has 1.4 million followers, with over 232 thousand tweets. Its KiniTV channel has over three thousand videos with a 30 million click-through rate. Generally, its Chinese and Tamil language news is a translation of English news. Since 19 February 2022, the *Malaysiakini* Chinese Facebook page has more than 1.8 million followers, 958,611 Likes and a daily average of 25 to 30 new posts, videos, hyperlinks and infographics. There is limited data on the demographics of *Malaysiakini*'s Chinese version due to the anonymity of its users.

## *Sin Chew Daily* (SCD)

*Sin Chew Daily* (SCD) is Malaysia's and Southeast Asia's highest-circulated and most-read Chinese language newspaper. It is owned by Tiong Hiew King and his family through Media Chinese International Limited. Since its first print in 1929, SCD has diversified its news presentation and distribution in the digital age through its online TV news, *Pocketimes*. SCD uses Facebook, Twitter, Instagram and YouTube to reach younger audiences—its Facebook page has 2.5 million followers and 2.1 million Likes. As a platform promoting rational discussions, its Facebook page extracts user comments to be published in their newspaper.

# INTERNAL REGULATION AND MODERATION ON THE SOCIAL MEDIA PLATFORMS

To examine the internal regulation and moderation practised by the three news entities via their Facebook pages, the discussion begins with AXTJ, followed by *Malaysiakini* and then SCD.

## *Ao Xiang Tian Ji* (AXTJ)

An advocate of free speech and expression, Ang Woei Shang does not censor his social media platforms, allowing for differing opinions and welcoming diverse interactions about Malaysia's political issues and current affairs. This is seen in his comments below:

> "You are free to speak, but you must be responsible for what you have said."

Ang would agree or disagree as he allows for differing opinions. Despite being bound by regulations (at least on "Everybody Talks Live"), audiences freely express their opinions. Scheduled for broadcast every Saturday at 10 p.m., those who wish to express an opinion must turn on their cameras to reveal their faces and identities, introduce themselves and be responsible for their comments. Once completed, the sessions are posted on his social media for audience comments. AXTJ manually chooses the "oldest comment" option to display the earliest comments first.

## *Malaysiakini*

According to a *Malaysiakini* senior journalist and social media manager, news is released on its website before being posted on social media without moderation. This allows *Malaysiakini* to remain neutral, independent and impartial. *Malaysiakini* provides two different platforms for users to post comments.[5] The first is on its website, where users must subscribe to comment under a news post. However, *Malaysiakini* can remove comments that include name-calling, profanity, personal attacks, impersonation and anti-social behaviour, including spamming and trolling. Users posting such comments could be permanently blocked, but their subscriptions remain active. If subscribers feel that their comments are unfairly blocked, they can email *Malaysiakini* to justify themselves. The *Malaysiakini* Facebook page cannot block users but can only filter comments based on a list of banned words. *Malaysiakini* utilizes the comment ranking by displaying the "most relevant" comments instead of "all comments".

## Sin Chew Daily (SCD)

The *Sin Chew Daily* (SCD) Facebook page is known as "Friends who like Malaysia Sin Chew Daily". It focuses on news stories that touch the audience's hearts, especially about Malaysian ethnic groups. According to an SCD gatekeeper, each branch office's editorial board of the printed version supplies news to the SCD online media editorial board, which then decides which news appears online. The same board occasionally advises the online media editorial board on what news is highlighted or posted quickly. The online media editorial board sometimes translates and writes their news and is monitored by an experienced editor from the print section. This editor is the gatekeeper and decides what news and angle to post on the SCD social media platforms. Based on the gatekeeper's feedback, the SCD Facebook page censors the audience's comments, thus curtailing freedom of speech and expression.

*Malaysiakini* and SCD practise self-regulation to minimize potential harmful content or user comments, but these moves curtail freedom of speech and expression. While these platforms and their users are seemingly not bound by the Printing Presses and Publications Act (PPPA), control is done through blocking, filtering and content removal using the Communications and Multimedia Act 1998, the Sedition Act 1948, the Defamation Act (1983 Revised) and the Security Offences (Special Measures) Act. The Evidence (Amendment) Act 2012 holds owners and editors of websites, providers of web-hosting services and owners of computers or mobile devices accountable for information published through their services or property.[6] Social media owners are thus liable for their news and user comments.

# CHINESE CYBER-COMMUNITY'S INTERACTION WITH THE MALAYSIAN MAINSTREAM PUBLIC

This section discusses the issues concerning the Malaysian Chinese cyber-community and their comments during Ismail Sabri Yaakob's 100-day in governance. The selected posts are those published the most in quantity during this period. Using content analysis, collected data was then analysed and categorized based on the following themes: political and political leaders' news on Malaysia, the new government and COVID-19 related news.

## Content Analysis on News about Politics and Political Leaders in Malaysia and Audience's Response

### *Political News*

Political elections, namely the Melaka by-election and the Sarawak state election, were the main political news during this period. For example, AXTJ focused on the Melaka by-election through its "RealTalk Live" and "Special Live" programmes. The episode of "RealTalk Live" on 1 November 2021 discussed the issues faced by the Democratic Action Party (DAP) and PH and why voters should support them. Ang interviewed Melaka assemblyman YB Allex Seah Shoo Chin on 20 October 2021. The interview received positive comments:

> "DAP needs this type of leader. To gain Malay support, you people (DAP) need to work harder, not bow to Anwar and allow a new leader to take charge." (*AXTJ audience*)

AXTJ also discussed the Sarawak state election. Generally, comments indicated disappointment towards PH, Anwar Ibrahim and DAP. The site also discussed the chances for the Gabungan Parti Sarawak (Sarawak Parties Alliance – GPS) political coalition to win the election:

> "08.12.2021, a new day or darker days for Malaysia. The world is watching whether [it is] worth investing in malaysia." [*sic*] (*AXTJ audience*)

> "There is not much surprise expected from the Sarawak State election as none of the political parties can challenge GPS. Suppose Pakatan Harapan could not perform this time. In that case, they will become the opposition in the upcoming election, and we will return to the political scenario before 2008." (*AXTJ audience*)

In an AXTJ post about the Sarawak election during an interview with the local radio station Ai FM on 25 November 2021, the audience stated:

"DAP must split with PKN." (*AXTJ audience*)

"For us to support them, the Lim father-and-son should step down first." (*AXTJ audience*)

On the SCD Facebook page, the Sarawak election had the most posts with headlines such as "Melaka Ends, Sarawak Begins War!" and "1206 nominations, 1218 votes". However, audiences were more concerned about COVID-19 than about the elections and they expressed their lack of confidence in the election.

Some of the users' comments:

投来做么。赢了又怎样。病毒可能会来第4波。。。好之为啦
(Translation: "Why should we vote? Who cares about who is going to win? There may be a fourth wave of the virus. . . Good Luck")
– username: Alex Lo

来，外围开盘赌希盟输剩多少 。。。 砂州选民，驱赶希盟回西马
(Translation: "Come, let us bet on how much Pakatan Harapan loses ... Sarawak voters, send Pakatan Harapan back to West Malaysia.")
– username: 张耀方

不然来个全国大选，反正已经没有什么分别？
(Translation: "Why don't we just run the national election? Anyway, there is no difference.") – username: Jay Ling

In an SCD post on 4 November 2021, DAP politician Lim Kit Siang stated that "the government hopes to eliminate DAP by using Malacca and Sarawak elections" and predicted that "the voter turnout in the election may be lower than 40%".

Some of the users' comments:

又要打悲情牌骗人出来投票？选情告急剧情又上映？
(Translation: "Want to play the sympathy card again to deceive people into voting? The plot of the election crisis is rereleased?") – username: Yong Zinn Horng

选条淋啦！你们中选每样都没有做到，讲就一流，讲到做到，呸，回家
睡啦。
(Translation: "Vote my dick! You did not keep any of your promises
once you were elected. First class in talking, do what you said! Go
back and sleep.") – username: Walter Chin

弄清楚，火箭是被你们两父子搞屎的！
(Translation: "Let us make it clear. You two, the father and son, make
the Rocket worse!") – username: Qi Yang. (*Rocket refers to the DAP.*)

A post about the Undi 18 initiative to grant eighteen-year-old
Malaysians the right to vote was posted on SCD on 9 November 2021.
The audience, however, disagreed with this policy:

18歲還沒夠思想成熟去投票，但是21歲符合參選資格，這三年都經歷了
什麼？
(Translation: "An 18-year-old is not mature enough to vote, but a
21-year-old is eligible to run for election. What have they experienced
in the past three years?") – username: Mengkeat Tan

### *Malaysian Politicians*

The three Facebook pages focused on the news about Malaysian
politicians. Ang invited politicians from various parties—such as DAP's
Tey Kok Kiew (1 November 2021), Anthony Loke (19 November 2021)
and Howard Lee (18 November 2021) and PKR's Ginie Lim (4 November
2021), Liew Chin Tong (16 November 2021) and Tian Chua—to his
AXTJ's programmes. Others invited include MCA's Chong Yew Chuan
(17 November 2021) and Saw Yee Fung (15 November 2021). Gerakan's
Fong Khai Ling was also interviewed.

In October 2021, Ang held a special edition interview with former
prime minister Mahathir Mohamad to discuss his ideology and thoughts.
The interview discussed the following:

1. On 22 October, Mahathir Mohamad shared his political ideology,
   why he joined politics, his observation of political changes and
   his ideas for a solid government.
2. On 27 October, he discussed Malaysia's issues with ethnicity,
   religion and language. To him, migrants to one country would
   never associate themselves with their original homeland.
   However, this does not happen in Malaysia as a sizeable number

of citizens from Chinese and Indian ancestry did not entirely severe ties with their homelands. To Mahathir, the Chinese in Thailand, Indonesia and the Philippines speak in their country's national language without portraying their Chinese identity. He pointed out that while many Malaysian Chinese speak Malay and learning the Chinese language is acceptable, he prioritizes speaking Malay.

3.  In response to the issues of vernacular schools and national unity, Mahathir Mohamad said that many Malay parents have chosen to send their children to Chinese schools because they are aware that Chinese is now a business language. However, he added that most countries have only one national language.

In response to Mahathir's comments, some audience stated:

"If we address ourselves as Malaysians ... no longer Malaysian Chinese or Malaysian Indian ... do we get the privilege as what the Malays get?" (*AXTJ audience*)

Another replied:

"You must be joking, so keep dreaming." (*AXTJ audience*)

"*Bahasa dan budaya tak pernah jadi halangan untuk* 'national integration'. But restrictive and over sensitive religious practice (of any religion for that matter) does." [sic] (*AXTJ audience*)

Other comments include:

"Now in my late 60s, having supported the 1980s theme Bersih, Cekap & Amanah and witnessing it rotted away by the doing of one selfish man. He is arrogant, opportunist and cruel for destroying and polarising a nation. He had destroyed the families and lives of many wonderful Malaysians during his years in power. I will witness the power of Karma befall his families in generations to come." (*AXTJ audience*)

"Every Malaysian has the right to learn and speak their cultural language — in the federal constitution. Please read the constitution, will you? Your videos are lies." (*AXTJ audience*)

"Who was the one who divide and rule." "The British?" "NO! It was the Old Man." [*sic*] (*AXTJ audience*)

Most disagreed with Mahathir Mohamad, with one stating that while some countries use only one national language, Sweden has four. Most comments also indicated how dishonest politicians could tarnish their images. One member reflected that this interview could have benefitted the audience. Ang replied in the thread that anyone can choose to follow or not to follow the interview. Mahathir Mohamad's statement on the issues of vernacular schools and national unity also caused extensive discussions. One commentator disagreed and stated that students in Chinese primary and secondary schools as well as national type schools learn both Bahasa Malaysia and English; there is no issue with communicating and reuniting with other students. People should be free to choose what language to use in their private time and space.

Another felt that removing vernacular schools did not mean abolishing the Chinese language:

"To standardise the education system means to standardise SPM and UEC, abolish vernacular schools but maintain the rights to learn their mother tongue, Chinese language and Chinese subjects." (*AXTJ audience*)

Some members of the audience had similar thoughts: one shared his experience as a Chinese primary school student who joined the national education system and had a good command of Bahasa Malaysia, which is the national language. However, it took much work in his first two years to comprehend the conversations between his Malay teachers and classmates. To him, the Malaysian education system has polarized society. One way to resolve this problem is to standardize the education system.

Another audience commented:

"... Malaysia was built by the Malay, Chinese, Indian and minority ethnic groups. They were part of the efforts for independence, and their cultures and languages are part of Malaysia. No ethnic group should request the people who contributed to the independence of Malaysia to throw away their culture and language. This is against multiculturalism principles." (*AXTJ audience*)

Besides Mahathir Mohamad, on 10 September 2021, *Malaysiakini* reported about Muhyiddin Yassin, who announced that the PN would return to the political battle in the 15th general election.

One audience commented:

还在发春秋大梦，想要回来当兽相啊？上届509大选是打着希盟旗帜，你们土团才能胜选，而之后就背叛自己的盟友和选民，你也才能硬坐上兽相位子的！这次大选少了希盟的票，污桶也不和你们土团联手，再加上你当兽相时期，搞到很多人家破人亡，民不聊生等等。。。搞不好你癌症复发的机率，都会比你们土团胜选来得高啦！

(Translation: "Still dreaming of spring and autumn, do you want to return to be a 'beast' minister? This election has lost the votes of Pakatan Harapan, and the 'dirty bucket' will not join forces with your bloc ... The odds of your cancer recurring are higher than winning the election!") – username: Vincent Chong

The comment above received 125 reactions (likes, laugh emoji, love emoji or angry emoji) and seven replies.

Other comments include:

先生，你越来越不受欢迎，别沉醉自我美好的感觉。
(Translation: "Sir, you are becoming less and less popular; do not indulge in your good feelings.") – username: KH Chia

我非常支持。有他来牵制巫统，有人反对吗？
(Translation: "I agree with him. He can contain UMNO. Is there any objection?") – username: Victor Lum

## Content Analysis on Posts about the New Government and COVID-19

### *The New Government*

One post on PH's feedback regarding Ismail Sabri's reform plan was put up on *Malaysiakini* on 11 September 2021. Upon forming the new government, Ismail Sabri had numerous meetings with the ruling and opposition leaders and proposed a reform plan, with Anwar describing it as a good start. This post received fifty comments and six shares.

Some of the comments from the audiences are as follows:

希门太好骗了。
(Translation: "Pakatan Harapan is so gullible.") – username: 李成文

你滚蛋就是反对党良好的开端。
(Translation: "You fuck off is a good start for the Opposition.")
– username: Kuchai Lim

尽是打嘴炮，废话王，忽悠希盟蓝眼支持者变成了你的专长，成事不足败事有余，续慕尤丁之后，沙比里更会爱你深深 #anyone not anwar #anwar out #undur anwar
(Translation: "It is all 'bullshit', the king of nonsense, and fooling the blue-eyed supporters of the PH has become your speciality. You are more likely to fail than succeed. After you continue to admire Muhyiddin, Sabri will love you even more." #anyone, not anwar #anwar out #undur anwar) – username: Apollo John

In a separate post on *Malaysiakini*, then health minister Khairy Jamaluddin declared two objectives: to reduce both severe COVID-19 cases and deaths in the next ninety-four days. Posted on 4 September 2021, the post received eighteen comments and two shares, with one comment stating:

Khairy比之前那个好上1百倍，巫统也好，不得不承认他是最好的之一。
(Translation: "Khairy is 100 times better than the previous one, as well as Umno. I must admit he is one of the best.") – username: Yoo Ng Seang

Another post on former prime minister Najib Razak and his meeting with Ismail Sabri with regards to improving the economy was posted on *Malaysiakini* on 7 September 2021. The post received 170 comments and 16 shares.

Some of the comments:

一个罪犯提醒一个傀儡首相别犯错，也只有马来西亚做到罢了！
(Translation: "A criminal reminds a puppet prime minister not to make mistakes. Only Malaysia can do that.") – username: Laipiaw Sim

提醒他吃钱要慢慢来，不要跟我犯同样的错误
(Translation: "Remind him not to make mistakes, eat slowly, do not eat like him, that is a mistake.") – username: Kam Lin Loo

盗贼和龟蛋讨论着如何偷国库及人民的血汗钱
(Translation: "Thieves and turtle eggs discuss how to steal national resources and people's hard-earned money.") – username: 叶和福

一个已被定罪的人 ，居然还能大摇大摆，自由的进进入入，马来西亚不累！

(Translation: "A convicted person can still be arrogant and enter freely. Malaysia *Boleh*!") – username: Geok Pin Chong

作贼的叫警察不要犯错？

(Translation: "The thief told the police not to make mistake?") – username: 刘建来

真的是蛇鼠一窝，马来西亚真的是完了。

(Translation: "It is a nest of snakes and rats. Malaysia is finished.") – username: Long Ah Long

The article on the meeting between Najib Razak and Ismail Sabri was also posted on SCD on 8 September 2021 with the headlines "Najib and Ismail meet for an hour", "Exchange for an hour on the topic of economy and Covid-19!" and "Unite for the beloved Malaysian family".

The post received 145 comments and 19 shares. Some comments are as follows:

请了几百个证人，拿出冒生命危险来作蹬，那么多的银行数据，又可以穿大衣到处乱跑，还可以给小弟指路，到底社会那里出了差错，搞不明。

(Translation: "Invited hundreds of witnesses, putting lives at risk, so much bank data, and still can run around in a coat, and can also give advice to the 'younger brother', what went wrong in society, I am perplexed.") – username: Steve Yeoh

還是納吉比較親民 為人民著想。

(Translation: "Still, Najib is closer to the people and thinks about the people.") – username: Bird Freedom

In a *Malaysiakini*'s post on 4 September 2021, Lim Guan Eng of DAP urged the government to rescue the economy and assist the small and medium enterprises (SMEs) facing closure.

The post received 248 comments and 57 shares:

大炮英！你上了位的那种嚣张啊，历历在目！做了官就不認實人了。

(Translation: "'Cannon Ying'! The kind of arrogance you had when you came to power is vivid in my eyes.") – username: Kho Francis

淋棍之前拿税务向华人开刀害到很多老板不爽。现在要努力争取回选票了！

(Translation: "This 'dickhead' had offended and slaughtered many 'Chinese Big Bosses'. Now it is time to work hard to get the votes back!") – username: Kien Hooi Tan

Settle你的city of dream 先啦。其他中小企业老板没有你这样幸运可以半价买豪宅。带mask就以为是 Iconic man ... 如果那时你有先行反贪污，反跳槽法令，现在你就不会这样了。

(Translation: "Settle your city of dream first. Other SME owners are not as lucky as you for buying a luxury house at half price. With a mask, you thought you were an Iconic man. If you had executed anti-corruption and anti-party-hopping laws in advance, you would not act like this now.") – username: Stanley Sim

In an SCD Facebook post on 5 September 2021, Lim Guan Eng criticized Ismail Sabri for appointing Muhyiddin as the chairman of the National Recovery Council. The post received 481 comments and 153 shares (with many comments removed).

One commented:

至少他派钱比你大方，你这里派30块那边加税收回来，淋棍吸血鬼。

(Translation: "At least he pays more generously than you. You gave away RM30 and charged more tax on people, 'dickhead' vampire.") – username: 陈治良

## COVID-19

In a *Malaysiakini* post on 1 September 2021, then health minister Khairy Jamaluddin announced that the government would treat COVID-19 as an epidemic. The post received 131 comments and 104 shares.

Some audience disagreed:

抗疫失败就与病毒共存。再看中国，新加坡如何抗疫。。。

(Translation: "Failure to fight the virus then survive with the virus. Let us look at how China and Singapore are fighting the epidemic ...") – username: 翁宗庆

这种人都可以做卫生部长。有没有为人民想先。如果凯里家人中covid死了。我才看你怎样说。

(Translation: "Such a person also can be the minister of health. There is no thinking for the people first. If Khairy's family died of COVID. I will see what you are going to say.") – username: TK Low

Another article on Saifuddin Nasution's criticism of Muhyiddin's appointment was posted on *Malaysiakini* on 4 September 2021. Saifuddin Nasution criticized how Muhyiddin, as the prime minister, failed in his fight against COVID-19.

The post received sixty-four comments and fifty-five shares. For example:

饭桶首相回锅做主席。
(Translation: "The rice bucket returns to the pot and becomes the chairman.") – username: 陈伟义 (*Rice bucket refers to useless people who know nothing but eat.*)

垃圾回收的政腐
(Translation: "garbage recycling government") – username: 刘建来

因为你家安华比丁丁没有用啊，当然是找丁丁比较有经验啦。
(Translation: "Because your Anwar is more useless than Din Din, of course, find the more experienced Din Din.") – username: Louis Leo. (*Din Din refers to Muhyiddin Yassin.*)

他妈的，安华是1997金融风暴的造孽者，还要当首相，真番薯。
(Translation: "Damn it, Anwar is the perpetrator of the 1997 financial crisis, yet he still wants to be the prime minister, what a sweet potato.") – username: Steven Wong. (*Sweet potato here refers to useless or dumb people as well.*)

A post about Lim Guan Eng's statement that Ismail Sabri, as the new prime minister, should "have the ability to deal with the epidemic and economic recession, as well as the determination to carry out system reform" was posted on SCD Facebook on 14 August 2021.

The post received 330 comments and 91 shares. One commented:

你們行動黨不可以再相信馬嗨丁，他的師傅就是老馬，還記得八十年代嗎？華社的訴求答應了，過後了都可以不算數的，千萬不可以相信這班牛鬼蛇神和魔鬼，再錯下去，人民對你們很失望了，一定要站穩立場，我們選民與你同在。

(Translation: "You DAP can no longer trust 'Cuntly Din'. His master is the Old Horse. Do you still remember the 80s? The demands of the Chinese community have always been agreed upon, but they never keep their promise. Never trust this bunch of devils and sneaky snakes. If you continue to make mistakes, people will be disappointed. It would be best if you were determined so the voters could be on the same side.") – username: Cecilia Lian. (*Old Horse refers to Mahathir Mohamad.*)

## DISCUSSION

The audiences of AXTJ Facebook page are active in their interactions. Most discussions were rational, with some disagreements occasionally. Ang Woei Shang would respond to Chinese, Bahasa Malaysia and English comments; he would reply to comments disagreeing with him and openly point out those using fake accounts. Unlike Ang, whose discussions are constructive, *Malaysiakini*'s Facebook posts have not attempted to create discussions with the audiences. SCD similarly never replies or reacts to audience comments. Audiences could contact the administrators using Messenger or email, and conversations are kept private.

Most comments in *Malaysiakini* are in Chinese, Cantonese and Hokkien. Other comments are in the form of animated graphics (GIPHY), pictures, screenshots and hyperlinks. The conversations in *Malaysiakini* depends on the issues discussed or the keywords used. For example, posts on COVID-19 received the least response and the fewest number of shares. However, those posts on Ismail Sabri and Khairy Jamaluddin received hundreds of comments due to the prominence of the source of the news. Examples of these posts include "The 100-day administration of the Cabinet has achieved 90% of the goal, and the prime minister called for continued efforts with the people" and "'All activities and meetings must be used', the prime minister called on the private sector GLC to promote Malay" (*Malaysiakini* 2021l, 2021k).

*Malaysiakini*'s followers commonly name-call and curse people, parties and organizations. For example, "If Khairy's family died of COVID, I will see what you are going to say." Sarcasm and terminologies also need to be understood through the context of the Malaysian Chinese community. For example, "Old Horse", "Chicken" and "Din Din" are direct translations of politicians' names, and "turtle eggs" refer to that served to a politician at a function in Sandakan (Chan 2015). Regarding political parties, "The Blue Eyes" refers to PKR and "Dirty Bucket" refers to UMNO. Chinese idioms and proverbs were occasionally used. For example, the phrase "Do not take the belly of a gentleman with the heart of a villain!" means not to speculate on a good man's intention with narrow minds. Foul language is common in comments posted on *Malaysiakini*. Examples include "You fuck off is a good start for the Opposition", "It is all 'bullshit', the king of nonsense ..." and "This 'dickhead' had offended and slaughtered many 'Chinese Big Bosses'. Now it is time to work hard to get the votes back!"

There are similarities between the audience comments on *Malaysiakini* and that on SCD. First, name-calling by SCD users commonly understood by Malaysian Chinese are 老马 "Old Horse", 鸡哥 "Chicken", 污桶 "Dirty Buckets" and 魏公公 "Eunuch Wei". "Eunuch Wei" ridicules politicians who are easily controlled and manipulated. Foul words used include 馬嗨丁 "Cuntly Din", 选条淋 "Vote my dick" and 淋棍吸血鬼 "Dick head vampire". "Vampire" refers to those who prey on others financially. As the oldest Chinese newspaper in Malaysia, SCD has the most followers, posts, comments, likes and shares. However, most comments on SCD were descriptive and lack constructive criticisms and deeper discussions.

Discussions on *Malaysiakini*'s Facebook page also focused more on individuals than on issues. For example, posts on the daily COVID-19 cases, vaccination rates and Undi 18 received very few or no comments and shares. However, the post "Guan Eng urges the government to rescue the market in various ways. Otherwise, nearly half of the SMEs will soon go bankrupt" was responded with out-of-context comments: "'Cannon Ying'! The kind of arrogance you had when you came to power is vivid in my eyes!" and "This 'dickhead' had offended and slaughtered many 'Chinese Big Bosses'. Now it is time to work hard to get the votes back!"

Discussion was more active when a post or thumbnail involves a prominent politician. However, there were differences between the Melaka and Sarawak by- and state election news, as well as Lim Kit Siang's comments. *Malaysiakini* used an image of the DAP flag while SCD used a photo of Lim Kit Siang. The use of a politician's photo could lead to either positive or negative comments.

One of the constructive comments by Eddie Teh in *Malaysiakini*'s post was hoping for a healthier democracy: "I do not like to see a political landscape that purely attacks and belittles opponents. When the other party does well, they should be supported and appreciated. Everyone should do it for the people of the country. Opposition parties should supervise and not oppose for the sake of opposition. When campaigning, you should show actual performance results and clear goals. Come on."

There were also more discussions about COVID-19 on SCD than on *Malaysiakini*. Audiences compared the number of cases in Malaysia with other countries and responded with comments such as "The little witch looks at the big witch. Malaysia is still open after 8000 cases" and "Malaysia is also half a catty, eight taels to laugh at Taiwan". Audiences used words, idioms or proverbs such as "half a catty, eight taels" to mock the subject. "Bulls, ghosts, snakes, gods and demons" represent a group of individuals deemed as evil. There was a sense of despair with comments such as "Why should we vote? Who cares about who will win? There may be a fourth wave of the virus. Good Luck", which demonstrates disappointment with the elections being held during the pandemic.

There are also critical differences in the posting styles. SCD typically uses a red byline as the headline. Unlike *Malaysiakini* and AXTJ, it does not always use the lead or first sentence of a news article as the post description. Instead, it uses sentimental sentences such as "Lim Guan Eng criticised Ismail for weakening his power" and "Melaka Ends, Sarawak Begins War!" On the other hand, *Malaysiakini* uses one or two sentences of a news lead to grab the audience's attention. The audience must subscribe to its website to read the full article, access the discussion and post comments.

## CONCLUSION

The three online platforms by AXTJ, SCD and *Malaysiakini* have provided the Malaysian Chinese cyber-community with an avenue to discuss sociopolitical matters. Although the posts and comments discussed in this chapter were limited to the first 100 days of the Ismail Sabri government, the social-political issues remain relevant. By allowing the second largest community in Malaysia to discuss these issues, Malaysian Chinese are able to play a role in forming societal policies. Their comments help to better understand the sentiments of the community regarding their support on the issues discussed. Although some platforms carry out some forms of restrictions on comments, others allow for discussions to be free and open, thus enabling the continued discourse of issues while preserving freedom of speech and expression. The emergence of social media at this juncture of the political landscape in Malaysia provides greater freedom of speech to the audiences. The Malaysian Chinese cyber-community has chosen to use social media to satisfy their needs and enable them to express their concerns on political, social and economic issues.

The political landscape during the first 100 days of Ismail Sabri's premiership played a determinant role in press freedom in Malaysia. The Chinese social media is represented by AXTJ, *Malaysiakini* and SCD Facebook pages. The leadership transition from Muhyiddin Yassin to Ismail Sabri was a period of political uncertainty in Malaysia. On the one hand, it took much work for the PN government to maintain unity due to the different ideologies of its coalition parties. Conversely, managing the COVID-19 pandemic remained a significant challenge for Ismail Sabri's government. The high unemployment rate and the impact of the pandemic on economic development added to the challenges faced by the new premier.

On the other hand, establishing these portals led to the rise of cybertroopers. In analysing these platforms, cybertroopers usually post repetitive comments which are posted on almost every post to disseminate political propaganda and disrupt discussions on these portals. They are usually hired to counter criticism or lead the discussion in a particular direction on social media platforms. There are methods to identify cybertroopers: these users usually do not have profile photos or any intro and background, have a weird, un-Malaysian name, and have no or a minimum number of friends. The above characteristics make it easy to identify cybertrooper comments. Fortunately, the presence of cybertroopers is not as strong as the most relevant comments always show the "Top Fans" of the news page. Thus, most users ignore cybertrooper comments as there are minimal reactions or discussions.

Secondly, most comments can only be understood under specific contexts. In other words, one needs to be familiar with the Malaysian Chinese social-political and cultural nuances and be able to read Mandarin. The direct translations of such comments would cause the essence of these discussions to be wrongly interpreted. An example is the comment "Cannon Ying!" Cannon is commonly used amongst the Malaysian Chinese community to describe someone as untrustworthy, who cannot keep a promise, lies or exaggerates. The Ying here refers to politician Lim Guan Eng. Another example is "I ate vinegar today, and it was super sour!" To eat vinegar means to feel jealous in Chinese.

## Notes

1. In 2022, the Malaysian Chinese community, comprising 22.8 per cent of the Malaysian population of 30.2 million citizens, experienced a decline in numbers from 23.0 per cent in 2021 (Soo 2022a).
2. *Bumiputera* could be translated as "sons of the soil". Originating from a Sanskrit word, *Bumiputera* categorizes the Malay majority and the Sabah and Sarawak indigenous communities (Lee and Ahmad 2015).
3. The Malaysian police have confirmed that the fight at Low Yat Plaza was not a racial incident (Rodzi and Cheng 2015).
4. For a detailed discussion about the Chinese pillars and cultural preservation, see Ng and Lee (2018, 2020).
5. On 9 June 2021, a few comments under the news, "CJ orders all courts to be fully operational from July 1", were found to be allegedly criticizing the Malaysian judiciary system (Malaysiakini 2020). Anonymous subscribers made the comments, and the court ruled that there is no excuse for a news agency to allow such comments, which might negatively affect society. Chief editor Steven Gan was charged for the incident, although the user comments were deleted forty-five minutes after posting. Despite politicians, news media, NGOs and international press speaking out on behalf of *Malaysiakini*, the ruling remained unchanged. *Malaysiakini* was found guilty and fined RM 50,000, but Steven Gan was found innocent (Karim 2021).
6. In February 2021, the Federal Court fined *Malaysiakini* RM $500,000 (US$120,000) for violating the Evidence Act. *Malaysiakini* was charged with criminal contempt in 2020 based on user comments criticizing the judiciary (Freedom House 2022).

# REFERENCES

Carvalho, Martin. 2015. "Ismail Sabri: Medan Mara Digital Mall Not a Racist Venture". *The Star*, 8 December 2015. https://www.thestar.com.my/news/nation/2015/12/08/ismail-sabri-yaakob-mara-digital-mall-not-racist-venture/.

Chan, Julia. 2015. "Ismail Sabri: I Honestly Didn't Know There Were Laws against Turtle Eggs". *Malay Mail*, 10 November 2015. https://www.malaymail.com/news/malaysia/2015/11/10/ismail-sabri-i-honestly-didnt-know-there-were-laws-against-turtle-eggs/1002497.

Chang, Peter T. C. 2018. "Ethnic Chinese Malaysia Are Celebrating China's Rise". *South China Morning Post*, 11 May 2018. https://www.scmp.com/comment/insight-opinion/article/2145521/ethnic-chinese-malaysia-are-celebrating-chinas-rise.

Channel News Asia. 2021. "Mahathir's Chopsticks Remark 'Simplistic, Offensive': Lim Guan Eng". 13 December 2021. https://www.channelnewsasia.com/asia/mahathir-chopsticks-chinese-malaysians-hands-lim-guan-eng-simplistic-offensive-2376401.

Department of Statistics Malaysia. 2021. "Population Size and Annual Population Growth Rate". https://v1.dosm.gov.my/v1/index.php?r=column/cthemeByCat&cat=155&bul_id=ZjJOSnpJR21sQWVUcUp6ODRudm5JZz09&menu_id=L0pheU43NWJwRWVSZklWdzQ4TlhUUT09#:~:text=Malaysia's%20population%20in%202021%20is,to%202.7%20million%20(2021)%20.

Freedom House. 2022. "Malaysia: Freedom in the World 2022 Country Report". https://freedomhouse.org/country/malaysia/freedom-world/2022.

Hakim Hassan. 2020. "What Happened to Low Yat's Contender, Mara Digital Mall?" *The Rakyat Post*, 24 January 2020. https://www.therakyatpost.com/news/malaysia/2020/01/24/what-happened-to-low-yats-contender-mara-digital-mall/.

Huang, Zach. 2015. "MDA and Comscore Release Rankings of Top Web Entities in Malaysia for July 2015". *Comscore*, 28 September 2015. https://www.comscore.com/Insights/Rankings/MDA-and-comScore-Release-Rankings-of-Top-Web-Entities-in-Malaysia-for-July-2015.

Karim, Khairah N. 2021. "Malaysiakini Guilty over Publication of Comments Criticising Judiciary". *New Straits Times*, 19 February 2021. https://www.nst.com.my/news/crime-courts/2021/02/666992/malaysiakini-guilty-over-publication-comments-criticising-judiciary.

Kim, Min-Sun, T. Youn-ja Shim, and Judith N. Martin. 2008. *Changing Korea: Understanding Culture and Communication*. http://ci.nii.ac.jp/ncid/BA86471536.

Lee, Seok Hwai. 2015. "Malaysia Minister Calls for Malays to Boycott Chinese Businesses". *Straits Times*, 2 February 2015. https://www.straitstimes.com/asia/se-asia/malaysia-minister-calls-for-malays-to-boycott-chinese-businesses.

Lee, Yuen Beng. 2012. *The Malaysian Digital Indies: New Forms, Aesthetics, and Genres in Post-2000 Malaysian Cinema*. Melbourne: The University of Melbourne.

──────. 2022. *Malaysian Cinema in the New Millennium: Transcendence Beyond Multiculturalism*. Hong Kong: Hong Kong University Press.

Lee, Yuen Beng, and Mahyuddin Ahmad. 2015. "Liberalisation of the Malaysian Media and Politics: New Media, Strategies and Contestations". *Media Watch* 6, no. 3: 296–308. https://doi.org/10.15655/mw/2015/v6i3/77892.

Lieber, Andrea. 2018. "Cyber Communities". In *Macmillan Handbook on Gender: Space*, edited by Aimee M. Cox, pp. 271–86. Farrington Hills, NC: Sage Publications.

*Malay Mail*. 2017. "Think Tank Predicts Chinese Malaysian Population May Drop Below 20pc by 2030". 21 January 2017. https://www.malaymail.com/news/malaysia/2017/01/21/think-tank-predicts-chinese-malaysian-population-may-drop-below-20pc-by-203/1297791.

──────. 2021. "PM Ismail Sabri Implements 100-Days 'Report Card' to Gauge Minister's Performance". 2 October 2021. https://www.malaymail.com/news/malaysia/2021/10/02/pm-ismail-sabri-peoples-view-on-ministers-among-methods-to-tally-100-days-s/2010172.

*Malaysiakini*. 1999. "About Malaysiakini". https://about.malaysiakini.com/.

──────. 2020. "CJ Orders All Courts to Be Fully Operational from July 1". 9 June 2020. https://www.malaysiakini.com/news/529385.

*Malaysiakini* [当今大马 (Malaysiakini Chinese Version)]. 2021a. 首相规定每名新部长，百日内需交出初步成绩 [The Prime Minister Stipulates That Each New Minister Must Submit Preliminary Results within 100 days]. Facebook, 27 August 2021. https://www.facebook.com/mkinicn/posts/pfbid0H1UFuu6hoSKmoM7yirZypDKuU6LbyHafHa3PVctijj6wYDZkSV47VjHcL4EdfKDhl.

──────. 2021b. 改把冠病视为地方流病，政府将放弃封锁简化SOP [The Government Will Abandon the Blockade and Simplify the SOP to Treat the New Crown Epidemic as an Endemic Disease]. Facebook, 1 September 2021. https://www.facebook.com/mkinicn/posts/pfbid0sckdJAmT57uftCjLbGYdinj478GHYFG6Gy2WBoiPTHobJQxWNd5vSPPPg9BQ9PSul.

──────. 2021c. 增42簇群1168人确诊，沙巴一园丘124人染疫 [1,168 Confirmed Cases in 42 Clusters, 124 Infected in a Plantation in Sabah]. Facebook, 1 September 2021. https://www.facebook.com/mkinicn/posts/pfbid0f3EDHsrjtLVUbuXU1C7oaj8PwQibZWQyZyPZ5dizmjfLhJ5Xhjrt2qaRu8RUdx4il.

_____. 2021d. 冠英力促政府多方救市，否则近半SME很快倒闭 [Guan Ying Urges the Government to Rescue the Market in Various Ways, Otherwise Nearly Half of SMEs Will Soon Go Bankrupt]. Facebook, 4 September 2021. https://www.facebook.com/mkinicn/posts/pfbid0TQdwhzrsLw 3nqKyJ37RVzfV1LENdkLFLWyaMVXggqiF9WuJaQZkgCqNwsmkUsr1ml.

_____. 2021e. 凯里百日新政两大目标：降重症与送院前死亡案例 [Two Goals of Khairy's 100-Day New Deal: Reduce Severe Illness and Death Cases before Hospitalization]. Facebook, 4 September 2021. https://www.facebook.com/ mkinicn/posts/pfbid02AGH9EijpwxBPWD4ddKYUvTkuud9LbPHszUvHMt PiueJd2UESyetBWK9mBVnEdX1cl.

_____. 2021f. 抗疫失败下台还任用？赛夫丁反对慕尤丁掌国复会 [He Failed in Anti-epidemic, Step Down and Still Be Appointed? Saifuddin Opposes Muhyiddin's Resumption of Parliament]. Facebook, 4 September 2021. https://www.facebook.com/mkinicn/posts/pfbid02GUzxe8dRMSfL5 sh1mSLpe1ZAzo9P68zuQWFm9ZCQXZNcGmUgrQcAiwpiJTRDKn9Kl.

_____. 2021g. 会晤依斯迈共商复苏策略，纳吉否认减少批评政府 [Meeting with Ismail to Discuss Recovery Strategy, Najib Denies Reducing Government Criticism]. Facebook, 7 September 2021. https://www.facebook.com/ mkinicn/posts/pfbid0jrb4WJUEexGySbMbTPwC4eRZFK6iTTG XiezESBLUZXkdiNqz2n4BXtRfi9F9eXTCl.

_____. 2021h. 慕尤丁下届大选再上阵，相信国盟可东山再起 [Muhyiddin Will Fight Again in the Next General Election, He Believes That the PN Can Make a Comeback]. Facebook, 10 September 2021. https://www.facebook. com/mkinicn/posts/pfbid02eoU3b7ryUbmtnNWXVNDUW1k1D7vgJA4P3DS 5qe3tSXvWpdZPcUYR5Uqz1a3rNmRTl.

_____. 2021i. 需说明改地方病政策变化，MHC促凯里立严谨KPI [It Is Necessary to Explain the Changes in Endemic Disease Policies, and MHC Urges Khairy to Set Strict KPIs]. Facebook, 10 September 2021. https://www. facebook.com/mkinicn/posts/pfbid02GhEN5bX5VL39yqfk6G9GWENH6bP 7mCn3dCdgoJdupCLMKD35VDmFmVXLzauxns4dl.

_____. 2021j. 希盟欢迎首相改革计划，但仍需磋商寻找"共识" [Pakatan Harapan Welcomes PM's Reform Plan, But Still Needs to Negotiate to Find "Consensus"]. Facebook, 11 September 2021. https://www.facebook.com/mkinicn/ posts/pfbid0rYHRTmnAN7sgpocuS8Ro2TNsPbKaUYTYzjtfytmKrYnia PzDCWJV1w3zMJsMh7LBl.

_____. 2021k. "活动会议都要用"，首相吁私人界GLC推广马来语 ["All Activities and Meetings Must be Used", the Prime Minister Called on the Private Sector GLC to Promote Malay]. Facebook, 29 November 2021. https://www.

facebook.com/mkinicn/posts/pfbid02TsW9H6uTyKYJ1taieLc7gBzis WrLdQsMgBzis5T7to95AmeASPvi2NkiY4f8QWV7l.

———. 2021l. 内阁百日施政达九成目标，首相吁继续与民努力 [The 100-Day Administration of the Cabinet Has Achieved 90% of the Goal, and the Prime Minister Called for Continued Efforts with the People]. Facebook, 9 December 2021. https://www.facebook.com/mkinicn/posts/pfbid02SoMy2Ypbt VuqCmuR98hqTUicUA4tXMaLA7Mm2DB36yWBKRHshZnE9WfWRM Wk46U6l.

Martin, P. A., Helmut K. Anheier, and Stefan Toepler. 2010. *International Encyclopedia of Civil Society*. 1st ed. New York: Springer.

Marzuki Mohamad, and Ibrahim Suffian. 2023. "Malaysia's 15th General Election: Ethnicity Remains the Key Factor in Voter Preferences". *ISEAS Perspective*, no. 2023/20, 24 March 2023. https://www.iseas.edu.sg/articles-commentaries/iseas-perspective/2023-20-malaysias-15th-general-election-ethnicity-remains-the-key-factor-in-voter-preferences-by-marzuki-mohamad-and-ibrahim-suffian/.

MCMC (Malaysian Communications and Multimedia Commission). 2020a. "Internet Usage Survey 2020: Infographic". https://www.mcmc.gov.my/ skmmgovmy/media/General/pdf/IUS-2020-Infographic.pdf.

———. 2020b. *Internet Users Survey 2020*. https://www.mcmc.gov.my/ skmmgovmy/media/General/pdf/IUS-2020-Report.pdf.

Michael, Edwin, and Yee Mun Chin. 2021. "The Role of Political Socialization on Facebook among Malaysian Chinese". *International Journal of Politics, Publics Policy and Social Works* 3, no. 9: 1–8. https://doi.org/10.35631/ IJPPSW.39001.

Mitra, Ananda. 2020. *Digital Communications*. Revised ed. New York: Chelsea House.

Müller, J. 2021a. "Active Social Media Users as Percentage of the Total Population in Malaysia from 2016 to 2023". *Statista*, 7 April 2021. https:// www.statista.com/statistics/883712/malaysia-social-media-penetration/.

———. 2021b. "Number of Facebook Users in Malaysia 2019-2028". *Statista*, 11 August 2021. https://www.statista.com/statistics/490484/number-of-malaysia-facebook-users/.

NapoleonCat. 2021. "Facebook Users in Malaysia: October 2021". https:// napoleoncat.com/stats/facebook-users-in-malaysia/2021/10/.

Net Ease. 2022. 中国发布世界华文新媒体影响力榜，新加坡只有两家上榜 [China Release the Most Influential Chinese New Media Ranking in the World, Only 2 Singapore Media Are Listed]. https://www.163.com/dy/ article/H2MU776O05148HD5.html.

Ng, Miew Luan, and Yuen Beng Lee. 2018. "Malaysian Chinese Language Newspapers and Cultural Identity: A Study of the Roles of Sin Chew Daily in Chinese Cultural Preservation and Nation Building". *Kajian Malaysia* 36, no. 1 (2018): 63–103.

_____. 2020. "Chinese Cultural Preservation, Identity and Community: Examining the Roles of Sin Chew Daily in Bridging Chinese Education, Cultural and Religious Rights of the Chinese Community in Malaysia". *Pertanika Journal of Social Sciences & Humanities* 28, no. 2: 1335–55.

*Oriental Daily Online*. 2016. 无可靠盈利模式 网媒主要困境 [The Central Dilemma of Malaysian Chinese Online Media Lack a Profitable System]. 1 February 2016. https://www.orientaldaily.com.my/news/nation/2016/02/01/125094.

Povera, Adib, Hana Naz Harun, and Tharanya Arumugam. 2020. "PM: Malaysia Has Suffered RM63 Billion Losses due to MCO". *NST Online*, 1 May 2020. https://www.nst.com.my/news/nation/2020/05/588982/pm-malaysia-has-suffered-rm63-billion-losses-due-mco.

Rahmat Khairulrijal. 2021. "Vernacular Schools Do Not Contravene Federal Constitution, Rules High Court". *New Straits Times*, 29 December 2021. https://www.nst.com.my/news/crime-courts/2021/12/758661/vernacular-schools-do-not-contravene-federal-constitution-rules.

Rodzi, Nadirah H., and Nicholas Cheng. 2015. "Nothing Racial in Low Yat Plaza Melee but Thuggery, Say Police". *The Star*, 12 July 2015. https://www.thestar.com.my/News/Nation/2015/07/12/Melee-Low-yat-not-racial/.

Similarweb. n.d. Malaysiakini.com Traffic Analytics & Market Share. https://www.similarweb.com/website/malaysiakini.com/#geography.

*Sin Chew Daily* [马来西亚星洲日报 Malaysia Sin Chew Daily]. 2021a. 台湾今增583本土病例 [Taiwan Reports 583 New Local COVID-19 Cases Today]. Facebook, 23 May 2021. https://www.facebook.com/SinChewDaily/posts/4707968689261535.

_____. 2021b. 首相应有能力抗疫救经济 [The Prime Minister Should Be Able to Fight the Epidemic and Save the Economy]. Facebook, 14 August 2021. https://www.facebook.com/SinChewDaily/posts/pfbid0XF4Frm9CmJvkmcgtDBxmfVM1Au5jrQqPEttuHb8dEMUjrabpL8YrgTG3G3FggwRgl.

_____. 2021c. 失望幕受委国复会主席。"首相不认真，不上心"[Lim Guan Eng: Disappointed, Muhyiddin Was Appointed Chairman of the National Resumption of Congress. "The Prime Minister Is Not Serious and Doesn't Care]. Facebook, 5 September 2021. https://www.facebook.com/story.php?story_fbid=5014077251984009&id=255057814552667&p=30&paipv=0&eav=AfbpOjrpk9H0OqpaVKKhfe1n0oCkaP70W0j5hha3FHgVmBVvUFhe3Z_Ld4Vs4p7X83c&_rdr.

———. 2021d. 依斯迈纳吉会晤一小时 [Ismail Sabri Meets Najib for One Hour]. Facebook, 8 September 2021. https://www.facebook.com/SinChewDaily/posts/5023289564396111.

———. 2021e. 首相规定每名新部长，百日内需交出初步成绩 [Prime Minister Mandates That Every New Minister Must Submit Preliminary Results within 100 Days]. Facebook, 4 October 2021. https://www.facebook.com/SinChewDaily/posts/5014077251984009.

———. 2021f. 林吉祥:政府内强硬派 [Lin Jixiang: Strong Faction within the Government]. Facebook, 4 November 2021. https://www.facebook.com/SinChewDaily/posts/pfbid02hxcVzEC8CDYLhZ9F4pecM83trc38pfW4XF5RCz6ckJszcswe47z8AEdQBdZgabpDl.

———. 2021g. 年满18岁自动登记为选民 [Automatically Register as a Voter When a Malaysian Turns 18]. Facebook, 9 November 2021. https://www.facebook.com/SinChewDaily/posts/pfbid0579te54PR5zqo46PBcpwzoLiaVRA8zfeAK1vR7gEuWi7useaBay437ZG5QEbsy7bl.

———. 2021h. 砂拉越选举 [Sarawak Elections]. Facebook, 24 November. 2021. https://www.facebook.com/SinChewDaily/posts/pfbid02EejoAwGi3nD2MdMJfz4QmTBuCxXoBP2zeK3svvQHiM51SpXzurwoLbezNbuAvNbNl.

———. 2021i. 砂拉越州选举1206提名1218投票 [Sarawak State Election 1206 Nominations 1218 Votes]. Facebook, 24 November 2021. https://www.facebook.com/SinChewDaily/posts/pfbid02EejoAwGi3nD2MdMJfz4QmTBuCxXoBP2zeK3svvQHiM51SpXzurwoLbezNbuAvNbNl.

———. 2021j. 确证持续下降 [Confirmed COVID-19 Cases Continue to Decline]. Facebook, 31 December 2021. https://www.facebook.com/SinChewDaily/posts/5138303682894698.

Soo Wern Jun. 2022a. "Statistics Dept: Malaysia's Population Rises to 32.7 Million in 2022 But Growth Rate Curtailed by Restrictions on Non-Citizens". *Malay Mail*, 29 July 2022. https://www.malaymail.com/news/malaysia/2022/07/29/statistics-dept-malaysias-population-rises-to-327-million-in-2022-but-growth-rate-curtailed-by-restrictions-on-non-citizens/20009.

———. 2022b. "Look in the Mirror before Making Accusations, Shahril Tells Muhyiddin". *New Straits Times*, 26 September 2022. https://www.nst.com.my/news/politics/2022/09/832898/look-mirror-making-accusations-shahril-tells-muhyiddin.

Statcounter. 2021. "Social Media Stats Malaysia: Jan-Dec 2021". https://gs.statcounter.com/social-media-stats/all/malaysia/2021.

Steele, Janet. 2023. *Malaysiakini and the Power of Independent Media in Malaysia*. Singapore: NUS Press.

Syed Jamal Zahiid. 2021a. "Facing Backlash, a 'Baffled' Ismail Sabri Says CNY Celebration SOPs Endorsed by Chinese Groups". *Malay Mail*, 5 February 2021. https://www.malaymail.com/news/malaysia/2021/02/05/facing-backlash-a-baffled-ismail-sabri-says-cny-celebration-sops-endorsed/1948707.

———. 2021b. "We Hear You: National Unity Ministry Says Will Relay Appeal for CNY Protocol Review to NSC". *Malay Mail*, 5 February 2021. https://www.malaymail.com/news/malaysia/2021/02/05/we-hear-you-national-unity-ministry-says-will-relay-appeal-for-cny-protocol/1947220.

Ting, Dorcas. 2021. "Trial Date Set for Defamation Case Filed by Yong against Tan Kai". *Dayak Daily*, 4 October 2021. https://dayakdaily.com/trial-dates-set-for-defamation-case-filed-by-yong-against-tan-kai/.

Wang, Victoria, John V. Tucker, and Kevin Haines. 2013. "Viewing Cybercommunities through the Lens of Modernity – The Case of Second Life". *The International Journal of Virtual Communities and Social Networking* 5, no. 1: 75–90.

Yiswaree, Palansamy. 2015. "After Ministers' Racial Boycott Call, Anti-Chinese Products Page Emerges on Facebook". *Malay Mail*, 6 February 2015.

# 5

# The Malaysian Indians' Newfound Voice in Cyber-Communities

Anantha Raman Govindasamy and
Kavitha Ganesan[1]

## INTRODUCTION

This chapter examines the role of cyber-communities in the consumption and dissemination of information relating to the political and socioeconomic discourse of Malaysian Indians. Numerous online platforms such as emails, blogs, online forums, online media and even text messages have played a crucial role in gathering and disseminating information which have reshaped the Malaysian Indians' perception of then ruling Malaysian government under Barisan Nasional (National Front – BN). In fact, the Hindu Rights Action Force (HINDRAF)[2] was successful in mobilizing Malaysian Indians against the ruling BN in 2007. This may be construed as the outcome of the synergy between these newly emerged online platforms which effectively disseminated information on the Malaysian Indians' marginalization that eventually resulted in the physical mobilization of the community in support of the HINDRAF leadership.

Since then, Indian based cyber-communities have played an important role in reshaping minority Malaysian Indians' public opinion on specific issues such as Tamil schools, urban poverty and Hindu temples as well as general problems relating to good governance, corruption, human rights and ethnic supremacy in Malaysia politics. In recent years, social media tools such as WhatsApp and Facebook have become increasingly popular not only as a source of information but also as a platform where issues pertaining to Malaysian Indians have been openly debated and reshaped especially among the younger generation. The outcome of this resulted in "politically savvy" Malaysian Indians actively participating in Malaysia's electoral politics.

One such huge change in mindset was observable during the 15th general election held in 2022 where the Indian voter turnout was high. In fact, the emergence of online communities and influence meant that vital information managed to infiltrate class demarcation, resulting in both elites and non-elites, as well as younger and older generation Indians, voting for change. Based on documentation and close observations of three Indian Facebook communities, this chapter argues that Indian online communities have increasingly become an alternative voice and continue to reshape public opinion while simultaneously cutting across class and age differences.

The first section of this chapter briefly looks at the arrival of Malaysian Indians and their association with print media from a historical perspective. More specifically, this chapter examines the role of Indian newspapers in the country and how they moulded the Malaysian Indian community's views on socioeconomic and political development. The second section looks at the rise of cyber-communities and how they challenged mainstream Indian media in reshaping the Malaysian Indian community's views on the question of marginalization. The final section examines the nature of Indian online groups through close observation of three Facebook groups during the 15th Malaysian general election and how such social media groups became the catalyst for Malaysian Indians' newfound voice.

## THE ARRIVAL AND SETTLEMENT OF INDIANS AND MEDIA DEVELOPMENT

This section explores Malaysian Indian mass media development under British Malaya and independent Malaya/Malaysia. It argues that the early growth of Indian mass media, particularly newspapers, was closely connected to the arrival and settlement of Indians as indentured labourers. On the other hand, in the post-independence period, Indian mass media such as newspapers played the role of transmitting official government policies rather than highlighting genuine problems faced by Malaysian Indians, which severely undermined the community's socioeconomic and political development.

At the end of the nineteenth century, the British government in Malaya systematically facilitated the arrival of Indians from India to overcome the acute shortage of labourers mainly in rural plantations. Although these labour-class Indians comprised of various sub-Indian ethnic groups such as Telegus, Malayalees, Kannadigas and Punjabis, they were nevertheless dominated by ethnic Tamils.[3] In fact, 90 per cent of labourers who came to Malaya in the 1920s and 80 per cent of those who arrived after the Second World War were Tamil-speaking Indians from Madras in South India.[4] The main characteristics of the Indian labour force in Malaya were poverty, ignorance and temporary nature (Stenson 1970). Ratnam (1965) went so far as to argue that Indian labourers were treated like an ordinary economic commodity by British administration policies.

Stenson (1970) further argued that under the British administration in Malaya, Indians in rural plantations were highly regulated in terms of movement and access to information from the outside world in order to maintain high plantation productivity. In fact, plantation Indians were given limited access to education, and reading materials in the form of magazines and newspapers were strictly scrutinized by the British to overcome labour uprisings in rural plantations. This isolated and controlled plantation environment managed to create a relatively docile plantation Indian community in Malaya.

In this context, the early Indian mass media development under the British administration in Malaya can be divided into three important phases. In the first phase, Straits Settlements States, mainly Penang and

Singapore, played an important part in the early informal development of Indian mass media. In fact, newspapers such as *Tangai Snahen*, *Penang Cnana Charian Daily News* and *Weekly Sun* were published in Singapore and Penang between 1876 and 1914 (Lent 1974).[5] These newspapers were intent on maintaining Indian culture and language roots in Malaya. More importantly, readership of these newspapers was limited to urban and middle-class Indians.

The second phase of Indian mass media development started in the 1920s with a focus on reformist and nationalist agenda. Lent (1974) argues that only from the 1920s, Tamil newspapers began to provide professional journalism by taking up important issues such as highlighting the plight of Malayan Indian labourers and closely observing the rise of Indian nationalism against the British rule in India. In fact, Tamil newspapers such as *Tamilaham* (1921), *Tamil Nesan* (1924) and later *Tamil Murasu* (1936) were very critical on labour policies in Malaya and took the position of discouraging Tamil migrants to Malaya as labourers (Karthigesu 1989).

The third phase of Indian mass media development started right after the Second World War until the creation of the Malayan Federation in 1957. During this period, Tamil newspapers played a crucial part in the post-war political development in Malaya. In fact, Tamil newspapers such as *Jananayagam*, which was linked to the left-wing Malayan Communist Party, regularly highlighted the anti-colonial views in their publications which have been largely used by plantation unions to mobilize plantation Indians against the British. Upon realizing this development, the British introduced strict press regulations and closely monitored the content of Tamil newspapers.[6]

In fact, Arasaratnam (1970) noted that the communist uprising forced major Tamil newspapers in Malaya to distance themselves from being critical of the British administration and as a result, they took a moderate view by focusing on the issues related to Malayan Indians' unity, culture and language development. For instance, newspapers such as *Tamil Nesan*, which was once the fiercest critic of the British administration in Malaya, took a rather moderate approach. Moreover, with the formation of the Malaysian Indian Congress (MIC), *Tamil Nesan* became the official mouthpiece of the party and promoted multiethnic cooperation with the United Malays National Organisation (UMNO) and the Malaysian Chinese Association (MCA) under BN.

In post-independent Malaya, the role of Indian mass media became complex and highly regulated, with Tamil newspapers being linked to political establishments; most became the "official spokesperson" for the government's policies rather than highlighting problems faced by Malaysian Indians (Karthigesu 1989). In fact, during the early years of independence, the Indian mass media failed to focus or galvanize views on the then emerging problems affecting the Indian community such as the repatriation of Malaysian Indians to India and the rampant subdivision of plantation estates, which resulted in a major displacement of Indian plantation labourers to urban areas.

Moreover, the emergence of complex ethnic-based bargaining in Malaysian politics in the post-independence era further marginalized the Malaysian Indian community. BN, which is a coalition of race-based political parties comprising UMNO, MCA and MIC dominated the post-independent Malaysian politics. Under BN rule, the New Economic Policy (NEP) was introduced in 1970 to economically empower the Malay majority ethnic group in Malaysia, which meant that ethnicity was used as the main priority in the wealth distribution policies. During this time Tamil newspapers such as *Tamil Murasu*, *Tamil Nesan* and *Tamil Malar* mushroomed and dominated the post-independent era with a daily circulation of around 35,000 to 40,000 (Lent 1974). These Tamil newspapers were the only source of information for the Malaysian Indian community and played a crucial role in promoting and transmitting the official version of the Malaya/Malaysian government. In fact, newspapers like *Tamil Nesan* were owned by MIC and promoted the ruling BN coalition's political narrative on issues such as the marginalization of Malaysian Indians by creating the perspective that only MIC can solve the problems relating to Malaysian Indians (Ramasamy 2019), although in reality policies such as the NEP severely undermine minority ethnic groups such as the Indians. As a result of this, Malaysian Indians firmly supported the ruling coalition BN, in particular, MIC throughout the 1960s to 1990s because of the limited alternative information available at that time.

## MALAYSIAN INDIAN MARGINALITY AND
## THE RISE OF INDIAN CYBER-COMMUNITIES

Malaysia began to embrace the Internet in the late 1990s. As argued by Pepinsky (2009), Malaysians were forced to adapt to the Internet as part of global modernization and globalization. By 2000, online media had been reshaped and began to challenge the dominance of government-controlled media in Malaysia by providing alternative information related to politics, economy and society.[7] In fact, the opposition political forces managed to capitalize on the use of online media to capture the imagination of Malaysians by providing alternative sources of information which challenged the official narrative of the Malaysian government on many issues. For Malaysian Indians, the emergence of online media played a crucial role in shifting their dogmatic opinion and views on the issue of Malaysian Indian marginality. In fact, as argued by Leong (2009) and Moten (2009), online media played an important role during the HINDRAF demonstrations in 2007, and subsequently during the 2008, 2013 and 2018 Malaysian general elections, which showed the shifting political loyalty of Malaysian Indians from the ruling BN government to opposition political parties.

As discussed previously, in the early years following Malaysia's independence, the majority of Malaysian Indians were cocooned in rural plantations. This isolated rural environment provided limited economic and educational development for the Malaysian Indian community. In fact, under the NEP (1970–90), Malaysian Indians emerged as the biggest losers when the policy primarily focused on eradicating poverty among the majority Malay community (Ramasamy 2004). In the 1990s, Malaysia witnessed rapid urbanization and economic growth. However, the wealth distribution process was largely marked by complex ethnic rivalry between the majority ethnic Malays and the Chinese and Indian minorities.

Malaysia's mainstream media, including Tamil newspapers, largely avoided critical examination of the problems relating to the Malaysian Indian community. National media, especially newspapers, were largely controlled by government proxies and propagated a common narrative which described Indians as a poor working-class community with a heightened percentage of social problems such as gangsterism and death in police custody. However, these mainstream newspapers rarely explored the root cause of the problems faced by the Indians in terms of failure of the governmental policy to uplift the community.

By 2000, nearly 85 per cent of Malaysian Indians are now dwellers in urban or semi-urban areas on the west coast of Peninsular Malaysia (Subramaniam 2004). During this time, Malaysian Indians, mainly poor urban working-class Indians, began to face complex problems relating to temples, estate housing and Tamil schools. These problems are deeply rooted in the Malaysian urbanization process from the 1960s to the 1990s, which saw plantation estates, where Indians were the main dwellers, systematically subdivided for urbanization; as a result, plantation Indians were forcefully displaced. Many of these plantation Indians ended up resettling in squatter settlements around poor corners of newly developed urban areas. Without a proper policy, urban developers, with the understanding of local administrations, allowed plantation markers such as temples to be patronaged by Indians.[8]

When Abdullah Badawi took over as the prime minister in early 2000, there was a drastic shift in the accommodation policy of allowing plantation temples in urban and semi-urban areas in Malaysia. The overzealous local administrators, including local council officers, were suddenly adamant about demolishing what they termed as "illegal temples" without proper negotiation with local Indian communities who prayed at these temples. In fact, the demolition of these Hindu temples that were mainly patronized by the working-class urban Indians was rampant in states like Selangor, Perak and Negeri Sembilan, especially between 2000 and 2006.[9]

The demolitions by state and local administrators shook the core sensitivity of marginalized Malaysian Indians as temples play a crucial role in sustaining the Indian identity in the country. Although many Indian non-governmental organizations (NGOs), including the Malaysia Hindu Sangam—a primary regulator of Hindu temples in Malaysia—voiced out their concerns on this issue and urged the government to take immediate action to halt the temple demolition exercise, the government sidestepped the issue by saying that local enforcement agencies can act based on existing local council law to prevent illegal buildings. More importantly, MIC, the sole Indian political representative in the then ruling BN government, was largely silent on the issue of temple demolition. Coverage by the mainstream media rarely highlighted the temple demolition issue and, in some cases, even blamed poor working-class Indians for building illegal structures on private or government land. Tamil newspapers in Malaysia also rarely highlighted temple demolition issues, and some newspapers like *Tamil Nesan*, took a neutral stand by promising that MIC would find an amicable solution to the problem faced by the Indians.

On the Internet, however, there was wide regular coverage of the temple demolition exercise. Malaysian Indian blogs to independent online media not only captured the plight of the Malaysian Indian community in defending temple demolitions but also for the first time, managed to link the temple demolition exercise to the larger issue relating to marginalization of the community in Malaysia. In fact, the development of the Internet in Malaysia provided a golden opportunity for Indian NGOs such as HINDRAF to emerge and galvanize support for various problems that affect the Malaysian Indian community.

HINDRAF, which was formed in 2006, is an umbrella body of nearly thirty Indian NGOs in response to the High Court's decision that Maniam Moorthy, a member of the first Malaysian team that successfully climbed Mount Everest, would be buried as a Muslim based on evidence that he had apparently embraced Islam earlier, although his family was unaware of this.[10] Although initially, HINDRAF was struggling to get the attention of working-class Indians, the then newly emergent Internet played a crucial role in its rise as one of the formidable forces in Malaysian politics. As a small NGO representing poor working-class Indians, HINDRAF realized that the only way to get wider attention and publicity on various problems faced by Malaysian Indians was to utilize the Internet as one of the platforms to promote its activities. In fact, YouTube was one of the initial online tools used by HINDRAF not only to highlight its activities, but also to systematically record and share issues such as temple demolition to a wider audience. As argued by Leong (2009), HINDRAF activism involved both conventional media methods such as manually preparing recorded VCDs on the issue of Indian marginalization and promoting the same issues on the Internet through blogs and YouTube.

When HINDRAF organized a demonstration in 2007, nearly 30,000 to 40,000 Malaysian Indians participated in the demonstration against the Malaysian government which was then headed by Abdullah Badawi. In fact, the success of this demonstration was undeniably fuelled by the newfound voice on the Internet which unified Malaysian Indians under a single agenda against the government. This 2007 HINDRAF demonstration significantly changed the perception of Malaysian Indians by the then ruling BN government and MIC. More importantly, online media played a crucial role in successfully disseminating information about the marginalization issues of Malaysian Indians to the wider, segregated Indian community.

The success of HINDRAF in utilizing the Internet to mobilize Malaysian Indians prompted the rise of the Malaysian Indian online community. The Malaysian Indian online community can be defined as a community where members share similar interests and interact primarily via the Internet using social networking sites such as Facebook, Twitter and Instagram as a virtual connecting tool to highlight various issues, discussions and feedback, including the framing of ideas concerning the socioeconomic and political development of Malaysian Indians.

In the aftermath of the HINDRAF rally, various Indian cyber-communities mushroomed as the Internet created an open and safe platform for Malaysian Indians to discuss and create a unified public opinion about the then ruling BN. As noted by Weiss (2013), BN's popularity among the non-Malay community continued to decline in the 2013 Malaysian general election, although then prime minister Najib provided various socioeconomic schemes, especially to Malaysian Indians. In fact, more than 80 per cent of Malaysian Indians overwhelmingly voted for opposition political parties in the 2013 Malaysian general election. The voting pattern among Indians continued in the 2018 Malaysian general election where Malaysian Indians played an important role in the formation of Pakatan Harapan (Alliance of Hope – PH) federal government in Malaysia.

## SELECTED CASE STUDY OBSERVATIONS OF MALAYSIAN INDIAN FACEBOOK GROUPS

This section examines Malaysian Indian social media specifically Facebook, which in recent times, not only has become the one-stop centre for Malaysian Indians to get the latest information on various developments relating to the community, but also has played an important part in reshaping Malaysian Indians' current response to various issues. As noted by Lee (2017), information from social media sites such as Facebook is widely shared in other personal or family cyber-communities through communication applications such as WhatsApp. More importantly, this has helped to create public opinion on various socioeconomic and political issues relating to the marginality of Malaysian Indians.

A profound change was noticeable during the Malaysian general elections. In the 2008 Malaysian general election, the aftermath of the 2007 HINDRAF demonstrations heavily dominated the Indian voters' shift from the then ruling BN to the then opposition Pakatan Rakyat (People's Alliance – PR). Such shifting patterns among the Indians continued in 2013 and were further consolidated in GE14 and GE15.

Based on selected observations of Malaysian Indian Facebook groups, namely the official Facebook groups of MIC, Malaysian Indian's Voice for Change and The Malaysian Indians Forum, the succeeding section explores the nature of the posts and discussions before, during and after the 15th Malaysian general election campaign period in 2022. The focus of this section is to understand the nature of the posts, the subject of discussion and the Facebook group members' feedback on the related subject. Finally, this chapter highlights how the Malaysian Indian online communities have become increasingly major players in reshaping the community's political affiliation.

## Types of Malaysian Indian Facebook Groups

Malaysian Indian Facebook groups can be broadly divided into three main types: personal groups; groups promoting Malaysian Indians' commercial or business activities; and groups relating to politics, history and the socioeconomic development of Malaysian Indians. In fact, Facebook groups relating to politics, history and socioeconomic issues are increasingly playing an important part in the Malaysian Indians' understanding of current issues pertaining to the community. More importantly, these Facebook groups not only have become one of the main sources of information but also have helped to create public opinion on various issues including those in the 15th Malaysian general election.

Personal Facebook groups, especially among young IT-savvy Malaysian Indians, still dominate as one of the main leisure forms for connecting friends and family members through updates on daily personal activities. But even on these personal Facebook groups, general issues relating to Malaysian Indians such as Tamil schools, Hindu temples, poverty and urban poor, as well as racial and religious discrimination have often been highlighted; these groups have become a platform for private discussion of such issues among the Malaysian Indian community. Thus, personal Facebook groups have also become a tool that has greatly reshaped the Malaysian Indians' public opinion.

The second type of Facebook group is mainly linked to business or economic promotional activities. In fact, groups such as the Malaysian Indian Community Centre use Facebook as the main tool for promoting small- and medium-sized Malaysian Indian businesses that produce products and/or provide services.[11] Moreover, several large Indian business entities, such as the Malaysian Indian Chamber of Commerce and the Malaysian Associated Indian Chambers of Commerce and Industry (MAICCI),[12] have also used Facebook to promote Malaysian Indian economy and business activities. MAICCI's main role is that of a middleman to promote various Malaysian government economic policies and create business opportunities for its members. These economic types of Facebook groups largely avoid critical posts and discussions on various economic policies pertaining to the Malaysian Indian community.

The third category of Facebook group relates to politics, history and the socioeconomic development of Malaysian Indians. This session focuses on discussing the socioeconomic development aspect. In fact, these types of Facebook groups have mushroomed since the HINDRAF uprising in 2007 as they create a free and safe platform for Malaysian Indians to share their views and idealism on Malaysian Indians' socioeconomic development. More importantly, these Facebook groups have a profound impact on creating Malaysian Indians' public opinions on various socioeconomic and political issues relating to their community.

One example is the Facebook group "History of Indian Labourers in Malaya" (https://www.facebook.com/groups/1778331939073375/), which functions not only as a reminder of Malaysian Indians' plantation roots, but also as a platform to criticize issues relating to plantation Indians, such as their displacement from plantation estates to the urban setting without proper government policy. Members in this Facebook group post various photos, documents and artefacts relating to Indian plantation workers from the British era to independent Malaysia. These posts constantly engage its group members to relook at the past to understand the current nature of Malaysian Indians as one of the most marginalized communities in Malaysia.

Facebook also plays an important role in connecting Malaysian Indians with various Indian political parties. In fact, all major Indian political parties have their own Facebook accounts to promote their political activities. Moreover, during election season, Facebook has become one of the best methods for Indian political parties to galvanize support from the Malaysian Indian community. Splinter factions from the HINDRAF uprising in 2007, such as the Malaysian Advancement Party (MAP)[13] and Malaysia Makkal Sakti Party (MMSP),[14] widely used Facebook as one of the key tools to promote their election manifestos. Both these relatively new Indian parties, headed by former HINDRAF activists, such as P. Waytha Moorthy and R. S. Thanenthiran respectively, use Facebook as one of the main platforms to promote their political activities, especially to young Malaysians. Other well-established Indian political parties such as MIC have also begun to use Facebook as one of the main promotion channels, especially during general elections. This will be explored in detail in the case study section below.

Meanwhile, Facebook groups such as The Enlightened Malaysian Indian Forum, The Malaysian Indians Forum and Malaysian Indian's Voice for Change play an important part in creating a "one-stop platform" for Malaysian Indians to get current news and information about the socioeconomic and political developments of their community. This type of Facebook group also allows Malaysian Indians to express their views and exchange ideas on various problems faced by their community. Thus, they increasingly function as an alternative source of information to the existing state-controlled mainstream media.

As Lee (2017) observed, Facebook has become a significant social media tool for the Malaysian public and political parties to debate

various issues to galvanize public opinion (see Table 5.1) as well as
to act as the main source of information (see Table 5.2).

TABLE 5.1
Malaysia Internet Users' Social Media Activities

| Account Ownership (%) | | | | | |
|---|---|---|---|---|---|
| Facebook | WeChat Moments | Instagram | YouTube | Google+ | Twitter |
| 96.5 | 60.2 | 46.7 | 42.1 | 30.9 | 26.5 |
| Frequency of Social Networking (%)* | | | | | |
| Site | Daily | Weekly | Monthly | Occasionally | Never |
| Facebook | 53.8 | 13.8 | 5.1 | 22.8 | 1.5 |
| WeChat | 31.7 | 9.0 | 2.4 | 14.7 | 2.5 |
| Instagram | 19.8 | 10.6 | 1.9 | 12.3 | 2.2 |
| YouTube | 13.5 | 10.1 | 2.8 | 13.9 | 1.9 |
| Google+ | 5.6 | 5.5 | 3.4 | 13.4 | 3.3 |
| Twitter | 8.3 | 3.6 | 2.2 | 9.0 | 3.6 |
| Time Spent on Social Networking Sites in a Day | | | | | |
| Time | ≤ 1 hour | 1–4 hours | 4–8 hours | 8–12 hours | > 12 hours |
| % Social Media Users | 40.4 | 41.6 | 11.1 | 3.1 | 4.1 |

Source: Malaysian Communications and Multimedia Commission, Internet Users Survey 2016.

TABLE 5.2
Malaysia Internet Users' Source of Information

| Internet Users' Source of Information | | | | | |
|---|---|---|---|---|---|
| Source of Information | Internet | People Around You | TV | Printed Media | Radio |
| % Internet Users | 90.1 | 75.0 | 67.0 | 65.9 | 50.7 |
| Types of Portal Accessed for Information | | | | | |
| Portal | Instant Messaging | Search Engine | Social Media | Online Video | News |
| % Internet Users | 90.4 | 87.2 | 86.9 | 69.5 | 65.5 |

Source: Lee (2017), abridged version.

## SELECTED OBSERVATIONS ON THREE FACEBOOK GROUPS DURING GE15: MALAYSIAN INDIAN CONGRESS, MALAYSIAN INDIAN'S VOICE FOR CHANGE AND THE MALAYSIAN INDIANS FORUM

Three Indian Facebook groups were selected as samples for observation, namely MIC, Malaysian Indian's Voice for Change and The Malaysian Indians Forum. MIC was selected because it is the oldest political party representing the Indian community in the BN government during the 2022 general election. The Malaysian Indian's Voice for Change and The Malaysian Indians Forum were selected based on their popularity among Malaysian Indians, with each having a membership of nearly 30,000 and are pioneer Facebook groups that highlight socioeconomic and political issues relating to Malaysian Indians.

The 15th Malaysian General Election (GE15) was conducted on 19 November 2022, and was one of the most closely contested elections by three major political coalition parties, namely PH, Perikatan Nasional (National Alliance – PN) and BN. Interestingly, for the first time in Malaysian politics, Indian social media groups, especially those on Facebook, played an important part in not only providing information about the contested political narratives during the general election, but also mobilizing voters during the campaign, in addition to convincing the Malaysian Indian community to take a clear stand on their political support.

### Malaysian Indian Congress

MIC's official Facebook group (https://www.facebook.com/MICMalaysia/) promotes the party's leadership and their official political activities. MIC widely used this Facebook group during GE15 to promote its political position to win back Malaysian Indian voters. Although MIC often claims to have more than a million registered members, its official Facebook group has just around 21,000 members. Moreover, responses and comments on various posts about current political issues in this Facebook group are limited, with no clear, critical discussions from its followers about statements or posts listed.

All close observations before, during and after GE15 revealed that this Facebook group was one of the main election campaign tools used to attract young Malaysian Indian voters. As part of the party's election campaign strategy, MIC used this Facebook platform to justify why a race-based party like itself is still relevant to Malaysian politics. Secondly, it helped the party to promote all the individual candidates taking part in GE15. Finally, MIC used this Facebook group, especially during the election period, to directly communicate with Malaysian Indians by highlighting various socioeconomic assistance that it offered.

For instance, in MIC's Facebook group posting on 18 November 2022, both the president and his deputy highlighted that the party is the only one that can defend and protect Malaysian Indians' interests in Malaysian politics. In a short video clip posted on this Facebook group, both top MIC leaders urged Malaysian Indian voters to vote for MIC and BN in GE15 to safeguard their community's interest. The MIC leaders argued that although there are a significant number of Indian politicians in PH, especially in the Democratic Action Party (DAP) and Parti Keadilan Rakyat (People's Justice Party – PKR), but in reality however, Indian politicians in these multicultural parties are controlled by the Chinese and Malays. Both MIC leaders claimed that only a race-based party like MIC that is led by Indians can deliver Malaysian Indians' expectations in terms of socioeconomic development.

Interestingly, some of the posts during the GE15 election campaign on this Facebook group touched on race and religious issues. On 18 November 2022, uploaded to this MIC Facebook group was an old video clip about the 1998 Kampung Rawa incident in Penang where Hindu and Muslim groups clashed. The caption to the video claimed that the current PH president, Anwar Ibrahim who was then deputy prime minister during the incident, had humiliated Malaysian Indians in the past and cannot be trusted as the future prime minister of Malaysia. Another video clip on the same issue was also posted on 17 November 2022, where the late MIC leader, Samy Vellu, accused Anwar Ibrahim of being the person responsible for the incident.

Secondly, the MIC's Facebook group was widely used to introduce its candidates and the party's election manifestos to Malaysian Indian voters. In fact, publicity about almost all of MIC's GE15 candidates in their respective constituencies were uploaded to the Facebook group to help their election campaign. This included MIC leaders such as P.

Kamalanathan (MIC-BN for Port Dickson), T. Mohan (MIC-BN for Hulu Selangor), Mohana Muniandy (MIC-BN for Hulu Langat), Sivarraajh Chandran (MIC-BN for Padang Serai), S. Vigneswaran (MIC-BN for Sungai Siput) and M. Sarawanan (MIC-BN for Tapah). Also noticeable in the Facebook group were several short video clips explaining in detail BN's GE15 election manifesto, including MIC's promises that if BN comes to power, the "Malaysian Indian Blueprint 2.0" would be implemented to enhance the community's socioeconomic activities.

Interestingly, observations on the comments and feedback from these Facebook followers indicated that most of the shared views were in line with MIC's official narrative. For instance, one of the issues that MIC champions is the need for race-based parties in Malaysia, and almost all these Facebook followers agreed that there is a need for race-based party like MIC to defend the Malaysian Indian community.

## Malaysian Indian's Voice for Change

This private Facebook group (https://www.facebook.com/groups/249092345125159) is one of the pioneers in advocating issues relating to Malaysian Indians. The group started in early 2000 and currently has nearly 35,000 followers. Like many other Malaysian Indian Facebook groups, the administrator and members regularly update this Facebook site with specific posts relating to socioeconomic issues and the political development of Malaysian Indians. This Facebook group also covers general information about development in Malaysia, but its main emphasis is to create a healthy debate on the issues related to Malaysian Indians. This group is akin to a "one-stop centre" for Malaysian Indians to get the latest important information about their community, and the issues covered since its formation are mainly about the marginalization of Malaysian Indians in various areas, such as education, culture, religion, economics and politics. In fact, its Facebook posts regularly cover various topics relating to Tamil schools, quotas for Malaysian Indians in public universities, religion and temples, death in police custody, urban poverty, MIC and MAP.

Prior to GE15 and during the campaign period, many articles relating to the general election were posted by the administrator and group members to galvanize Indians to go out and cast their votes.

Another general observation on this Facebook group was that the administrator and group members asked Indians to vote wisely to safeguard Malaysian Indians' future in Malaysia. In fact, almost all of the uploaded information before and during the GE15 campaign period were pro-PH, with most articles coming from online news media such as *Free Malaysia Today*, *Malaysiakini* and *Star Online*.

The GE15 coverage of the Malaysian Indian's Voice for Change Facebook group included ongoing issues relating to the community's political leadership in Malaysia. For instance, news from StarOnline. com about the MIC president announcing his intention to contest the Sungai Siput parliamentary constituency during the party's annual meeting on 11 October 2022 was posted on the Facebook group. Another interesting post on this Facebook page was the decision by Waytha Moorthy, former minister and president of MAP (a splinter group of HINDRAF), to support BN ahead of GE15. Some argued that MIC has already lost touch with the Malaysian Indian community and that it would be a sure defeat for the MIC president if he contested in Sungai Siput. Others felt that Waytha Moorthy's intention to support BN was a technical move by the former HINDRAF leader to protect his position if BN came to power after GE15. They also thought that Waytha's move to support BN was not unexpected as he had done so in 2013 just before the general election by supporting then prime minister Najib Razak.

The GE15 campaign period from 5 to 18 November 2022 was well covered in this Facebook group. Besides advising Malaysian Indians to go out and vote, members of this group also advised their own community to choose wisely to safeguard their future in Malaysia. More specifically, it covered three important issues during the campaign period in GE15: the importance of Malaysian Indian votes, political parties and Indian candidates, and issues relating to Malaysian Indians such as education and poverty.

At the beginning of the GE15 election campaign period, there were videos that were trying to create awareness by urging Malaysian Indians to go out and vote. For instance, on 8 November 2022, a video entitled "PRU15: *Apa Perlu Anda Tahu*" (GE15: What You Need to Know) was uploaded to this Facebook page, and on 11 November 2022, another short video clip entitled "*Cara Mengundi Pos*" (Ways of

Postal Voting) was also uploaded to create awareness for Malaysian Indians to go out and vote in GE15. Generally, observations of responses from group members show that they were asking Malaysian Indians to forget what happened after the 2018 general election and continue to vote to preserve a united Malaysia.

## The Malaysian Indians Forum

According to the Facebook group's introductory statement (https://www.facebook.com/groups/malaysian.indian), the group's objective is to specifically understand Malaysian Indian's marginalization by providing a platform to debate, brainstorm and agree to disagree on various issues pertaining to the community without jeopardizing the existing social harmony in Malaysia. Since this Facebook group's creation, it has attracted 28,000 members, making it one of the most active Indian Facebook groups in Malaysia.

Unlike other Malaysian Indian Facebook groups, this group's GE15 coverage was rather comprehensive and can be divided into three main time periods: pre-, during and post-GE15. Among the main issues that emerged were Indian political parties such as MIC, Indian candidates and leadership, as well as race and religion.

The pre-GE15 posts were dominated by discussions about MIC which had its annual general assembly meeting in mid-October 2022 that was officiated by UMNO President Ahmad Zahid Hamidi. One of the crucial questions raised by the Facebook group members was MIC's survival in GE15 as the party had claimed it could win back the Malaysian Indians' votes based on the state election results in Melaka and Johor where BN secured a major win against PH and PN respectively; the party believed that the wins showed that it had won back the support of Malaysian Indians. During the GE15 election campaign, there was a post on 11 November 2022 that focused on UMNO Deputy President Mohamad Hasan's statement that BN was confident of winning back Malaysian Indian voters. However, the Facebook group members had contradictory views; they felt that MIC had lost the support of the Malaysian Indian community, although many thought that PH could have done better for them. Based on various posts in the Facebook group, they also felt that having Mahathir Mohammad as the prime minister was not a good idea for the Malaysian Indian community. For instance, in response to the post about MIC's annual general meeting in October 2022, members uploaded a video clip entitled "Nesa Holdings" and "Maika Holdings", in reference to the scandalous collapse of Nesa and Maika Holdings, two MIC ventures that were supposed to help poor Malaysian Indians (Pillai 1992).

This Facebook group also highlighted the issue of race relations during GE15. For instance, on 13 November 2022, there was a post entitled *"Parti-Parti Yang Bermain Rasis"* (Parties That Play Racism) and on 14 November 2022, the group's administrator posted an article from Malaysiakini.com about the urgent need for a race relations act in Malaysia. Facebook group members agreed that there was an urgent need for the new government to implement a race relations act to maintain Malaysia's multicultural landscape. Other group members also suggested that Malaysian Indians needed to go out and vote in GE15 to strengthen the non-Malay position and avoid extremist groups from taking over the nation.

Generally, the responses to PH-related posts in this Facebook group were positive, although there was dissatisfaction in some areas such as policies regarding the future of the Malaysian Indian community and the selection of GE15 Indian candidates in PH coalition parties, namely PKR and DAP. For instance, many Facebook group members doubted PKR's selection of R. Ramanan, an ex-MIC member, as the parliamentary candidate for the Sungai Buloh constituency; they were sceptical about his capability to defend Indian and PH values. The group members were also unhappy with DAP's decision to replace Charles Santiago and Kasthuri Patto as candidates in GE15 and questioned why highly educated and qualified Indian candidates were dropped by PH parties in favour of less credible Indian candidates. However, despite the misgivings, PH was still the best choice based on general responses from Facebook group members.

One of the main post-GE15 issues highlighted in the Facebook group was about Indian representation in the newly formed unity government under Prime Minister Anwar Ibrahim. The posts which had headings such as "Cabinet post for Indian – just one minister, the question on fairness" and *"Komposisi Kaum Kerajaan Perpaduan"* (Racial Composition of Unity Government) showed that the group members were concerned about Malaysian Indian representation in the unity government under Anwar Ibrahim. A close observation of the comments section on this issue is that group members did not have a major problem with the lack of Indian participation in the unity government; they even argued that Indian representation in past governments did not change anything for Malaysian Indians. Nevertheless, there was a small number of Facebook group members who were disappointed by the lack of Indian representations in the newly formed unity government, saying that "Anwar has revealed his true colours" by undermining the non-Malays.

## CONCLUSION

This chapter has thus so far highlighted the role of cyber-communities in reshaping Malaysian Indians' views with specific observations on three Facebook groups, namely MIC, Malaysian Indian's Voice for Change and The Malaysian Indians Forum. The GE15-related posts and discussions were very much in line with the outcome of GE15, whereby nearly 80 per cent of Malaysian Indians voted for the multiethnic PH coalition, firmly moving away from the old ethnic narratives played by MIC during the GE15 election campaign period. Social media, such as Facebook, played an important part in this political shift among Malaysian Indians. Unquestionably, cyber-communities played an important part in the political shift of the Malaysian Indian community from MIC-BN to opposition parties in Pakatan Rakyat and its successor PH. Social media platforms, such as Facebook, have given newfound voice and space for Malaysian Indians to freely exchange issues relating to socioeconomic and politics which has manifested in the community's support for political parties in PH.

From a broader perspective, as argued by Anuar (2000), Brown (2005) and Leong (2009), social media such as Facebook will continue to play an important role in galvanizing Malaysian public opinion in electoral politics. Moreover, as argued by Pepinsky (2009) and Lee (2017), Malaysians are increasingly turning to online media as an alternative source of credible information. More importantly, social media platforms such as Facebook have given ordinary Malaysian citizens a voice in the nation's political narrative. For minority communities such as Malaysian

Indians, social media provides a clear platform to exchange ideas, and this newfound voice for Indians will empower this community to freely participate in the future of Malaysian politics.

## Notes

1.  The main author of this chapter leads the Democracy Studies Research Group, while the corresponding author leads the Gender and Postcolonial Studies in Southeast Asia Research Group. Both research groups are based at the Centre for the Promotion of Knowledge and Language Learning, Universiti Malaysia Sabah.

2.  Hindu Rights Action Force (HINDRAF)—a loose coalition of more than thirty Malaysian Indian non-governmental organizations—was formed in 2006 mainly to defend the rampant demolition of Hindu temples under the Abdullah Badawi administration in Malaysia. In 2007, HINDRAF organized a major rally that largely contributed to the shift of working-class Malaysian Indians' support for the ruling Barisan Nasional to the opposition political parties in the 2008 Malaysian General Election.

3.  Sandhu noted in 1931 that nearly 87 per cent of South Indians and 82 per cent of all Indians in Malaya were Tamils. See Sandhu (1993), p. 160.

4.  Malaysian Indians make up an estimated 6.9 per cent of the nation's total population while the other major ethnic groups such as Malay/Bumiputera and Chinese make up 69 per cent and 22 per cent, respectively. See Department of Statistics Malaysia (2019).

5.  Lent noted that the early development of Tamil newspapers was mainly to fulfil the cultural needs of the migrant Indians. See Lent (1974).

6.  Ramasamy highlighted that the rise of left-wing unionism in plantations in the 1930s was the direct outcome of the British plantation policies in Malaya. See Ramasamy (1994).

7.  Internet World Statistics noted that in December 2013, a total of 20,140,125 people (i.e., 67.0 per cent) of Malaysians were using the Internet. There were also 13,589,520 Malaysian Facebook users as of December 2012. See Zanuddin et al. (2017).

8.  Subramaniam noted that in 2000, almost 85 per cent of the Malaysian Indian population lived in urban or semi-urban areas. See Subramaniam (2004).

9.  The state government of Selangor (2008) revealed that ninety-six Hindu temples have been demolished by the local authorities during 2004 to 2007. For more information, see Perumal and Lim (2008).

10. Maniam's body tussle between his Hindu wife and the Islamic authority has gained great media attention between Malays and non-Malays in Malaysia. See Fauwaz (2005).

11. The mission of this Facebook group is to promote Malaysian Indian economic activities. See https://www.facebook.com/MalaysianIndian CommunityCentre/.

12. The role of this Facebook group is to facilitate various Indian chambers of commerce in Malaysia. For more information, see https://www.facebook.com/myMAICCI/.

13. See Malaysian Advancement Party (MAP), https://www.facebook.com/advancementparty/.

14. See https://www.facebook.com/makkalsakti.

## REFERENCES

Abbott, Jason, and John W. Givens. 2015. "Strategic Censorship in a Hybrid Authoritarian Regime? Differential Bias in Malaysia's Online and Print Media". *Journal of East Asian Studies* 15, no. 3 (2015): 455–78. http://www.jstor.org/stable/26335200.

Ampalavanar, Rajeswary. 1993. "The Contemporary Indian Political Elite in Malaysia". In *Indian Communities in Southeast Asia*, edited by K. S. Sandhu and A. Mani, pp. 237–65. Singapore: Institute of Southeast Asian Studies.

Anuar, Mustafa. 2000. "Malaysian Media and Democracy". *Media Asia* 27, no. 4: 183–90.

Arasaratnam, Sinnappah. 1970. *Indians in Malaysia and Singapore*. Bombay: Oxford University Press.

Baradan, K. 2000. "Still No Entry for Pandithan". *The Sun*, 27 July 2000.

Brown, Graham. 2005. "The Rough and Rosy Road: Sites of Contestation in Malaysia's Shackled Media Industry". *Pacific Affairs* 78: 39–56.

Crouch, Harold. 1996. *Government and Society in Malaysia*. Ithaca: Cornell University Press.

Department of Statistics Malaysia. 2016. "Current Population Estimates, Malaysia, 2014–2016". https://v1.dosm.gov.my/v1/index.php?r=column/ctheme&menu_id=L0pheU43NWJwRWVSZklWdzQ4TlhUUT09&bul_id=OWlxdEVoYlJCS0hUZzJyRUcvZEYxZz09.

———. 2019. "Current Population Estimates, Malaysia, 2018–2019". https://v1.dosm.gov.my/v1/index.php?r=column/pdfPrev&id=aWJZRkJ4UEdKcUZpT2tVT09Snpydz09.

Fauwaz Abdul Aziz. 2005. "Heavy Security at Everest Heros Burial". *Malaysiakini*, 28 December 2005. http://www.malaysiakini.com/news/45075.

Jayasooria, Denison. 2018. "Battling the Hearts and Minds of Indian Voters in GE14". *Malaysiakini*, 3 May 2018.

Karthigesu, Ranggasamy. 1989. "The Role of Tamil Newspapers in Ethnic Cultural Continuity in Contemporary Malaysia". *Sojourn: Journal of*

*Social Issues in Southeast Asia* 4, no. 2: 190–204. http://www.jstor.org/stable/41056775.

Kaur, Amarjit. 2006. "Indian Labour, Labour Standards, and Workers' Health in Burma and Malaya 1900–1940". *Modern Asian Studies* 40, no. 2: 425–75. http://www.jstor.org/stable/3876491.

Lee, Cassey. 2017. "Facebooking to Power: The Social Media Presence of Malaysian Politicians". *ISEAS Perspective*, no. 2017/74, 5 October 2017.

Lent, John A. 1974. "Malaysian Indians and Their Mass Media". *Southeast Asian Studies* 12, no. 3: 344–49.

Leong, Susan. 2009. "The Hindraf Saga: Media and Citizenship in Malaysia". *ANZCA09 Communication, Creativity and Global Citizenship.*

Letchumanan, A. 2013. "GE13: Wooing Indians with 'Nambikei'". *The Star*, 16 April 2013. https://www.thestar.com.my/news/nation/2013/04/16/ge13-wooing-indians-with-nambikei/.

Liu, Yangyue. 2014. "Controlling Cyberspace in Malaysia: Motivations and Constraints". *Asian Survey* 54, no. 4: 801–23. https://doi.org/10.1525/as.2014.54.4.801.

Malaysian Communications and Multimedia Commission. 2017. Internet Users Survey 2016. https://www.skmm.gov.my/skmmgovmy/media/General/pdf/IUS2015-Appendix_281216_final-20171016.pdf.

Milne, R. S. and Diane K. Mauzy. 1999. *Malaysian Politics under Mahathir.* London and New York: Routledge.

Moten, Abdul Rashid. 2009. "2008 General Elections in Malaysia: Democracy at Work". *Japanese Journal of Political Science* 10, no. 1: 21–42.

Muzaffar, Chandra. 1993. "Political Marginalization in Malaysia". In *Indian Communities in Southeast Asia*, edited by K. S. Sandhu and A. Mani, pp. 211–36. Singapore: Institute of Southeast Asian Studies.

Pepinsky, Thomas B. 2009. "The 2008 Malaysian Elections: An End to Ethnic Politics?" *Journal of East Asian Studies* 9, no. 1: 87–120. http://www.jstor.org/stable/23418684.

Perumal, Elan, and Lim Chia Ying. 2008. "Applicants for 54 places of Worship Approved". *The Star*, 29 October 2008.

Pillai, M. G. G. 1992. "Crisis in Malaysian Indian Congress". *Economic and Political Weekly* 27, no. 34: 1789–89. http://www.jstor.org/stable/4398778.

Rajaratnam, Usha Devi. 2009. "Role of Traditional and Online Media in the 12th General Election, Malaysia". The Journal of the South East Asia Research Centre for Communications and Humanities (SEARCH) 1, no. 1: 33–58.

Ramasamy, P. 1994. *Plantation Labour, Unions, Capital, and the State in Peninsular Malaysia.* Kuala Lumpur: Oxford University Press.

_____. 2004. "Nation-Building in Malaysia: Victimization of Indians?" In *Ethnic Relations and Nation-Building in Southeast Asia*, edited by Leo Suryadinata, pp. 145–67. Singapore: Institute of Southeast Asian Studies.

_____. 2019. "A Tale of 2 Newspapers, and Its Lesson to Others". *Free Malaysia Today*, 10 October 2019. https://www.freemalaysiatoday.com/category/opinion/2019/10/10/a-tale-of-2-newspapers-and-its-lesson-to-others/.

Ratnam, K. J. 1965. *Communalism and Political Process in Malaysia.* Singapore: University of Malaya Press.

Sandhu, K. S. 1993. "The Coming of the Indians to Malaya". In *Indian Communities in Southeast Asia*, edited by K. S. Sandhu and A. Mani, pp. 151–89. Singapore: Institute of Southeast Asian Studies.

Stenson, Michael R. 1970. *Industrial Conflict in Malaya: Prelude to the Communist Revolt of 1948.* Petaling Jaya: Oxford University Press.

Subramaniam, Nagarajan. 2004. "A Community in Transition: Tamil Displacement in Malaysia". PhD thesis, University Malaya.

Weiss, Meredith L. 2013. "Malaysia's 13th General Elections: Same Result, Different Outcome". *Asian Survey* 53, no. 6: 1135–58. https://doi.org/10.1525/as.2013.53.6.1135.

Zanuddin, Hasmah, Jen Sern Tham, Fauziah Ahmad, Badrul Redzuan Abu Hassan, Julia Wirza Mohd Zawawi, Norliana Hashim, and Muhammad Badri Ishak. 2017. "Burying the News for the Public: Agenda Cutting of the Tamil Newspapers and MIC Candidate Facebook during the 13th General Election". *Jurnal Komunikasi: Malaysian Journal of Communication* 33: 55–72.

# 6

# Social Media, Politics and Identity in Sabah and Sarawak

James Chin

## INTRODUCTION

Social media has become an influential platform for political discourse and engagement in Malaysia. It has played a significant role in shaping political narratives, mobilizing supporters and fostering political activism (Leong 2019; Chin 2003).

In recent years, social media platforms like Facebook, WhatsApp, Telegram, Twitter (now known as X), TikTok and YouTube have been widely used by Malaysian politicians, political parties and activists to connect with the public and convey their messages. Social media provides a more accessible and immediate channel for politicians to communicate directly with their constituents, bypassing traditional media outlets. Social media is also used by marginalized communities to create their own voice in Malaysia because these communities are often ignored by the mainstream media (Loh and Chin 2023).

Overall, social media has become the most significant factor in shaping political conversations in Malaysia. It provides a platform for citizens to voice their opinions, engage with political figures and mobilize support for various causes. However, the challenges of misinformation and government regulations continue to influence the dynamics of politics on social media in the country.

This chapter highlights the political social media in Sabah and Sarawak, two states often ignored by scholars working on Malaysia. It is largely based on my observation and participation in many political social media groups on Facebook, WhatsApp and Telegram during 2021–23.[1] All these groups were started and administered by Sarawakians and Sabahans. This chapter is divided into three parts. The first part deals with the political social media community in Sarawak, followed by the social media community in Sabah. The second part discusses the key themes in Sarawak, namely Gabungan Parti Sarawak, state nationalism and secession, Abdul Taib Mahmud, the issue of native customary rights (NCR) and Dayak marginalization; followed by the key themes in Sabah, namely political instability and "Kataks", the issue of Pendatang Asing Tanpa Izin (PATI), marginalization of Kadazan, Dusun, Murut and Rungus (KDMR) and non-Muslims, and territorial claims by Sulu. The final part deals with common themes in both states, namely the controversy over the Malaysia Agreement (MA63) and the political marginalization of non-Muslim *Bumiputera*.

## PLATFORM

The increase in social media usage in both Sabah and Sarawak is driven by two key factors. First, smartphone prices have dropped dramatically over the past five years. In 2023, a basic smartphone package[2] with Internet access was available for around RM300 and an unlimited data plan was available for around RM25 per month. Many telcos in Malaysia offer cheap plans for home internet in the region of RM200 a month for broadband access.

It must be said that the number of users who engaged in political discussion in both states are rather limited. Age plays an important role when it comes to political discussion and speech. Older users prefer Facebook while younger users prefer Twitter when it comes to public feeds. However, both groups prefer to use private WhatsApp and Telegram groups when it comes to more direct and often controversial issues that they do not wish to share with the public. In general, we see a clear shift from public groups on open platforms like Facebook to private Facebook groups that require membership. Of course, for WhatsApp groups, the administrator must add the user to the group.[3]

One common feature is that the founder or administrator of a group will "reset" the group if too many members exit the group in a short time frame, usually after a huge controversy over a post or a heated disagreement among the vocal members. The reset is done by creating a new group or pausing the group before renaming the group and adding new members.

The number of participants in each group varies. Some groups are large with the largest one having 80,000 participants (Facebook) while the smallest one has only about 250 members (Telegram). But what is clear is that in almost every group, a small minority accounts for more than 70 per cent of the postings. These active participants post every few hours, with some averaging about three posts a day. Although it is assumed that these active users are retirees, this may not be true. In several groups where I am a member, the most active users are individuals who can access social media at any time. Some are business owners, others are senior professionals such as engineers and lawyers who have control over their time, and a significant number of them are civil servants. There are, of course, retirees who are active, but they are not the majority. Although many politicians are in these groups, including incumbent elected assemblymen and members of parliament, they tend to be inactive. It is likely that those in government are using these groups to get feedback on what the public thinks about their parties and the performance of the government. The elected assemblymen and members of parliament have their own exclusive WhatsApp and Telegram groups, usually along party lines. More serious discussions take place in these groups and some "inside" information is shared among these participants.

The main themes for discussions in the political social media groups in Malaysia are contemporary politics, state of the economy and cost of living. However, there are unique discussion themes in groups consisting mainly of Sabahans and Sarawakians. In the next section, I will discuss some of the key themes in Sarawak and Sabah and the common theme found in both states: the Malaysia Agreement (MA63) and the political marginalization of non-Muslim *Bumiputera*.

## KEY THEMES IN SARAWAK

Among the key political themes in Sarawak groups are:

### 1)  Gabungan Parti Sarawak (GPS)

Gabungan Parti Sarawak (GPS) is the ruling coalition in Sarawak. GPS has ruled Sarawak since 1970. For the period 1970–2018, GPS was known as Sarawak Barisan Nasional (SBN). It changed its name to GPS after the federal Barisan Nasional lost power in the 2018 general elections.

The discussion in the past two years (2021–23) is often critical of GPS's stranglehold on Sarawak politics. In the 2021 Sarawak state election, GPS won 76 of 82 seats, thus effectively making Sarawak a single coalition state with no real opposition. By the end of 2023, defections towards GPS saw the opposition left with only two seats. Most of the discussion were related to the need for a strong opposition to ensure that GPS is accountable to the polity. In particular, many participants are concerned that Abang Johari, the Sarawak premier, may hold too much power and misuse the massive state reserves (around RM30 billion) for prestigious projects such as a Sarawak airline and a monorail system.

There are comments that GPS does not practise "power sharing" in the coalition. In theory, GPS consists of the following parties: Parti Pesaka Bumiputera Bersatu (PBB), Sarawak United Peoples' Party (SUPP), Parti Rakyat Sarawak (PRS) and Progressive Democratic Party (PDP). In practice, PBB has enough seats to rule as a single-party government and it tends to dominate the decision-making process, often at the expense of the two smallest parties, PRS and PDP. PBB's president is automatically Sarawak's premier and its deputy president is often made Sarawak's deputy premier.

### 2)  State Nationalism and Secession

Sarawak is a state with the highest level of political autonomy from federal control and interference. The reason for this is twofold. First, the main coalition parties of the Barisan Nasional (BN)— United Malays National Organisation (UMNO), Malaysian Indian Congress (MIC) and Malaysian Chinese Association (MCA)—do not have branches in Sarawak. The BN coalition governed Malaysia as a federal government from independence until 2018. In contrast, all parties or coalitions that have governed Sarawak since independence in 1963 have been Sarawak-based parties. Similarly, all of Sarawak's chief ministers since 1963 have belonged to political parties based in Sarawak. Therefore, the federal parties have no political influence on the ground. Second, when Mahathir was in power at the federal level (1981–2003), he struck a political deal with Sarawak's longest-serving chief minister, Taib Mahmud. He promised not to open a branch of UMNO in Sarawak during his tenure. MIC and MCA have simply followed UMNO's example in this matter. Hence at the grassroots level, there is no link between the federal BN and the local Sarawak parties that controlled the Sarawak government (Chin 2004, 2021).

The absence of UMNO meant that Sarawak politics has always had a strong sense of nationalism. This became even more pronounced during the Adenan Satem administration (2014–17) when it was made clear that Sarawak exists for its residents and that no Malaya-based political party was welcomed in Sarawak. Adenan had great success in the 2016 Sarawak state election, using state nationalism as a central theme in his campaign.

This strong state nationalism is reflected in the social media group posts. Many posts urged the Sarawak state government to ban Malaya-based political parties from entering Sarawak (which is not legally enforceable) and prevent "toxic" Malaysian political culture from flowing into Sarawak. The "toxic" political culture refers to the Ketuanan Melayu Islam (Malay Islamic Supremacy) ideology that dominates Malayan politics. Many participants in the Sarawak group compared this ideology to Sarawak's good ethnic relations; they attribute the good ethnic relations to a lack of sharp divisions between Muslims and non-Muslims in the absence of the Ketuanan Melayu Islam ideology (Chin 2018).

Many of the same participants also believed that given the evolving nature of Malaysian politics and the strength of Parti Islam Se-Malaysia (PAS) in Malayan politics (Chin 2023), Sarawak would be better off seceding from the Malaysian federation in the long run.

Many are worried about PAS's avowed aim of turning Malaysia into an Islamic state eventually.

Many used the failure of the Malaysian Agreement of 1963 (MA63) as the basis for their withdrawal from the federation (more on this later). Many contributors have supported secession, arguing that Sarawak can continue to exist as an independent state, often citing Singapore and Brunei as successful and rich small states. A common argument, which is factually false, is that if Sarawak were to be an independent state, its oil and gas resources would be enough to sustain its economy. Some support the idea of an independent federation of Borneo consisting of Sabah, Brunei and Sarawak, or just Sabah and Sarawak.

## 3)  Abdul Taib Mahmud

Another topic that comes up regularly is the late governor of Sarawak, Abdul Taib Mahmud, who passed away in February 2024. Nearly all the posts relate to allegations of massive corruption during his more than three decades as the chief minister of Sarawak (1981–2014). He is estimated to have made billions of dollars from logging concessions he gave to his entourage and cronies (Straumann 2014). His alleged multibillion assets are often discussed along with a list of his possessions outside Sarawak. The most popular source of information related to Taib Mahmud is the Sarawak Report (www.sarawakreport.org), a website originally set up to expose his misdeeds and details of his overseas holdings. Quite a number of contributions relate to Taib Mahmud's Middle Eastern second wife, Ragad Waleed Al-Kurdi. Many contributors compared her extravagant lifestyle to that of Rosmah Mansor, the wife of disgraced former Malaysian prime minister Najib Razak. Other posts relate to Ragad and her two sons' acquisition of citizenship and status as Sarawak's indigenous Melanau within a short time (Siah 2018). There is a lot of outrage in Sarawak due to the large number of stateless indigenous people who cannot obtain Malaysian citizenship despite being born and reside in Sarawak. It is not uncommon for such a stateless person to wait decades before they can be granted Malaysian citizenship (Laeng, Sim, and Lim 2021).

One of the reasons Taib-related posts are popular on WhatsApp and Telegram groups is that similar claims cannot be posted on public forums without being prosecuted. Under Malaysian law, anyone who publicly criticizes the governor can be prosecuted under the Sedition Act. Participants in these groups have the false impression that postings in these private groups are safe from law enforcement. It is more likely that the police purposely took no action against these participants so that Taib's massive wealth do not gain attention in the mainstream media, which would not cover allegations of Taib's kleptocracy.

## 4)   Native Customary Rights (NCR) and Dayak Marginalization

The issue of native customary rights (NCR) to land, or commonly referred to as "native title", and the lack of political power in the Dayak community are major themes in political social media groups dominated by the community (Jalli and Chin 2023). Outrage over Sarawak government's refusal to recognize native titles is high, as many of the NCR's claims are not recognized or rejected by the government after a lengthy process. In many cases, the disputed NCR land is simply licensed to logging or plantation companies, often leading to direct conflict between the private company and the landowner. Stories and photos showing the police or gangsters taking the side of the company against the native owners are common.

Numerous posts refer to the NCR as an inalienable right of the Dayak community, and the state's refusal to recognize native titles is often linked to corruption. The link between timber barons and the grab for native land is a consistent theme, and the person most often blamed is Taib Mahmud (Colchester 1993).

Another recurring theme is the poor political leadership of the Dayaks and their inability to get the state to recognize native titles, despite holding high positions in the Sarawak government. Many posters use derogatory terms, such as "traitors", on Dayak ministers. Some of these Dayak ministers have been in office for more than two decades, and many have been accused of secretly profiting from the unresolved NCR issue. Photos purported to show the palatial mansions of the corrupt Dayak ministers are regularly posted.

Many posters argue that the Dayak's inability to fight for native title is due to the political marginalization of the community. Many argue that Taib Mahmud's "divide and conquer" policy means that the Dayak community can never unite politically under a single leader or political party (Chin 2017). Other posts accused the Dayak leaders themselves of "killing" other Dayak political leaders out of personal rivalry.

Many posts refer to the first chief minister of Sarawak, Stephen Kalong Ningkan, who was an Iban Dayak. Sarawak's second chief minister, Tawi Sli, was also an Iban Dayak. Since the 1970s, all Sarawak chief ministers have been of Muslim origin. Posters often ask why Dayaks cannot become the chief minister again, even though they make up the majority of Sarawak's population. Related to these posts are questions regarding the position of the governor of Sarawak. Participants regularly asked why the state's two highest political offices (governor and premier[4]) are occupied by Muslims. In fact, all governors of Sarawak have been Muslim since independence, including those who converted to Islam prior to taking the office. Many Dayaks questioned the verbal 1970 political agreement in which the posts of chief minister and governor were split between the Muslim and Dayak communities. In other words, if a Muslim holds the post of chief minister, the post of governor should be given to a Dayak. The idea was not to concentrate power within the same community. Anger has also been directed at incumbent governor Taib Mahmud, with many young Dayaks blaming him for Dayak's political marginalization and the NCR issue.

## KEY THEMES IN SABAH

In Sabah, many of the key political themes are different from Sarawak. There are also issues related to PATI (illegal migrants) which are non-issue in the Sarawak context.

The key themes found in Sabah social media groups are:

### 1)   Political Instability and "*Kataks*"

In contrast to Sarawak and GPS's political dominance, the opposite is true for Sabah. In Sabah, there are many political parties centred on individuals, and elections and defections result in a change of government making the political environment unstable. For the decade 2013–23, Sabah had three different chief ministers (Musa Aman, Shafie Apdal and Hajiji Noor). Since independence in 1963, Sabah has had sixteen chief ministers while Sarawak only had six. Political instability has slowed development, making Sabah one of Malaysia's poorest states (Asadullah, Joseph, and Chin 2023). One reason the government keeps changing is because "*Katak*" politicians are ubiquitous. *Katak* means "frog" in the local language, but on social media the word refers to a politician who changes parties (i.e., "jump" from one political party to another).

Many posts have accused Sabah's *Katak* politicians of being responsible for the overthrow of the state government and for political instability (Golingai 2023). Many of the social media posts in the past two years (2021–23) relate to the constant shifting of political loyalties, creating political instability. The two most recent state governments were formed after several rounds of defections. Ironically, in groups where the *Katak* politicians are subscribers, their supporters openly defend their *Katak* movements as a political necessity as this is what their voters want. There is no way to verify if this is true, but the usual reason given is that they are forced to defect to a government party because they need development funds to support their constituents. Another typical reason is that it is within one's democratic right to join or leave a political party.

## 2) Pendatang Asing Tanpa Izin (PATI) (Illegal Migrants)

Pendatang Asing Tanpa Izin (PATI) is a big issue in many Sabah groups. Sabah's proximity to the southern Philippines and the shared maritime borders have made Sabah vulnerable to illegal migration from the Mindanao region. The Mindanao region, which is located at the most southern part of the Philippines, is Muslim dominated and the Muslims have been fighting for a separate homeland from the largely Catholic Philippines. The armed rebellion against Manila was intense in certain periods from the 1960s to the 1980s.[5] The undocumented migrants enter Sabah through irregular means, mostly by boat. The journey is short, usually a few hours only. Following the conflict in the Mindanao region, Sabah experienced its first wave of immigration in the 1960s. They were followed by successive waves in the 1970s and 1980s.

PATI became a contentious political issue because many of them obtained citizenship in Malaysia because of "Project IC". Project IC, also called Project M (Mahathir), involved the federal Malaysian government granting them citizenship outside the normal regulations, particularly if they are Muslims. This project aimed to change Sabah's demographics for political reasons. Sabah was a non-Muslim majority state prior to Project IC. With the massive number of PATI, it has become a Muslim-majority state in less than a generation (Sadiq 2005). Most experts believe that at least one-third of Sabah's population is made up of unauthorized immigrants who obtained Malaysian citizenship covertly (Frank 2006). The sheer number meant that Muslim-majority constituencies are now the biggest block in Sabah's seventy-three-seat assembly. In other words, it has been impossible for the native non-Muslim *Bumiputera* to win Sabah elections without Muslim support since the late 1980s (Welsh, Somiah, and Loh 2021).

Many PATI-related social media posts fall into two broad categories. First, many believe there is no political solution to resolve the PATI problem as long as the federal government do not want to deport these new Muslim citizens or admit that they were behind this illegal scheme. Many non-Muslim Sabahans think that the federal government wants Sabah to remain under Muslim hands so that it is easier for them to control Sabah. And if there any moves to secede from Malaysia, the Muslim population will put up resistance.

Second, there are those who think the illegal immigrants should be deported if their citizenship was obtained via Project IC. Not only is this unrealistic given that many of these illegal immigrants have settled in Sabah for over twenty years, many of them also have children born in Sabah. To make matters worse, the Philippines does not want to accept children born in Sabah as Filipinos. Some posters believe another way to solve the PATI issue is to issue a "Sabah IC" that allows the state to distinguish between "genuine" Sabahans and "instant" Sabahans (Chan 2022; *Free Malaysia Today* 2022). Many of the posters take the view that a Sabah IC was a bad idea as it is an indirect recognition of their citizenship status.

Many of the postings attack the federal government for its inability to protect the east coast of Sabah. Although the federal government established the Eastern Sabah Security Command (Esscom) in 2014 to stop illegal movements between the east coast of Sabah and the Mindanao region, it is largely a failure with the movement of people and goods continue unabated.

Overall, there is a sense of hopelessness when it comes to the PATI issue. Many posters, including retired politicians, do not seem to have any workable solutions in the short or long term.

## 3) Marginalization of Kadazan, Dusun, Murut and Rungus (KDMR) and non-Muslims

The marginalization of the largest non-Muslim indigenous groupings—Kadazan, Dusun, Murut and Rungus (KDMR)—is a popular theme. Similar to the Sarawak Dayaks, the KDMR feel that they are being marginalized in politics in favour of the Muslim majority. Often, the marginalization is linked to two issues: PATI (see above) and religious persecution. The overwhelming majority of the KDMR are Christians, mainly Roman Catholics and Borneo Evangelical Church (Sidang Injil Borneo or SIB). From independence to the 1980s, the KDMR were the majority in Sabah's population. Project IC changed Sabah to a Muslim-majority state. There are many posts asking why a Christian Kadazan cannot be the governor. Legally there is no religious requirement for the ceremonial position of state governor but in practice, all the governors since independence have been Muslims, including converted Muslims. The underlying cause of this debate is the concern that the Muslims, via Project IC, have now dispossessed the indigenous people of Sabah. The greatest fear is that Muslims, with the support of the federal government, will "import" the ideology of Ketuanan Melayu Islam (Malay Islamic Supremacy) to Sabah, and the KDMR will never regain any real political power in the future (Chin 2015). This fear is reinforced by the strong presence of UMNO in Sabah politics. One post that keeps appearing is the call for the federal government to lift the ban on the book, *Peter J. Mojuntin: The Golden Son of the Kadazan* (Sta Maria 1978). Mojuntin was a Catholic state minister who had complained to the prime minister about the persecution of the Catholic Church by Mustapha Harun, the then chief minister of Sabah. In more recent times, the Muslims agitated for the removal of Joseph Pairin Kitingan as chief minister of Sabah from 1985 onwards, in part because he was a Catholic Christian (Chin 1999). In 2022, there was a serious attempt by KDMR groups to nominate Pairin to be Sabah's first non-Muslim governor since he is retiring from active politics. The

Muslim chief minister simply ignored the call by renewing the term of the incumbent (Santos 2022).

Another recurring post refers to the "Batu Sumpah" (Oath Stone). The Oath Stone is a monument in Keningau, Sabah erected to commemorate the merger of the Crown Colony of North Borneo with the former colony of Sarawak and states of the Federation of Malaya to form the new federation of Malaysia. The inscription on the Oath Stone says in part *"Ugama Bebas Dalam Sabah"* or Freedom of Religion in Sabah. In other words, a promise was made that there will not be an official religion in Sabah. However, this promise was broken in the early 1970s when the chief minister, Mustapha Harun, engineered a constitutional amendment to the Sabah constitution making Islam the official religion of Sabah (Lasimbang et al. 2020). Many posts called on the Sabah government to repeal the law and return Sabah to a secular state. Almost all argued that making Islam the official religion of Sabah is a breach of the Malaysia Agreement of 1963.

## 4) Territorial Claims by Sulu

The Sulu claim on Sabah refers to the historical territorial dispute between the Philippines and Malaysia over the ownership of the state of Sabah. The claim is based on the assertion by the heirs of the Sultanate of Sulu, a historical Muslim state in the southern Philippines, that Sabah was part of their ancestral territory and should rightfully belong to the Philippines as they never ceded Sabah. The Sultan of Sulu merely "leased" Sabah in 1878 to the British North Borneo Company, in return for an annual payment in perpetually. This lease was later transferred to the British government, which eventually granted Sabah to Malaysia upon its formation in 1963.

The Sulu claim asserts that the transfer of Sabah to Malaysia was illegitimate and that the descendants of the Sultan of Sulu should have sovereignty over the territory. Supporters of the claim argue that the lease was only temporary and did not confer permanent ownership. The conflict between the heirs and the Malaysian government has sparked sporadic tensions and occasional violence over the years, most notably when "Royal Sulu" army launched an invasion of Sabah in 2013, resulting in casualties on both sides in Lahad Datu. In 2019, the surviving heirs filed an arbitration lawsuit against the Malaysian government in Spain for failing to pay the annual cession payment of about five thousand ringgit (RM5,000). The Malaysian government suspended the annual payments after a 2013 raid. In an unprecedented ruling, a French arbitration court awarded US$14.9 billion in damages to the heirs (Telling 2022; Che, Shirodkar, and Sebag 2023). The ruling was widely reported in Malaysia and became a hot topic among Sabahans. Many social media posts accused the federal government of allowing this to happen, amid reports that the Malaysian government did not take part in the arbitration process even when it was aware of it. The prevailing opinion in the posts was that Sabah's sovereignty as a Malaysian state was undisputed and that Malaysia should settle the issue with the Philippine government rather than with the Sultan's successors. Posts about Sulu's allegations have surfaced regularly throughout 2022 and 2023 since the Malaysian government took active legal action and successfully overturned the arbitration decision in Europe.

## COMMON THEME: MALAYSIA AGREEMENT 1963 (MA63)

If there is one common theme among social media posts in Sabah and Sarawak, it is the historical grievances over the Malaysia Agreement 1963, or more commonly referred to as "MA63". The Malaysia Agreement 1963 is an agreement that was signed on 9 September 1963 between the Federation of Malaya, Singapore, Sabah (then known as North Borneo) and Sarawak. The agreement laid the foundation for the formation of Malaysia as a federation, incorporating these territories. The controversy surrounding the Malaysian Agreement 1963 revolves around several key issues relating to Sabah and Sarawak's status, autonomy and rights in the federation. The basic complaint is that Putrajaya had not honoured the "twenty-point" safeguards written into the Malaysia Agreement. The safeguards essentially granted Sabah and Sarawak a high degree of autonomy—from control over immigration to religion to the state civil service—from Putrajaya. In practice, Putrajaya centralized as much power as possible under the federal system and tried its best to control Sabah and Sarawak by ensuring Muslims were always in control there, despite ethnic Malays being a minority in both states (Chin 2019a).

In social media, the most commented MA63-related topics were

1) **Status of Sabah and Sarawak**: there are concerns among many Sabahans and Sarawakians that the terms of the agreement have not been fully upheld, leading to marginalization and neglect by the federal government since independence. In the past two years (2021–23), there were many posts related to the following:

   a) The 2021 federal constitutional amendment: The Constitution (Amendment) Act 2022 amended the Constitution of Malaysia to restore Sabah and Sarawak as founding members of the Malaysian federation and to give effect to the Malaysia Agreement of 1963, which was previously not mentioned in the constitution. While may posts celebrated this amendment, after a similar amendment failed in 2019 (Chin 2019b), other posts claimed it was a pyrrhic victory as it did not use the term "equal partner", nor does it give any additional resources to Sabah or Sarawak. In other words, it was mostly symbolic.

   b) The change of title from Sarawak chief minister to Sarawak premier: this was made in early 2022 to reflect the constitutional amendment. The rationale was that the political status of the chief minister of Sarawak was higher than that of the chief minister of the other states in the federation. Sarawak was an "equal partner" in the founding of the federation and therefore the status of the top state political office should reflect this (Ten 2022). While most social media posts supported the name change, many also pointed to Sabah's refusal to change the prime minister's appointment (Doksil 2022). Most of the postings claimed that Hajiji was afraid to change his title because he may not have the support required to change Sabah's constitution, which would be needed if he wanted to use the title "premier". In 2024, Hajiji announced that Sabah will amend its state constitution and change the title to premier.

2) **Oil and gas resources**: there are many posts regarding the ownership of oil and gas resources. Both Sabah and Sarawak are major oil and gas producers but under the Petroleum Development Act 1974 (PDA 1974), Petronas, the national oil company, owns all the oil and gas resources. In return, each state receives a paltry

5 per cent royalty. To add insult to injury, both Sabah and Sarawak are under-developed. Many posts claimed that the massive profits from oil and gas were "stolen" by the federal government for use in Malaya's development.

3) **Immigration and citizenship**: another contentious issue is related to the control of immigration and citizenship in Sabah. Under MA63, Sabah and Sarawak have absolute control over their own immigration but, as mentioned above, the federal government's Project IC makes a mockery of the promise when it comes to Sabah. This is a major issue in social media in Sabah.

4) **Political autonomy**: according to MA63, both states should enjoy a high degree of political autonomy. This is mostly true for Sarawak, but not for Sabah. The federal government has repeatedly intervened in Sabah's internal politics, particularly through UMNO. Many posts on social media in Sabah lamented that UMNO is too influential and wished they could be like Sarawak and keep UMNO out of Sabah. Many posts also praised GPS as a powerful coalition that has successfully countered federal influence. Sabah's ruling Gabungan Rakyat Sabah (Sabah People's Alliance – GRS) coalition has openly said it sees GPS as a political model. Many posters agreed with this and even suggested that GPS and GRS collectively challenge the federal government on MA63 (Peter 2022). Many postings call for a Borneo bloc consisting of all Sabah and Sarawak MPs to support MA63.

5) **Sabah's 40 per cent claim**: under MA63, the federal government was required to pay a special grant annually to Sabah in accordance with Article 112C and Section 2 of Part IV in the Tenth Schedule of the Federal Constitution. The special grant, being two-fifths of the total revenue raised from Sabah, is commonly referred to as Sabah's 40 per cent entitlement. This 40 per cent entitlement was an important part of the financial provisions to provide for the development needs of Sabah since Sabah was far behind Malaya in 1963. The federal government, however, stopped the payment after 1974. In 2022, the Sabah Law Society (SLS) filed a judicial review against the federal government as public interest litigation. This created a lot of excitement in social media as many Sabahans saw this as a way to force the federal government to meet its MA63 commitment (Fong 2023).

## COMMON THEME: POLITICAL MARGINALIZATION OF THE NON-MUSLIM *BUMIPUTERA*

Another common theme found in social media groups in Sabah and Sarawak is political marginalization of the non-Muslim *Bumiputera*. Most of the discussion centres on the loss of political power since Sabah and Sarawak became states in the Malaysian federation. When North Borneo (present day Sabah) and Sarawak became part of the Malaysian federation in 1963, the biggest ethnic group in Sabah was the Kadazan, while in Sarawak it was the Iban Dayak. This is reflected in the political system. The first chief minister of Sabah was Donald Stephens, a Kadazan, while in Sarawak it was Stephen Kalong Ningkan, an Iban. Both groups are still predominantly non-Muslims today.

By 1970, both Kadazan and Ibans were out of power. Federal intervention by the Muslim-led federal government saw both Sabah and Sarawak installing Muslim chief ministers (Chin 2015, p. 83). Since then, the federal government has tried to ensure that both states are under Muslim control. In Sarawak, the federal government was much more successful. Since 1970, all the chief ministers have been Muslim. In Sabah, from 2003 onwards, all chief ministers are Muslim. Moreover, the federal government's Project IC has turned Sabah into a Muslim-majority state. There is deep resentment in both states that the biggest native groupings, the Ibans in Sarawak and the Kadazan in Sabah, will never occupy the office of the chief minister as long as the federal government is led by Muslims (Chin 2019c).

Many of the postings pointed to an unwritten "Gentlemen's Agreement" that the top two political positions in the state—state governor and the chief minister—were to be divided between the Muslims and the non-Muslim *Bumiputera*. In other words, for example in Sarawak, if the chief minister was a Muslim, then the state governor, a ceremonial post, will be appointed from the Iban or wider Dayak community.

The fact that the governor's position has been monopolized by Muslims since independence in 1963 suggested that the Gentleman's Agreement was never taken seriously by the Muslim leadership, both at the state and federal levels. The reason given by Muslim leaders is that the governor is expected to lead Islam-related ceremonies, which cannot be performed by a non-Muslim. However, this is untrue as the non-Muslim governor can delegate such ceremonies to the Muslim chief minister. There is no reason why Islamic ceremonies must be presided by a Muslim governor. Legally, the Sabah Constitution, like the Sarawak Constitution, does not prohibit a non-Muslim from the post. In fact, the only legal requirements are that the candidate must be a natural-born Sabahan or Sarawakian and be appointed by the Yang di-Pertuan Agong (King) after consultation with the chief minister.[6] Many Sabah Muslims also gave the excuse that a non-Muslim cannot be appointed the governor because the governor is supposed to be the head of Islam in the state. This was untrue because the Yang di-Pertuan Agong is the head of Islamic matters in Sabah.

The postings on this issue in both Sabah and Sarawak usually conclude that the non-Muslim *Bumiputera* are too weak politically to enforce this unwritten agreement or that the unwritten agreement is urban myth. Others pointed to the inability of the Dayaks and Kadazan to place one of their own in the governor's office because they are politically divided and hence are dominated by Muslims. This issue blew up spectacularly in 2022 when senior members of the Kadazan community wanted to nominate Joseph Pairin Kitingan, the Huguan Siou (traditional paramount chief of the Kadazans) and ex-chief minister, to be the next Sabah governor. The move received widespread support among the non-Muslim population in Sabah (*Daily Express (Sabah)* 2022). Despite the public lobbying on social media and in the press, the incumbent was reappointed for a fourth term as governor. In social media, the reaction was muted, suggesting political disappointment and realization that as long as the Muslims are in power, it will be very difficult for them to even contemplate appointing a non-Muslim *Bumiputera* to the symbolic position of governor.

## CONCLUSION

The influence of social media on the opinions of ordinary people in Sabah and Sarawak, as in any other parts of the country, can vary and is subjected to different factors. However, social media platforms provide individuals with an avenue to express their opinions and engage in discussions on topics that are relevant only to Sabah and Sarawak. The leading political issue in both states in the past two years (2021–23) is undoubtedly related to MA63. While social media platforms can amplify the voices of ordinary people and provide a platform for diverse perspectives, Sabahans and Sarawakians are united on how the federal government has not adhered to the spirit of MA63 and has marginalized Sabah and Sarawak for most of the past fifty years.

Many of the closed social media groups in Sabah and Sarawak suffer from the echo chamber effect, where people are more likely to interact with and follow others who share similar opinions. This is especially true of WhatsApp and Telegram groups where members are normally screened before being admitted to the group. This can lead to a skewed perception of public opinion, as users may primarily encounter viewpoints that are aligned with their own, rather than a representative range of diverse opinions.

There is also the issue of vocal minority versus silent majority. In political discussion in all these groups, a small but vocal group will dominate the discussions, while a larger silent majority may have different or more nuanced perspectives, which is not heard of or only in a single posting.

The most obvious problem with these groups is that they are prone to online manipulation and disinformation. Most of the postings offer information as "facts", when in reality, they are merely information forwarded from another source, or worse, from fake news.

In summary, all major political issues posted on social media groups in Sabah and Sarawak are directly tied to the unique identities of the states. They do not share the same religion, history, language, origins, demographics and culture as the people of the peninsula, and this is reflected in their postings. The MA63 posts only reinforced their identity as Sabahans or Sarawakians, and they have a distinct identity apart from just being Malaysians.

## Notes

1.  Much of the information here were gathered/observed during the period 2020–23. The author was a member of more than two dozen groups, many of which are closed groups. Only groups using mostly English and Bahasa Melayu were monitored. The author was co-administrator for the most popular

Facebook group dedicated to contemporary Sarawak, and was co-administrator for a dozen Whatsapp groups. Twitter was not monitored for this chapter because there are only a few closed-lists on Twitter dealing with politics in Sabah and Sarawak. The rapid change in social media applications means that the social media platform described here may change in the coming year, but the themes described in this chapter will probably outlast the platform.

2. A "package" deal usually means that the user must sign up for two years with one particular network.

3. Whatsapp played an important role in the 2018 general elections, see Johns (2020).

4. From 2021 onwards, the chief minister was renamed as the premier of Sarawak.

5. The Mindanao issue is complex and lies beyond the scope of this chapter. For details, see Montiel, Rodil, and de Guzman (2012).

6. Article 2 of the Sabah Constitution.

## REFERENCES

Asadullah, M. Niaz, Jeron Joseph, and James Chin. 2023. "The Political Economy of Poverty Reduction in Malaysia". *Progress in Development Studies* 23, no. 2: 127–51.

Chan, Julia. 2022. "Sabah IC Motion to Be Brought to State Assembly in March, Says GRS Component Party". *Malay Mail*, 22 February 2022.

Che, Jenny, Ravil Shirodkar, and Gaspard Sebag. 2023. "Malaysia Wins Court Fight over Sulu Heirs' $15 Billion Award". *Bloomberg*, 6 June 2023.

Chin, James. 1999. "Going East: UMNO's Entry into Sabah Politics". *Asian Journal of Political Science* 7, no. 1 (June): 20–40.

———. 2003. "Malaysiakini.com and Its Impact on Journalism and Politics in Malaysia". In *Asia.com*, edited by K. C. Ho, Randy Kluver, and C. C. Yang. London: Routledge.

———. 2004. "Autonomy: Politics in Sarawak". In *Reflections: The Mahathir Years*, edited by Bridget Welsh, pp. 240–51. Washington, D.C.: John Hopkins University Press.

———. 2015. "Exporting the BN/UMNO Model: Politics in Sabah and Sarawak". In *Routledge Handbook of Contemporary Malaysia*, edited by Meredith Weiss, pp. 83–92. London: Routledge.

———. 2017. "The Politics of Native Titles in Sarawak". *New Mandala*, 11 March 2017. https://www.newmandala.org/politics-native-titles-sarawak/.

———. 2018. "Sabah and Sarawak in the 14th General Elections 2018 (GE14): Local Factors and State Nationalism". *Journal of Current Southeast Asian Affairs* 37, no. 3: 173–92.

_____. 2019a. "The 1963 Malaysia Agreement (MA63): Sabah and Sarawak and the Politics of Historical Grievances". In *Minorities Matter: Malaysian Politics and People*, edited by Sophie Lemiere, pp. 75–92. Singapore: ISEAS – Yusuf Ishak Institute.

_____. 2019b. "Commentary: The Ghost of Borneo, Talk of Secession Are Back to Haunt Malaysia". *Channel News Asia*, 10 April 2021.

_____. 2019c. "'Malay Muslim First': The Politics of Bumiputeraism in East Malaysia". In *Illusions of Democracy: Malaysian Politics and People*, edited by Sophie Lemière, pp. 201–20. Amsterdam: Amsterdam University Press.

_____. 2021. "Borneo Brews Another Malaysian Reality". *Asialink*, 8 December 2021.

_____. 2023. "Anwar's Long Walk to Power: The 2022 Malaysian General Elections". *The Round Table: The Commonwealth Journal of International Affairs* 112, no. 1: 1–13.

Colchester, Marcus. 1993. "Pirates, Squatters and Poachers: The Political Ecology of Dispossession of the Native Peoples of Sarawak". *The Political Ecology of Southeast Asian Forests: Transdisciplinary Discourses* 3, no. 4/6: 158–79.

*Daily Express (Sabah)*. 2022. "The Case for a Non-Muslim Sabah TYT". 9 October 2022.

Doksil, Mariah. 2022. "Hajiji: Sabah Won't Change 'Chief Minister' Title to 'Premier'". *The Borneo Post*, 1 March 2022.

Fong, Durie Rainer. 2023. "Sabah Lawyers to Pursue Judicial Review of 40% Special Grant in Court of Appeal after Stay Decision". *The Star (Malaysia)*, 3 February 2023.

Frank, Sina. 2006. "Project Mahathir: 'Extraordinary' Population Growth in Sabah". *Südostasien aktuell: Journal of Current Southeast Asian Affairs* 25, no. 5: 71–80.

*Free Malaysia Today*. 2022. "Sabah IC Not Solution to Migrant Problem, Says Warisan Veep". 11 April 2022.

Golingai, Philip. 2023. "Sabah's Political Gamblers". *The Star*, 15 January 2023.

Jalli, Nuurrianti, and James Chin. 2023. "Native Customary Rights Land Titles and Thwarting Deforestation: Digital Acts of Resistance among Sarawak's Indigenous Peoples". In *New Media in the Margins: Lived Realities and Experiences from the Malaysian Peripheries*, edited by Benjamin Y. H. Loh and James Chin. Singapore: Palgrave Macmillan.

Johns, Amelia. 2020. "'This Will Be the WhatsApp Election': Crypto-Publics and Digital Citizenship in Malaysia's GE14 Election". *First Monday* 25, no. 12. https://doi.org/10.5210/fm.v25i12.10381.

Laeng, Jenifer, Natasha Sim, and Lim Huck Hai. 2021. "For Some in Sarawak, Quest for Citizenship Is Unending". *The Borneo Post*, 18 July 2021.

Lasimbang, Jannie, Peter Saili, Noorita Saul, Adrian Banie Lasimbang, Clare Taunek Simbat, and Grelydia Gillod Keningau. 2020. "Uphold Three Sworn Promises of Batu Sumpah". *Malaysiakini*, 31 August 2020.

Leong, Pauline Pooi Yin. 2019. *Malaysian Politics in the New Media Age: Implications on the Political Communication Process*. Singapore: Springer Nature.

Loh, Benjamin Y. H., and James Chin, eds. 2023. *New Media in the Margins: Lived Realities and Experiences from the Malaysian Peripheries*. Singapore: Palgrave Macmillan.

Montiel, Cristina J., Rudy B. Rodil, and Judith M. de Guzman. 2012. "The Moro Struggle and the Challenge to Peace Building in Mindanao, Southern Philippines". In *Handbook of Ethnic Conflict: International Perspectives*, edited by Dan Landis and Rosita D. Albert, pp. 71–89. Boston, MA: Springer.

Peter, Anthea. 2022. "Jeffrey Credits Sarawak, Hopes GRS Will Emulate GPS". *Daily Express (Sabah)*, 29 May 2022.

Sadiq, Kamal. 2005. "When States Prefer Non-citizens over Citizens: Conflict over Illegal Immigration into Malaysia". *International Studies Quarterly* 49, no. 1: 101–22.

Santos, Jason. 2022. "Kadazandusun Group Wants Joseph Kitingan to Be Next Sabah Governor". *The Vibes*, 28 September 2022.

Siah, Francis Paul. 2018. "Sarawak Must Clarify 'Melanau' Status of Taib's Wife". *Malaysiakini*, 7 February 2018.

Sta Maria, Bernard. 1978. *Peter J. Mojuntin: The Golden Son of the Kadazan*.

Straumann, Lukas. 2014. *Money Logging: On the Trail of the Asian Timber Mafia*. Basel, Switzerland: Bergli Books.

Telling, Oliver. 2022. "The Sultan, His Family and a \$15bn Dispute over Oil in Malaysia". *The Financial Times*, 17 July 2022.

Ten, Marilyn. 2022. "Abdul Karim: 'Premier' Instead of CM Because Sarawak's Different from Other States in Malaysia". *The Borneo Post*, 15 February 2022.

Welsh, Bridget, Vilashini Somiah, and Benjamin Y. H. Loh, eds. 2021. *Sabah from the Ground: The 2020 Elections and the Politics of Survival*. Singapore: Strategic Information and Research Development Centre (SIRD)/ISEAS – Yusof Ishak Institute.

# 7

# Online Christian Communities in Malaysia

Clarence Devadass, Pauline Pooi Yin Leong and Meng Yoe Tan

## CATHOLIC SOCIAL TEACHINGS AND THEIR ONLINE COMMUNITIES

It is often thought that the Church's role is only in the spiritual realm and therefore it has no role to play in social and political life. There is sometimes a tendency to keep "sacred" and "secular and temporal" affairs apart because the fundamental principles are considered different. However, the spiritual and sacred affairs are matters experienced in the context of real-time and space just as how social and political affairs are experienced. Therefore, issues of justice and the common good are within the realm of that which are both sacred and spiritual.

The involvement of Malaysian Christian communities in the political and social spheres is not something new in Malaysian society. As in biblical times, the Church's mission in being the prophetic voice in society today by addressing social issues with great clarity and urgency, demanding action and situating itself as a community must be seen as a congruent part of the faith and not as opposing parts of the Christian faith and identity. Though the awakening may have been delayed, Malaysian Christians have been involved in public life and policies in the last three decades. Contrary to what many may think, "the separation of Church and state does not require division between belief and public action, between moral principles and political choices, but protects the right of believers and religious groups to practice their faith and act on their values in public life" (Fay, n.d.).

In the past, the Church and the State shared a close bond with each other, especially when the Christian emperor appeared as God's representative on earth. As the Western empires expanded, close bonds between both parties meant the imperial Church enjoyed privileges while the empire received approval from the Church's hierarchy. Nevertheless, the American and French revolutions at the end of the eighteenth century resulted in separation between the Church and the State whereby the government had to maintain neutrality towards religion, which meant that it could and should not recognize or favour any religion. This was the prevailing view of many Christians during the nineteenth and twentieth centuries that the Church should only occupy itself with spiritual issues, and not become involved with temporal issues. Thus, anyone who spoke against political establishments was frowned upon by the institutional Church despite its early history where it was involved in the governance of the state and its people; it was considered not the "work" of the Church.

However, the dawn of industrialization in the late nineteenth century changed the world and the lives of its people. The growing disparity between workers and wealth became a grave concern for Pope Leo XIII, leading him to write the ground-breaking encyclical *Rerum Novarum* (Of New Things) in 1891 where he upheld the rights to private property, rejected socialism and communism, while defending worker dignity and the principle of labour over capital, whereby people are more important than property. This unprecedented pronouncement from a pope took the Church by shock. Since then, the Church's social vision has grown and become an integral part of its teaching and preaching: "At the heart of the Church's proclamation there also must be [actions] on behalf of justice and participation in the transformation of the world. [These actions] appear to us as a constitutive dimension of the preaching of the Gospel, or, in other words, of the Church's mission for the redemption of the human race and its liberation from every oppressive situation" (World Synod of Catholic Bishops 1971, para. 6).

Gradually, these teachings came to be known as Catholic Social Teachings (CST), comprising Catholic doctrine that relates to matters dealing with the collective aspect of humanity. It is primarily intended to assist believers in the process of reflection so that the criteria for judgement and directives for action can be achieved. The Catholic Church's social vision is in fact founded on Scripture. In truth, social agenda is one of the life cores of the Church, in both the Old and New Testaments of the Bible. In the Old Testament, the Israelites sought to build a just society based on the covenant between God and His people. Any injustices were scorned by God and considered a transgression of the covenant. In the New Testament, at the very outset, Jesus sets His mission as liberating humanity from social evils brought about by sin. It is clear then that a social agenda within the Church for the common good of society cannot be considered as not well-founded.

Over the years, there are several major themes that form the core of CST. These are not economic or political programmes, but offer a powerful way of thinking about what common good requires:

1. *Life and Dignity of the Human Person*: human life is at the core of CST and since it is sacred, it requires respect and protection from the moment of conception till death.

2. *Call to Family, Community and Participation*: since the human person is a social being and family is the basic unit of society, family and community are the contexts in which social responsibility, respect, solidarity and other values for the building of God's kingdom are to be promoted.

3. *Rights and Responsibilities*: given that human dignity is at the core of CST, protecting the rights and responsibilities is one of the CST themes. The right to life characterizes the dignity to which human life must be afforded.

4. *Option for the Poor and Vulnerable*: care and concern for those on the margins of society are also at the heart of the Church's mission. Solidarity with the poor and vulnerable is an integral part of CST.

5.  *The Dignity of Work and the Rights of Workers*: this theme is what launched the Church into a more systematic approach towards concern for life and faith. In affording dignity and protecting the rights of workers, the Church sees the way in which humanity can be directed towards the destiny intended by God, our Creator.

6.  *Solidarity*: faith in God must correspond with human action, especially when there are injustices. In that sense, the light of faith must inspire a unity of the human race that brings about solidarity.

7.  *Care for God's Creation*: environmental stewardship, as described in the biblical creation accounts, imposes fundamental moral and ethical dimensions to the faith. In short, care for God's creation is a requirement of the Christian faith.

Seen from this perspective, the Church's invitation to its followers to be concerned and involved in issues that affect the common good of humanity is consistent with the teachings of Jesus Christ. The social mission of the Church has deep biblical roots that cannot be ignored. Being involved in the common good must be at the heart of one's Christian identity. The Christian social agenda is neither founded on personal identity nor group power. It is not about social activism but about building a society where people can be good, a society where people can love and take care of one another, and where they can find God. In the words of Pope John Paul II in his encyclical *Sollicitudo rei socialis* (1987), "The teaching and spreading of the social doctrine are part of the Church's evangelising mission. Since it is a doctrine aimed at guiding people's behaviour, it consequently gives rise to a 'commitment to justice' according to each individual's role, vocation, and circumstances."

The online environment has provided Christians in Malaysia—Catholics and Protestants alike—a space to deepen their faith experiences through prayer, reflection and the exchange of religious knowledge. Through live-streamed services, online forums and social networking platforms, members engage in virtual worship, share spiritual insights and build meaningful connections that shape their religious identity. The digital arena allows individuals to explore and develop their personal religious narratives, contributing to a diverse and evolving landscape of Internet Christianity in Malaysia. Nevertheless, cyberspace is also a place for Christians to discuss sociopolitical matters that affect the practice of their faith, especially in a Muslim-majority country. It is in this context that the chapter examines the narratives of online Christian communities—Catholics and Protestants—in Malaysia when discussing sociopolitical issues that affect them.

Using the digital ethnographic approach, which is a method of "representing real-life cultures through combining the characteristic features of digital media with the elements of story", we examined two Catholic and two Protestant online communities (Underberg and Zorn 2013). The purpose of ethnography is to holistically characterize the cultural membership in a community (Singer 2009), whether online or offline. Digital ethnography is a method for enhancing understanding of meanings within the technological environment, and the cultural experiences that enable and are enabled by digital media (Hine 2000). Digital ethnographic studies involve experiential observations of specific chatrooms, online discussion groups or virtual sites where the available texts and graphics are processed and examined for their meanings. The aim of digital ethnography is to understand relational and behavioural patterns and orders in cyberspace (Kaur-Gill and Dutta 2017).

We will first examine two Catholic online communities: Catholics at Home (https://www.catholicsathome.org/about), a podcast service which went on air on 1 April 2020 after Malaysia had its first COVID-19 lockdown in March 2020; and a private Facebook group whose members are mainly Malaysian Catholics.

Catholics at Home (CAH) has four main objectives: firstly, to provide a brand-new platform for everyone to unite as one community and discuss daily issues and trending topics from a Catholic's point of view; and secondly, to create a convenient alternative for Catholics to stay in touch with the current updates of the Church due to the then ongoing pandemic. Thirdly, CAH aims to help Malaysian Catholics understand the diversified religions and traditions that are being freely practised by all races in Malaysia, and in so doing bring Malaysians closer as one united family who share the same love for one another, which is its last objective. To reach as many Malaysian Catholics as possible, CAH is present on all major online platforms such as Facebook, YouTube, Spotify and Instagram. It has 6,800 followers and 4,700 likes on its Facebook account while its YouTube channel has 6,700 subscribers. Its Instagram account is less active with 831 followers only. While the topics that it has covered focus on various aspects of the Catholic faith, such as praying at home during the pandemic and spiritual matters, CAH also covered sociopolitical issues such as the role of Christians in nation-building, helping the poor during the pandemic, youth as catalysts for change and the social responsibility of Christians to participate in general elections.

For example, on 16 September 2023, which is Malaysia Day, CAH invited former Member of Parliament (MP) for Batu Kawan constituency, Kasthuri Patto, to explore the concept of nation-building and how faith and community contribute to the country's growth and unity.[1] The topic of Catholics and nation-building was discussed in conjunction with the 2023 Merdeka Day celebrations in August through a Tamil podcast with Rev. Fr. George Harrison who spoke about the crucial role of the Catholic faith in inspiring positive changes and contributing to the country's growth.[2] The same topic on Christians and nation-building in Tamil was also covered in February 2022 when podcast host Mr Stephen John spoke to Rev. Fr. Bonaventure Rayappan about the Church's involvement in nation-building, especially in education, healthcare and poverty eradication, and how lay Catholics can contribute to build not just a nation, but also a society for the sake of the future. In fact, the topic of nation-building has always been covered by CAH since its inception in 2020. CAH had two podcasts to celebrate Merdeka Day and Malaysia Day. The first was about Unity in Diversity where Rev. Fr. Clarence Devadass talked about the expression of Malaysia's diversity in race, culture and religion, and how it can be a strength as well as a weakness. The podcast discussion also explored what Catholics could do to promote harmony in the spirit of nation-building. The second podcast also featured Fr. Clarence Devadass as well as two guests—La Salle Brother Augustine and Victor Tuan (a retiree from the Royal Malaysian Air Force)—who reminisced about their past memories growing up in Malaysia and what they hoped to see in the future.

In its podcasts, CAH has also featured politicians such as former deputy minister of women, family and community development, Hannah Yeoh, who was invited to speak about the increase of domestic violence during the COVID-19 movement restrictions, and how society can help to overcome this crisis.[3] Another issue that emerged during the COVID-19 pandemic was the rise in poverty rates which has affected everyone, especially the poor and the vulnerable. The podcast in July

2021 had Hartini Zainudin, a child activist and co-founder of Yayasan Chow Kit which helps disadvantaged children and teenagers, and Arnaud Marolleau, vice president of The Giving Bank, discussed the precarious position of the marginalized as a result of the pandemic and how the Malaysian community can respond and reach out to their fellow citizens.[4] In addition to the health and economic crisis, Malaysia was also rocked by various political crises with changes in government that affected the nation's stability. There was a feeling of despair as citizens helplessly watched the chaotic politicking that occurred. To make sense of the situation, CAH invited Batu Kawan MP Kasthuri Patto and then chairman of Bersih 2.0, Thomas Fann, to unpack the political circumstances and discuss what ordinary citizens could do to voice out their unhappiness and turn their despair into hope.[5] CAH also talked to three youths as catalysts for change in society: Heidy Quah, a social activist from Refuge for the Refugees; Adrian Oh, a volunteer at the COVID-19 vaccination centre; and Fabian Lee, the coordinator of the Catholic Church's Kuala Lumpur Archdiocesan Single Adults and Youth Office.

In the run-up to the 15th general election (GE15) in November 2022, CAH had a podcast in August 2022 to discuss why Catholics should vote in the general election by inviting political scientist Professor Wong Chin Huat from Jeffrey Cheah Institute on Southeast Asia, and Thomas Fann, former chairman of Bersih, the Coalition for Clean and Fair Elections.[6] The podcast's blurb stated that the Catechism of the Catholic Church speaks about the right to vote as a moral obligation (CCC 2240) and that as good stewards of God's gifts and faithful citizens, it is important to participate in elections and exercise the right to vote, which is a gift from God that cannot be taken for granted. Closer to GE15, CAH organized another podcast on the topic of "Voting as Catholics" where Rev. Fr. Clarence Devadass was on hand to answer frequently asked questions such as: To vote or not to vote? Who do I vote for? How to choose which government I want? What difference would I make? Do I have to do this?[7]

An older, online Catholic community is a private Facebook group whose members are mostly Malaysian Catholics. Its 36,000-plus members are managed by three administrators cum moderators. Most of the postings relate to the Catholic faith and Church matters such as masses, prayers, liturgy, priests, feast days, saints and gospel reflections, with a few core members driving the publication of content, including one of the administrators. Engagement and discussions are mostly minimal with less than thirty members either "liking" or "loving" the post and/or less than ten members stating their agreement and support by commenting "amen".

Nevertheless, whenever sociopolitical issues that relate to the Malaysian Catholic community are posted, the engagement level increases. For example, in 2018, a member posted a picture of controversial Muslim preacher Zakir Naik and a link to an online petition to lobby for his deportation from Malaysia back to his home country India for making a statement that criticized the building of churches in Malaysia which he claimed to be an Islamic state, adding that their religion and worship is wrong. This riled up many Malaysian Christians who were upset by his denigration of their faith and the post garnered 213 comments, with many of them signing the online petition and supporting the call for deportation. Members also reposted a reflection from a priest regarding the issue and content to debunk Zakir Naik. Other issues that the group members discussed included a protest in 2011 by purported members of a Malay rights non-governmental organization that called on the government to ban Christian teachers from teaching in Malaysian public schools. In 2014, group members were also upset by the publication and distribution of a book titled *Pendedahan Agenda Kristian* (Exposing the Christian Agenda) published by the Selangor Islamic Religious Council (MAIS) to some 1,000 students who attended a seminar at Universiti Teknologi Mara (UiTM). The book allegedly warned Muslims about "tricks" by Christians to sway Muslims from their faith which causes apostasy, and that Christian proselytization is a well-planned mission by a "mastermind". The issue emerged again when former chief justice Tun Abdul Hamid Mohamad claimed that Christians in Malaysia plan to use the word "Allah" as a political ruse to "confuse" and "convince" Muslims to convert to Christianity and cause a schism between the Malays and *Bumiputera* in Sabah and Sarawak (Shazwan 2014), which upset group members to the extent that the administrator had to remind them not to name call or use profanity, failing which she would delete the comment. The group members were again upset when Gerakan Pembela Ummah (Movement to Defend the Muslim Community), a coalition of Malay-Muslim groups, said that the Christian Federation of

Malaysia (CFM) was seeking to place as many Christians as possible in national political leadership positions, as part of its evangelism to the Malay-Muslim community, which is a major threat. CFM's chairman, Archbishop Julian Leow, denied the allegations, stating that Malaysia is a democracy, and its leaders are elected by the people during general elections, and criticized the attempt as a means to promote feelings of ill-will and hostility among Malaysians.

One major issue that emerged between 2008 and 2015 which was highlighted by members include the government's ban on the use of the word "Allah" which ended up in the courts. Muslims in Malaysia commonly use the word "Allah", which is an Arabic term referring to God, to pray. However, Christians in Sabah and Sarawak also use "Allah" in their Malay-language bibles and religious publications, as well as in their prayers. Muslim pressure groups in Malaysia argued that they have exclusive use of the word "Allah", citing a 1986 government prohibition that prevented its use for non-Muslims. Nevertheless, Christians who predominantly communicate in Malay, disputed this as they claimed they have used "Allah" to describe God for centuries. Two legal cases ensued due to this: a Malaysian woman who was detained at Kuala Lumpur International Airport for possessing compact discs that contained the word "Allah" in her luggage; and Catholic weekly newspaper *The Herald*, which challenged the government's ban to use "Allah" in its publication. In 2015, the woman won the case as the court declared that the seizure was unlawful, and the items were returned to her, and in 2021, she was allowed to use the word "Allah" in her religious practice. *The Herald*, however, was unsuccessful as the Federal Court affirmed the Court of Appeal's decision that the use of the word "Allah" was not essential to the Christian faith and could confuse Muslims; this can threaten national security and public order.

While most supported the Catholic Church's decision to take legal action against the government, there were some who felt uncomfortable and questioned the need to challenge the authorities on the use of the word "Allah" when other words such as "Abba" or "Tuhan" can also be used. They felt that Catholics in Peninsular Malaysia do not use this Arabic word in their prayers, so there is nothing that can be gained from this lawsuit; Christianity is about love for others and not alienating people. The constant posts and discussions on this matter led to some members expressing their unhappiness that the Facebook group was becoming a political movement instead of focusing on the Catholic faith, and that the Catholic Church should just give up the legal action and allow Muslims to use the word "Allah" exclusively because that has minimal impact on their faith. There were also concerns that the court case was being "hijacked" by the then opposition parties for their political agenda to agitate the government, and there were calls to stop politicizing the issue as they felt that the situation was getting out of hand.

Others responded by referring to scholars who stated that "Allah" is of Christian Syriac origin and was used by the people to refer to God long before Prophet Muhammad's time, and that it is within the constitutional right of Christians to practise their religion freely. They also said that secular authorities should not be allowed to dictate the Church's liturgical language, which is part of the freedom to practise one's religion. Also, there are bibles, hymns, songs and religious books that use the word "Allah", especially by Christians—Catholics and Protestants—in Sabah and Sarawak, and that those who do not use Bahasa Malaysia during prayers, masses or services do not understand its importance. They also pointed out that "Allah" has historical context and has been used by all Abrahamic faiths and East Malaysian Christians for many generations, and that Christians in Peninsular Malaysia should support their right to worship instead of turning their backs on them. In fact, Muslims in Sabah and Sarawak do not have any issues with Christians using the word "Allah" in their religious practices. One member also shared an article which explained why the word "Allah", which means God, cannot be replaced with "Tuhan", which means Lord. Another member was concerned that "turning the other cheek" and moving on may eventually affect the right to practise their religion in the future, adding that "it's not about winning, it's about being heard". East Malaysians from Sabah and Sarawak came to the forefront and said that they, as well as *The Herald* and other Christian publications, have been using "Allah" for a long time without any problems, and that it was the Home Ministry that banned its use for Christians and behaved aggressively to the Church while politicizing the issue to win votes. Thus, the Catholic Church is just defending its right through the legal process for justice, not just victory alone.

The content of the posts is not exclusively Catholic. Occasionally, there are posts on other Christian groups but mostly in relation to sociopolitical matters. For example, in 2019, one of the group members posted a news report that the Sarawak state government approved a 1.2-ha land for the building of a church and a community centre in Kuching by the Borneo Evangelical Mission (BEM). This post received twenty-nine comments that were supportive of the move by the Sarawak state government, which shows that the Catholic community was also happy with their Protestant brethren's good fortunes as part of Christian solidarity in a country where Christians are a minority.

Members of this Catholic Facebook group were also very concerned about the abduction of Pastor Raymond Koh in 2017, and posted news articles and content which showed the closed-circuit television (CCTV) of the incident. Prior to his abduction, Pastor Koh ran a non-governmental organization that focused on helping people with HIV/AIDs, recovering drug addicts and single mothers with children. During the incident on 13 February 2017, CCTV footage showed several men emerging from three black SUVs and forcing Pastor Koh to pull over just as he was exiting a highway in a Malaysian suburb. There were several posts about his disappearance and calls to join several candlelight vigil and prayers for Pastor Koh. SUHAKAM, Human Rights Commission of Malaysia, subsequently conducted an investigation and concluded that Pastor Koh was a victim of enforced disappearance by the country's police due to his alleged proselytization of Muslims, which is illegal under Malaysian laws (Leong 2019).

On the issue of Bersih protests, most of the group members were supportive of the movement for free and fair elections. Bersih, which means "clean" in Malay, is a civil society coalition of eighty-four non-government organizations pushing for electoral reform in Malaysia. The second rally, also known as the Walk for Democracy, was held on 9 July 2011 to protest against alleged vote rigging and other electoral abuses (*The Straits Times* 2015). The authorities were threatening to use hardline approaches to stop the protest from materializing. Members posted prayers for the safety of the protestors, and one even posted information on three Catholic churches that would be open for anyone, Catholic or non-Catholic, to seek refuge during the protest. The members also shared information on how to participate in the rallies and safety measures that people could take when they go to the protest. Nevertheless, there were a few comments that religious institutions such as churches should not mix with politics and concerns that the protestors might interrupt the mass if they entered the church's compounds, but these received rebuttals from other members.

Three more Bersih rallies were held subsequently in 2012 (Bersih 3.0), 2015 (Bersih 4.0) and 2016 (Bersih 5.0). News articles, photos and Facebook posts from third parties were also reposted into the Malaysian Catholic Christians group. There were posts asking for volunteers to assist St. John's Cathedral in Bukit Nanas as it was opening its doors to provide rest and refreshments to those attending the Bersih 4.0 rally and to maintain overall safety. In fact, photographs of Archbishop Emeritus Tan Sri Datuk Murphy Pakiam and Bishop Bernard Paul attending the Bersih 5.0 rally were also reposted by the administrator into the group. In fact, when Bishop Bernard was criticized for his support of the Bersih movement by a political party aligned to Barisan Nasional, the administrator posted information from the Catechism of the Catholic Church, paragraph 2246 which states: "It is a part of the Church's mission to pass moral judgments even in matters related to politics, whenever the fundamental rights of man or the salvation of souls requires it." She added that Catholics must form their conscience in full accord with the authoritative teaching of the Church in all areas of their lives, which includes the political arena. This post received 120 likes and 46 comments that mostly supported her position while criticizing the political party.

Group members also posted about general elections, often fasting and praying for peace in the country. During the 12th general election in 2008, a member published a post to recruit people to sign up as an election observer to independently monitor the electoral process, where they would receive training under a human rights organization. Group members also posted calls for prayers for a safe, clean and fair election, which they also did for the 13th and 14th general elections in 2013 and 2018 respectively. During the 14th general election, Kuala Lumpur Archbishop Julian Leow called for twenty-four hours of prayer and fasting; he also issued a statement and a video calling on the Catholic faithful to exercise their civil and moral rights to vote as part of their engagement and participation in the nation's democratic process. He reminded Catholics of the Church's social teachings, one of which is the dignity of the human person. Some members also posted about various forums during the campaign period that people could attend, as well as guidelines on the voting process as part of voter education.

Group members also supported the Kuala Lumpur Archbishop Julian Leow when he backed the Sabah Council of Churches' Christmas message in 2016 in which its president Rev. Jerry Dusing said that truth needs to be established by the authorities and those in government on sociopolitical issues such as the 1Malaysia Development Board scandal and purported Islamization efforts that affect religious freedom. When asked about the trend of political and religious leaders who included political messages in their religious greetings, he said that "asking people to own up to what is happening is a normal request, especially when public money is in question", adding that people should speak up and question. He added, "I believe we have to distinguish between politics and political parties. We are not with political parties. The church is not with political parties. But we are involved in politics. Politics in the sense of speaking out against what is not right, speaking of the values of justice, of what is right, and what is wrong."

During the campaign period before GE15 in 2022, the group's administrator reposted a statement from Kota Kinabalu Archbishop John Wong who called on Catholics to fulfil their right and responsibilities as citizens and in the upcoming general election for a better nation and a better future for the next generation. There was also a post exhorting Catholics to pray during Holy Hour for the nation and the general election, either in person at the chapel or virtually through Zoom. In the midst of the GE15 campaign period, the group's administrator reposted a statement from the Christian Federation of Malaysia (CFM) in response to allegations made by former prime minister Muhyiddin Yassin during GE15 campaigning where he urged the public not to vote for the Pakatan Harapan coalition as it was allegedly supported by Jews and Christians who were pushing for a Christianization agenda in Malaysia. CFM stated that politicians should not make statements that cause strife and cast seditious aspersions to win support from a particular race or religious group, which can disturb the nation's peace, harmony and well-being of its citizens. It urged the authorities to swiftly and effectively take appropriate action so that such irresponsible statements do not recur.

Other issues that have been discussed by group members include the plight of Catholic missionary schools in Malaysia, which have educated hundreds and thousands of students, including prominent figures such as former prime minister Najib Razak and former Bank Negara governor Tan Sri Dr Zeti Aziz. These schools are under the administration of the Education Ministry, but they receive insufficient financial support such that their buildings have become dilapidated, thus affecting the safety of the students and teachers. Group members were also concerned about the bid by Convent Bukit Nanas in 2017 to renew its land lease, which was rejected by the Federal Territories Land and Mines Office, so that it could be gazetted as a fully aided government school. The school's board of governors and trustees decided to take legal action and challenged the authority's decision; petitions were also initiated to preserve the school both as an institution of learning and as a national heritage site. Finally, in 2021, the Prime Minister's Office agreed to extend the lease by another sixty years, taken into consideration the school's contribution to the education of the nation. The closure of some missionary schools such as Convent Pulau Tikus and Convent Light Street in Penang, as well as St. Thomas School in Kuantan were also discussed by group members who were concerned about the fate that would befall other missionary schools which are part of Malaysia's education tapestry. The most recent issue that caught the attention of group members was the statement issued by the Catholic Bishops' Conference of Malaysia (CBCM) about the Education Ministry's directive to organize a Palestine Solidarity Week in schools to support Palestinians in Gaza. CBCM stated that schoolchildren are minors and should not be dragged into politics. It expressed its shock to see videos on social media where schoolchildren are being exposed to toy guns, violence and hatred by their teachers, which runs counter to the values espoused by Rukun Negara (National Principles), which is about building unity and harmony for a strong, stable and prosperous nation.

It is clear from the observations of the content and discussions in these two Catholic online communities that while online and social media is mainly used to discuss matters of faith and spirituality, conversations about sociopolitical issues that affect the fundamental right to freely practise one's religion also emerge whenever incidents of such a nature occur. As a result of the Catholic teachings on social justice and Church leadership, Malaysian Catholics are aware of the sociopolitical issues that affect their freedom of religion, as well as their Christian duties and obligations to participate in the country's democratic and electoral process. While the Catholic Church is apolitical and non-partisan, its clerical leaders remind the flock of their moral duty to vote and participate in nation-building as Malaysian citizens. Furthermore, the Church has also taken the lead in bringing awareness of sociopolitical issues to the forefront by inviting politicians and civil society activists to speak in podcasts. Members of the clergy have also discussed about the intersection between faith and the role of Christians in contributing to the country. On issues where the Catholic Church believes that the fundamental right to practise their faith has been affected, its leaders have issued statements on these issues and engaged with the authorities in an effort to find a solution. Only when all else fails, then legal action is taken as a last resort. The statements and actions by the Catholic Church leadership often form the basis for discussions in Catholic online communities who are mostly supportive. While there is a small minority who believe that the Catholic Church should just focus on spiritual matters relating to faith and religion, most of the flock endorse the actions of the Church in taking a stand whenever their religious freedom is impacted by the state's actions. Malaysian Catholics also use social media networks to mobilize actions such as going to vote, joining protest movements, signing online petitions, in addition to prayers and fasting as a community for peace. Social media has enabled the Malaysian Catholic community to be informed about their faith and also be faithful Christians and loyal citizens.

## PROTESTANT ONLINE COMMUNITIES

To broaden the discussion beyond the Catholic Church community, it is worth looking at how other Christian communities, such as the Protestant Christian community in Malaysia, engage in political discourse on social media. The following sections provide descriptions of two Facebook groups, comprising a significant cohort of Malaysian Protestant Christians, and the forms of political discourse that take place within these groups. The sections highlight the contextual background of both groups, throughout which their similarities and differences will be illuminated. For the purposes of focused discussion, specific attention will be given to the activity surrounding the events of Bersih

4 in 2015 where both groups experienced consistent levels of activity. The analysis of these sections focuses on how political discourse and spirituality intersect and are moderated, and how spiritual authority and preferred ideology are established in an online environment where freedom of expression is encouraged.

For context, Bersih 4 was the fourth in a series of planned public rallies organized by Bersih, which is the Coalition for Clean and Fair Elections, to demand reforms to the electoral process in Malaysia. The rally took place over two days from 29 to 30 August 2015, primarily in three cities in Malaysia—Kuala Lumpur, Kuching and Kota Kinabalu. According to the organizers, the rally drew an estimated 500,000 participants over the two-day period and was largely peaceful (Buang 2015). As the previous iterations of Bersih rallies gained public prominence and were among the largest held in Malaysia, debates and discussions branched out beyond the issue of elections to broader concerns about the Malaysian government, particularly the premiership of Najib Razak, during which all the rallies took place.

Interest in the rallies was high, and in the case of Bersih 4, both the Facebook groups featured in this section—Friends in Conversation (FIC)[8] and the End Time Watchmen (ETW)[9]—actively engaged with their respective communities in the lead-up to the protest. Key opinion leaders of both groups, including founding members and group administrators, took very different stances. All of FIC's Facebook posts on Bersih 4 focused on rallying support for the cause and encouraging participation, while most of ETW's posts focused on discouraging members from attending the rally. Both groups' approach to the rally is, while different, useful in gaining a snapshot of how political discourses emerge in online Christian communities, and how related issues are negotiated by the members of the Malaysian Christian community. The following sections describe key characteristics of both online communities, and then conclude with some observations on the nature of political discourse in online Christian groups.

## Characteristics of the Community

The first group is called Friends in Conversation (FIC). The Facebook group was formed in 2010 and as of February 2022, has 161 members. In the welcome post, the group founder, a pastor of the Lutheran church, envisioned the group to be like "safe spaces for dangerous conversations". Although there are no apparent restrictions to membership, the low membership, along with the "closed" status of the group suggests there is at least some level of exclusivity towards Malaysian Christians who are interested in intellectual engagement on a variety of theological and sociopolitical issues that impact the Malaysian church. A general survey of activity in the group suggests that the membership is interdenominational, though predominantly composed of Malaysian Protestants.

The second group featured in this section is the End Time Watchmen (ETW). Formed in 2015, the group has over 1,200 members. It is worth noting that out of that number, most of the membership was accumulated within the first few days of the group's formation when the group founders added members from their respective networks of Facebook friends. The composition of the group is more varied than FIC's, and it has members from outside Malaysia who are actively engaging with the content posted on the group. That being said, like FIC, the group is also interdenominational and comprises mainly Malaysian Christians with different theological interests.

## Online Presence, Objectives and Strategies

Although there are differences in the membership and demographics, both groups share broadly similar aims, which are to freely engage and discuss issues, be they theological or sociopolitical, that affect the Christian community within Malaysia and beyond. Both groups allow a range of topics to be posted and deliberated on—prosperity gospel; megachurches; speaking in tongues; lesbian, gay, bisexual and transgender (LGBT) rights; Malaysian politics, and more. However, beyond the relative freedom to discuss all kinds of topics, their approach to these aims is different. A starting point to identify these differences are the stated objectives of the group on their respective Facebook pages.

In the "About" section of FIC's Facebook page, it states that "This Facebook group is hosted by FIC to facilitate reflective and constructive conversations on faith, spirituality, community, and society between those who confess to belong to the Christian faith and tradition. The aim of this Facebook group is to provide a safe space for exploration and dialogue, undergirded by friendship and humility." For ETW, their stated aim is "widespread end time false teaching calls for discernment. To overcome deception, we need to be like the Bereans—scrutinize every teaching against God's Word". In practice, the group permits discussion on any issues with the purpose of allowing the community to scrutinize, debate and engage one another to identify false teachings. While FIC's stated aims are within the context of "safe space" and "exploration", ETW's approach is grounded in "scrutiny" and "overcoming deception". This is more clearly elucidated in the group's official editorial guidelines, where the stated aim of the group is to "correct false teaching". This raises the question: who does the correcting, and in a space where subjective discussions take place, who is the final authority on what constitutes correct Biblical interpretation? These questions apply also to FIC, even if there is no distinct right or wrong approach stated in their aim.

## Internal Regulation and Moderation

The above question draws from the broader discussion on how authority is negotiated and claimed in online communities. This is a subject of ongoing interest in the field of online religion, with Campbell (2007), Radde-Antweiler (2012), Cheong (2012) and Tan (2020) all discussing various dimensions of the subject. One way to observe how authority is established in a social media group is to consider the formal and informal rules of the group and how they are enforced. This approach is inspired by an aspect of du Gay and Hall's work on the circuit of culture (du Gay et al. 2013). One factor that determines the success of any cultural artefact being widely adopted by a community is its producer's ability to negotiate with both formal regulations like legal restrictions and cultural objections on a personal and everyday level.

Similarly applied, in the cases of FIC and ETW, there are two ways to consider internal regulation and moderation. Formal regulations in online communities like forums and social media groups often take the form of easily accessible text such as pinned posts or shared documents. This is no different for both Facebook groups here. FIC has detailed communication guidelines in the "About" section of the page. The fourteen points provided are divided into two sections. The first focuses on the recommended attitude towards the group, with guidelines including "a preference for self-critique", "a bias for the vulnerable, marginalised and disadvantaged" and "an expectation that you will find certain views expressed to be disagreeable, but that's ok". The second set of guidelines relates to the way members should communicate, such as "stay on topic", and "be constructive, polite and fair". Similarly, ETW has a set of formal editorial guidelines uploaded in a PDF format for all members to read. The guidelines are also divided into two sections: "allowed content" and "disallowed content". Both sections are tied directly to the aforementioned aim of correcting false teaching, with an emphasis on posting content that "identifies/corrects false teachings using the Bible", "query with regard to strange/suspect doctrine, teachings, prophecies or practice", and to avoid "discussion/debate merely for the sake of intellectual or theoretical discussions". It also covers posting of "cute content, prayers, photos of church functions", and a preference to not name individuals and churches when discussing false teachings.

One can analyse how conversations and comments are moderated and engaged upon, and whether preferred ideological positions emerge in these discourses, including how these discourses are reinforced, and by whom. By identifying what are the preferred ideological positions that emerge in the day-to-day narrative of these groups, we can observe how "less formal and more abstract rendering of a particular pattern and order of signifying practices ... appear to be 'regular' or 'natural'" (Leve 2012, p. 8). The flurry of activity in the lead-up to Bersih 4 serves as a good example of the exercise of codifying and controlling practices related to the regulatory aspects of the circuit of culture (Champ 2008, p. 87).

In FIC, there were a total of seventeen posts about the rally authored by three different members. All of the articles, except one, were strongly supportive of the rally. The one exception was an article listing down the pros and cons of participating in Bersih 4 which took a relatively neutral tone. These posts covered a range of topics from criticizing the Malaysian Anti-Corruption Commission's lack of effectiveness in deterring corruption in the country, the government's mishandling of the 1Malaysia Development Board (1MDB) funds and a call for the president of Transparency International Malaysia to resign. The posts also reinforce what Bersih stands for and assert that Bersih participants are, in fact, good Malaysian citizens. An analysis of these posts reveals that firstly, the authors did not make religious or spiritual arguments about why people should support the rally. Instead, as described above, the posts served to express opinions about the rally by highlighting various associated issues from within the political context of the event. Another point to note is that the three authors contributing posts on the group's Facebook wall are active members who regularly publish posts in the group. All the posts received a small number of "likes", and very few had comments, none of which was about opposing the participation of the rally. It is difficult to infer why these posts did not generate much engagement—it could possibly mean there is already a consensus on the subject matter, or an unwillingness to engage with the authors on the topic. Regardless, in both scenarios, the apparent dominant ideological position is that participation in the public rally is encouraged with no resistance.

In ETW, all the posts related to Bersih 4 in the group were authored by one of the group's founding members and de facto leader, Pastor Simon.[10] In contrast to FIC, Pastor Simon took a negative position to the rally in most of these posts, generally acknowledging the discontent that many felt about the state of the country but suggesting that taking to the streets to protest may not be the best way Christians could represent themselves on the matter. However, one post generated a lively discussion, accumulating seventy-nine comments. In that post, Pastor Simon explained why he opposed the Bersih protests, claiming that participants were neglecting the dangers that it would cause to the public. He also accused would-be attendees as ignorant about the protest, thinking it would be fun. In the same post, he pleaded for church leaders to do something about the indifference of church members and stated that those who are not attending the rally were possibly doing more biblical things that bring the knowledge of Jesus Christ to others.

This post was met with disagreement by a few people. A member, Siu, immediately responded to the post asserting that the people who were attending the rally "are doing a serious and important thing", and that they are "standing up for justice and righteousness in our nation". Another member, Xavier, who is not from Malaysia, responded to the post by asking members to pray for the safety of rally-goers and drawing comparisons to how President Marcos's leadership in the Philippines came to an end because of a civil uprising. Two leaders of the group, Pastor Simon and Ross, responded to the above comments, asserting that Malaysia's situation cannot be compared to the Philippines', and that "flippant protest attitudes" is a problem. Pastor Simon also quoted the Bible, saying that there were occasions when God withheld His punishment on corrupt and sinful nations, perhaps implying that it was not for people to take to the streets of their own will.

The above is notable because it revealed the preferred ideological position of the leaders of the ETW Facebook group. In a separate but related post, Siu also commented by saying that Bersih 4 is in line with the "scriptural call for justice and righteousness in our land". However, another of ETW's co-founding leader, Bob, responded by asking where such a scriptural call was made in the Bible, and asked for examples of when such protests led to justice and righteousness in the land. He also further queried Siu on whether protesters "really give glory to the Father" when attending the rally. In both scenarios, there was no resolution to these disagreements. In summary, the group leaders who actively engaged on the topic were all anti-protests, and firmly engaged with members who supported the rally. Also, there were no other members who published posts related to the rally in the group during that period. While it is difficult to infer the reasons for this, it is possible to see a clear establishment of the group's preferred ideology about Bersih 4 through the primary content and engagement with members.

## ADVANTAGES AND DISADVANTAGES OF ONLINE COMMUNITIES

Through observation of the above groups, there are several interrelated features of online communities that can both serve as advantageous and disadvantageous in the context of community building and engagement.

Firstly, on social media platforms, new types of communities with diverse demographics can emerge easily. Although both groups observed are "Christian" communities, the diversity lies in having different types of Christians, with different denominations, doctrinal leanings, theological interests and age groups, engaging with one another in a shared space. Coupled with the groups' relative freedom to discuss different topics, this leads to an organic and dynamic space with new content and new threads of engagement that would otherwise be hard to organize in an offline environment.

This freedom, however, does not necessarily translate to a more democratic space. While the democratization of Internet spaces can mean that there are more opportunities for people to express their views, this does not necessarily equate to more productive conversation, a phenomenon that is well documented. Back in 1998, in an early work by Hill and Hughes on cyber-activism and online politics, *Cyberpolitics: Citizen Activism in the Age of the Internet*, the authors looked at how Internet users participated in the political process in various forums and online platforms. They noted then that:

> We found very little data to support the supposition that the Internet changes people's minds politically. Rather, reading web pages seem to be an act of self-selection; people go online to find out more information about a subject, not to be transformed. Likewise, debate and information-based discussed in the usenet newsgroups and political chat rooms serves to reinforce pre-existing ideological positions, not to change them (Hill and Hughes 1998, p. 183).

The above notion that the Internet serves only to reinforce ideological positions has been repeatedly noted as a concern in the field of communications and media studies (Kitchens, Johnson, and Gray 2020; Guo, Rohde, and Wu 2020). Terms like "echo chambers" and "filter bubbles" are commonly used to describe social media environments "built around the ability of users to follow like-minded individuals" (Rhodes 2022, p. 5) where Internet users are repeatedly exposed to messaging that they agree with. When interacting beyond their circles, particularly on sociopolitical issues, online spaces often exacerbate political division in various ways (Brändle, Galpin, and Trenz 2022; Wakefield and Wakefield 2022). This is true in the case of both FIC and ETW as well. In all the posts relating to Bersih 4, despite several back-and-forth comments, there were no texts that indicated acceptance of opposing views, or concession of a particular point. Responses were always a restating of one's opinion, affirming the view of another commenter who shares the same positions, and critiquing and problematizing the opposing positions on the subject.

Another issue that online communities face is the difficulty in sustaining a high level of community engagement over a long period. As of the writing of this chapter, both groups still exist: FIC is no longer active, while ETW is limited to one member publishing occasional posts with little feedback and comments. This could be due to several reasons. One obvious factor is that without a sustained effort to engage members, particularly when key group members stop contributing content, groups naturally decline into inactivity over time. Another possible factor is that Facebook's membership is declining, with members opting to interact on other platforms such as WhatsApp, Telegram and TikTok (Naughton 2022). These sites are opportunities for further research on the subject.

## INTERACTION WITH THE MALAYSIAN PUBLIC SPHERE

As described above, both FIC and ETW welcomed a broad range of topics for discussion. The subject of Malaysia or Malaysia-specific topics do not regularly feature in the day-to-day activities that take place in these groups. While there are ongoing discussions on controversial topics within the global Christian community, such as the doctrine of salvation, speaking in tongues, and LGBT rights, signifiers of Malaysian-ness would be difficult to identify, although this does not make the community any less Malaysian.

However, issues that captured the broad interest of everyday Malaysians were actively engaged by members. As described above, both observed Facebook groups were active in posting views on Bersih 4, and in the case of FIC, previous iterations of Bersih rallies also saw significant engagement in the group. Also in both cases, the topic of Bersih 4 gradually disappeared in the days after the rally and the group members returned to debating other issues impacting Christianity at large.

## THE CHRISTIAN ONLINE COMMUNITY
## AND ITS FUTURE

There are some observations that could potentially inform the way in which online communities are studied, particularly in the context of online religious communities' engagement with Malaysian politics.

Firstly, online Christian communities provide new avenues for engaging in political discourse in Malaysia. Social media has allowed new groups with specific demographics to gather and communicate with one another. In many ways, Internet platforms can effectively facilitate Christian interdenominational discourse simply through their ease of access. These platforms also allow relatively private discourses among like-minded minorities, such as the Malaysian Christian community, to talk about sensitive sociopolitical issues in Malaysia. However, as noted in the findings above, there are limitations to how members interact with one another and with issues in online communities. Even in seemingly laissez-faire environments where all members and almost all topics are allowed, there are preferred ideologies that dominant figures seek to impose. Members with differing opinions do comment, but they are systematically rebutted until they stop engaging on the subject. One also cannot ignore the institutional presence, such as religious leaders (pastors, priests) within these groups, and the possible shift in power relations due to them.

To conclude, online communities, particularly those with specific interests, are in a state of reinvention. FIC is inactive now, while ETW, despite still having more than a thousand members, has only one or two members actively posting content. Online communities are very conducive for robust engagement on issues, even hot-button social issues within the Malaysian political realm. However, online communities are difficult to sustain as people lose interest, or when it clearly becomes less democratic than it promises. However, these micro-communities are an important affordance of the Internet and are likely to continue emerging in newer platforms such as WhatsApp and Telegram, which allow for even more private and insular communities with stricter membership admissions. As to how these evolutionary changes to online communities intersect with the public sphere and the offline world, it is a question that requires further investigation over the long term.

## Notes

1. Archdiocese of Kuala Lumpur, "Nation Building, Malaysia Day Special", 16 September 2023, https://www.youtube.com/watch?v=rA1qmUMka1g &list=PLVXTknFCbxELnNMl4uHuapZukBpECoGU2&index=7&t=1851s.

2. Archdiocese of Kuala Lumpur, "Catholics and Nation Building", 25 August 2023, https://www.youtube.com/watch?v=HWB4O28SI34&list=PLVXTknFCbxELnNMl4uHuapZukBpECoGU2&index=10&t=722s.
3. Catholics At Home, "Silent Screamers — Domestic Violence and How to Help", 28 February 2021, https://www.youtube.com/watch?v=P_FNm8dgipc&list=PLOvvYIjAk31hSbscihwQClopuxsLP1OzE&index=50.
4. Catholics At Home, "Poverty in the Pandemic", 10 July 2021, https://www.youtube.com/watch?v=YZWlnqgULh4&list=PLOvvYIjAk31hSbscihwQClopuxsLP1OzE&index=61.
5. Catholics At Home, "Malaysia: Where Do We Go from Here?" 14 August 2021, https://www.youtube.com/watch?v=8A5jIc2cYgk&list=PLOvvYIjAk31hSbscihwQClopuxsLP1OzE&index=65.
6. Catholics At Home, "GE15: Why Bother Going to Vote?" 19 August 2022, https://www.facebook.com/CatholicsAtHome/videos/1340022606535479/.
7. Catholics At Home, "Voting as Catholics: #GE15", 12 November 2022, https://www.facebook.com/CatholicsAtHome/videos/370999315217030.
8. "Friends in Conversation" is the real name of the group. The founder of the group opted for it to not be anonymized.
9. "End Time Watchmen" is not the real name of the group. It has been anonymized due to the relatively public nature of the group.
10. All individual social media usernames in this article are pseudonym.

## REFERENCES

Brändle, Verena K., Charlotte Galpin, and Hans-Jörg Trenz. 2022. "Brexit as 'Politics of Division': Social Media Campaigning after the Referendum". *Social Movement Studies* 21, no. 1–2: 234–53. https://doi.org/10.1080/14742837.2021.1928484 (accessed 10 November 2023).

Buang, Shakira. 2015. "500,000 Were at Bersih 4, Says Organiser". *Malaysiakini*, 31 August 2015. https://www.malaysiakini.com/news/310565 (accessed 10 November 2023).

Campbell, Heidi. 2007. "Who's Got the Power? Religious Authority and the Internet". *Journal of Computer-Mediated Communication* 12, no. 3: 1043–62.

Champ, Joseph G. 2008. "Horizontal Power, Vertical Weakness: Enhancing the 'Circuit of Culture'". *Popular Communication* 6, no. 2: 85–102. https://doi.org/10.1080/15405700801977426.

Cheong, Pauline H. 2012. "Authority". In *Digital Religion: Understanding Religious Practice in New Media Worlds*, edited by Heidi A. Campbell, pp. 72–87. London and New York: Routledge.

du Gay, Peter, Stuart Hall, Linda Janes, Anders K. Madsen, Hugh Mackay, and Keith Negus. 2013. *Doing Cultural Studies: The Story of the Sony Walkman.* 2nd ed. Thousand Oaks, CA: SAGE Publications Ltd.

Fay, William P. "Catholics in Political Life". n.d. United States Conference of Catholic Bishops. https://www.usccb.org/issues-and-action/faithful-citizenship/church-teaching/catholics-in-political-life (accessed 20 March 2022).

Guo, Lei, Jacob A. Rohde, and H. Denis Wu. 2020. "Who Is Responsible for Twitter's Echo Chamber Problem? Evidence from 2016 U.S. Election Networks". *Information, Communication & Society* 23, no. 2: 234–51. https://doi.org/10.1080/1369118X.2018.1499793.

Hill, Kevin A., and John E. Hughes. 1998. *Cyberpolitics: Citizen Activism in the Age of the Internet.* Lanham, MD: Rowman & Littlefield Publishers.

Hine, Christine. 2000. *Virtual Ethnography.* Thousand Oaks, CA: SAGE Publications.

John Paul II, Pope. 1987. *"Sollocitudo rei socialis".* http://www.vatican.va/content/john-paul-ii/en/encyclicals/documents/hf_jp-ii_enc_30121987_sollicitudo-rei-socialis.html (accessed 15 March 2022).

Kaur-Gill, Satveer, and Mohan J. Dutta. 2017. "Digital Ethnography". In *The International Encyclopedia of Communication Research Methods*, edited by Jörg Matthes, Christine S. Davis, and Robert F. Potter. https://doi.org/10.1002/9781118901731.iecrm0271.

Kitchens, Brent, Steven L. Johnson, and Peter H. Gray. 2020. "Understanding Echo Chambers and Filter Bubbles: The Impact of Social Media on Diversification and Partisan Shifts in News Consumptions". *MIS Quarterly* 44, no. 4: 1619–49.

Leong, Trinna. 2019. "Malaysian Police behind Pastor and Activist Disappearance: Human Rights Commission". *Straits Times*, 3 April 2019. https://www.straitstimes.com/asia/se-asia/malaysian-police-behind-pastor-and-activist-disappearance-human-rights-commission.

Leve, Annabelle M. 2012. "The Circuit of Culture as a Generative Tool of Contemporary Analysis: Examining the Construction of an Education Commodity". Paper presented at the Joint Australian Association for Research in Education and Asia-Pacific Educational Research Association Conference (AARE-APERA 2012) World Education Research Association (WERA) Focal Meeting, Sydney, New South Wales, 2–6 December 2012. https://eric.ed.gov/?id=ED544487.

Naughton, John. 2022. "For the First Time in Its History, Facebook Is in Decline. Has the Tech Giant Begun to Crumble?" *The Guardian*, 6 February 2022. https://www.theguardian.com/commentisfree/2022/feb/06/first-time-history-facebook-decline-has-tech-giant-begun-crumble.

Radde-Antweiler, Kerstin. 2012. "Authenticity". In *Digital Religion: Understanding Religious Practice in New Media Worlds*, edited by Heidi A. Campbell, pp. 88–103. London and New York: Routledge.

Rhodes, Samuel C. 2022. "Filter Bubbles, Echo Chambers, and Fake News: How Social Media Conditions Individuals to Be Less Critical of Political Misinformation". *Political Communication* 39, no. 1: 1–22. https://doi.org/10.1080/10584609.2021.1910887 (accessed 10 November 2023).

Shazwan, Mustafa Kamal. 2014. "Ex-CJ: 'Allah' Row a Ploy to Divide Country". *Malay Mail*, 24 January 2014. https://www.malaymail.com/news/malaysia/2014/01/24/ex-cj-allah-row-a-ploy-to-divide-country/605537.

Singer, Jane B. 2009. "Ethnography". *Journalism & Mass Communication Quarterly* 86: 191–98. https://doi.org/10.1177/107769900908600112.

*Straits Times*. 2015. "What You Need to Know about Malaysia's Bersih Movement". *Straits Times*, 27 August 2015. https://www.straitstimes.com/asia/se-asia/what-you-need-to-know-about-malaysias-bersih-movement.

Tan, Meng Yoe. 2019. "Facebook and the Mediatization of Religion: Inter-/Intrareligious Dialogue in Malaysia". In *Mediatized Religion in Asia: Studies on Digital Media and Religion*, edited by Kerstin Radde-Antweiler and Xenia Zeiler, pp. 71–88. London: Routledge. https://www.amazon.com/reader/B07L6VN1YB/ref=rdr_sb_li_hist_1&state=11111.

_____. 2020. *Malaysian Christians Online Faith, Experience, and Social Engagement on the Internet*. 1st ed. Singapore: Springer.

Underberg, Natalie M., and Elayne Zorn. 2013. *Digital Ethnography: Anthropology, Narrative, and New Media*. 1st. ed. Austin, TX: University of Texas Press.

Wakefield, Robin L., and Kirk Wakefield. 2022. "The Antecedents and Consequences of Intergroup Affective Polarisation on Social Media". *Information Systems Journal* 33, no. 3: 640–68. https://doi.org/10.1111/isj.12419.

# Index

1MDB (1Malaysia Development Berhad), 61, 64–65, 227

www.ingramcontent.com/pod-product-compliance
Lightning Source LLC
Chambersburg PA
CBHW041255040426
42334CB00028BA/3026